SACRED LEAVES OF CANDOMBLÉ

SACRED LEAVES OF CANDOMBLÉ

African Magic, Medicine, and Religion in Brazil

Robert A. Voeks

UNIVERSITY OF TEXAS PRESS   AUSTIN

⊗The paper used in this publication meets the minimum
requirements of American National Standard for
Information Sciences—Permanence of Paper for Printed
Library Materials, ANSI z39.48-1984.

Library of Congress Cataloging-in-Publication Data
Voeks, Robert A., 1950–
Sacred leaves of Candomble : African magic, medicine,
and religion in Brazil / Robert A. Voeks. — 1st ed.
        p.   cm.
Includes bibliographical references (p.   ) and index.
ISBN 0-292-78730-8 (c : alk. paper) — ISBN 0-292-78731-6 (pbk. : alk. paper)
1. Candomble (Cult)   2. Plants—Religious aspects—Candomble (Cult)
3. Medicine, Magic, mystic, and spagiric—Brazil—Bahia (State) I. Title.
BL2592.C35.V64   1997
299′.673—dc21   96-51297

To the memory of Pauline Janette Voeks

CONTENTS

FIGURES

NOTE ON ORTHOGRAPHY

The Candomblé lexicon is derived from the Portuguese, Yoruba, Ewe, Ijesha, Kimbundu, and, to a lesser extent, Tupi languages. For spelling and diacritics of terms specifically related to Candomblé, I follow Olga Cacciatore's *Dicionário de cultos Afro-Brasileiros* (1977). Note that she employs a Portuguese orthography of African lexemes. As a supplemental source for African terms not covered in her dictionary, I rely on Ruy Póvoas's *A Linguagem do Candomblé* (1989). Spelling of Portuguese vernacular plant names follows for the most part L. A. Silva, G. Lisboa, and T. Santos, *Nomenclatura Vulgar e Científica de Plantas Encontradas na Região Cacaueira da Bahia* (1982). General Portuguese words follow A. B. de H. Ferreira's *Pequeno Dicionário Brasileiro da Língua Portuguêsa*, while Tupi orthography conforms to T. Sampaio's *O Tupi na Geografia Nacional* (1955).

For clarity, the origins of terms—Portuguese, African, or Tupi—are distinguished by type style throughout the text. Portuguese terms are <u>underlined</u>; African terms, regardless of the specific linguistic group, are **boldfaced**; and Tupi terms are ***italicized and boldfaced***. Botanical binomials are in *italics*. Word origins follow Megenney's *A Bahian Landscape* (1978), Mendonça's *A Inflência Africana no Portugûes do Brasil* (1935), and various other sources.

PREFACE

The once politically innocent field of nature-society relations finds itself increasingly caught in a vortex of competing intellectual and political agendas. Ethnobotany, the study of plants and people, is no exception. This change is due at least in part to the prevailing view that the earth is in the midst of a biological and cognitive cataclysm of unprecedented proportions. As the last native forests and fields are bulldozed or burned, the potential contribution of native plants to the development of new foods, fuels, fibers, and medicines is forever eliminated. As the last traditional societies are seduced by the Western worldview, the accumulated plant knowledge of unknown millennia is forever forgotten. Nature-society discourse is also caught in the emerging consensus— too long in coming—that the strategies and ultimate objectives of environmental conservation in the developing world are inexorably tied to cultural survival. According to this view, nature conservation efforts will be successful in the long term as a result of, not in spite of, local participation and guidance. Such grassroots-directed efforts challenge the standard "top-down" imposition of temperate-zone models of conservation, such as the creation of parks and reserves that treat locals as conservation liabilities rather than assets. At least in the tropical realm, understanding the time-tested linkage between plants and people constitutes the linchpin upon which the long-term success of these efforts turns.

Sacred Leaves of Candomblé is a study of Candomblé ethnobotany—the source, diffusion, use, classification, and meaning of Afro-Brazilian sacred leaves. This work traces its origin to a seemingly insignificant field observation. While collecting data in a second-growth forest in Bahia, Brazil, I noticed a patch of an unfamiliar herb along a path. I asked my friend, a local botanist, if he knew the name of the plant. He glanced at it, told me the name, but suggested by his tone that it wasn't a terribly interesting species. "It's not a native," he noted, but rather "just a weed from Africa." Most importantly, he went on to say that it was used to do **macumba**, or African black magic, by followers of Candomblé, an Afro-Brazilian religion in the region. I filed this nugget away for several years, convinced that this innocuous little weed someday would have a story to tell.

Originally expecting to document the origin and use of a few African plants in Brazil, I discovered in short order that the story of the Candomblé flora not only was rich and complex, but was in many respects a metaphor for the African American diaspora. Neither can be comprehended without understanding the subtle interplay between history, geography, culture, and political economy. Neither has been examined to the extent that its complexity and continuity would warrant. And neither can be interpreted as an orthodox expression of African traditions and beliefs or an anachronistic residue of neo-European domination.

While much of this book is descriptive in nature, at least three themes emerge that are at variance with prevailing streams of thought in the biological and human sciences. First, this book is not about the highly touted medicinal potential of pristine tropical rainforests. Rather, it underscores the intrinsic medicinal worth of *peopled* tropical landscapes, of *disturbed* forests and fields and the healing flora they harbor. Like the territories from which African forced immigrants were uprooted, the world in which they arrived had witnessed centuries of exploitation—some destructive, some not. Their ethnobotany was never born exclusively of West Africa's primary forests, nor was it to be so in Brazil. Rather, their plant knowledge was based on the fruits of human-derived landscape change, an ethnobotany adapted to and modified by fire, machetes, cattle hooves, and monoculture. The sacred leaves of Candomblé are, with few exceptions, sacred shrubs, sacred weeds, and sacred cultivars. Depending on your perspective, this feature either undermines any botanical interest in the Afro-Brazilian pharmacopoeia or, on the contrary, suggests that a significant portion of the "tropical pharmaceutical factory" should be sought in disturbed as opposed to primary forests.

Second, this book is not about victims of the African slave trade, men and women forever hobbled by the chains of historical oppression. It is about victors, empowered African slaves and their descendants who steadfastly refused to succumb to European cultural dominance. In no case are their successes more visible than in the area of religion and healing. Faced with seemingly insurmountable obstacles—economic, political, and geographical—New World Africans somehow managed to sow and nurture the seeds of their traditional beliefs in an alien landscape. The eventual outcomes of these efforts vary from region to region. Nevertheless, African-derived systems of religion, medicine, and magic exhibit a remarkable degree of consistency and continuity, and their practitioners maintain a striking sense of self-esteem and pride.

Third, this book is not about African religious orthodoxy, nor does it in any way support the notion that syncretic Afro-Brazilian belief systems are somehow less pure than those of their Yoruba forebears. Rather, it is about the inevitable osmosis of ideas and innovations between cultures in intimate and extended contact. In Brazil, Africans and their descendants were able to forge a successful New World belief system exactly because they were willing to absorb, eagerly and without apology, relevant spiritual and folk medicinal practices from their European captors and their Amerindian coworkers. Given the limitations of geography and the harsh reality of slave existence, rigid adherence to immutable beliefs and practices was neither feasible nor advantageous. Most importantly, African traditions and beliefs were retained as oral knowledge—compendia of hero legends and healing recipes passed from person to person, from generation to generation. Perhaps ironically, it was the inherent flexibility and fallibility of oral transmission that allowed Africans and their descendants to accommodate what was new and alien, to bend with the winds of social domination, but not break. Rather than a weakness, this malleability proved to be a potent defense against spiritual obliteration. The results, both in Africa and the Americas, were bodies of wisdom perceived by adherents to be religiously conservative, but at the same time supremely adaptable to new cultural and physical environments.

Field research for this project was carried during June–August of 1988, July 1990–January 1991, July–August 1991, and January 1992. I worked in and around the cities of Salvador, Ilhéus, and Itabuna, Bahia. My primary methods included extended interviews and participant observation, as well as field excursions to spiritual gardens, vacant lots, secondary habitats, and primary rainforest. I witnessed dozens of ceremonies and healing rituals and was spiritually cleansed myself on several occasions. Acceptance into Candomblé circles, which is generally closed to outsiders, was greatly facilitated by the friendships

I made in and outside the Candomblé community. It also helped, curiously enough, to bring my young sons to ceremonies. Because children have a special place in Brazilian society, suspicion of this strange red-headed gringo with his funny accent and endless questions was greatly diminished by the sight of my children fiddling with the drums and chasing sacrificial chickens around the temple.

Just as the scope and content of this project evolved over my years of association with Candomblé priests and priestesses, so too did my perception of its practitioners and its role in Brazilian society. I admit to being attracted, in the beginning, to Candomblé's exotic nature—spirits, trance, witchcraft, and the sort. The occult forces have their obvious appeal. Over time, however, as Candomblé appeared less and less arcane and mysterious, I developed a healthy respect for many of its leaders. These are men and women of considerable intelligence and charisma, people limited in their upward social mobility only by their race and class. I also learned that leadership, unfortunately, is motivated as much by ambition and lust for power as it is by altruism. Counted among the ranks of Candomblé healers are unscrupulous charlatans as well as men and women of unquestioned integrity. Differentiating between the two is not always an easy task, either for ailing clients or for enthusiastic researchers.

Rather than focus on the knowledge of a single Candomblé healer, I chose to work with adherents representing all of the major Candomblé traditions—Ketu, Ijexá, Jeje (Vodun), and Candomblé de Angola. These included a total of four Candomblé priests (pais-de-santo) and two priestesses (mães-de-santo), as well as innumerable followers of the faith. Although this survey approach enabled me to document similarities in ethnobotany and healing properties across the range of Candomblé "nations," it did not afford the level of idiographic detail associated with the works of others, such as William Bascom, Lydia Cabrera, and Pierre Verger.

The list of people who contributed to this book, either directly or indirectly, is considerable. To all, I wish to state my sincerest appreciation. I am particularly grateful to Pai Ruy do Carmo Póvoas, who introduced me to the meaning of the leaves, and to Pierre Fatumbi Verger, who unselfishly shared his insights into Yoruba religion and plant classification. I also thank the Candomblé priests and priestesses who were willing to reveal a portion of their plant knowledge, including Pai Pedro, Mãe Maria de Loudres, Pai Vicente Paulo dos Santos, Mãe Esmeralda, Pai Terinho, and Pai Balbino Daniel de Paula. Several spiritual herb dealers, especially Edson Souza (Caboclo) and Djalma Santana, generously provided a different perspective of the Candomblé healing flora. Plant collection benefited from the assistance of Eduardo, Tônia, Dona

Antônia, and Orlando. I also thank Dr. Armando Bandeira for his introduction to the world of Candomblé, as well as Wayt Thomas, Peter Sercombe, Susan Thomas, and an anonymous reviewer of this manuscript for their insightful comments and criticisms.

For introducing me to the forests and people of Bahia, the staff at the Centro de Pesquisa do Cacau herbarium deserve special thanks, especially André Mauricio de Carvalho, Sergio G. da Vinha, Luis A. M. Silva, and Talmon Soares dos Santos. I belatedly thank Hilgard O'R. Sternberg, James J. Parsons, Larry Price, and Herbert Baker for cultivating my initial interest in humans as agents of environmental change. The maps and graphics were kindly produced by Kelly Donovan. Finally, I thank Janira Barcellos Voeks, who took many of the photographs used in the text and helped me appreciate the aesthetic side of Candomblé.

Funding for this project was generously supplied by grants from the National Geographic Society (no. 4247-90) and the National Science Foundation, Geography and Regional Science Division (no. SES 9110306), a National Endowment for the Humanities Summer Stipend Award, a Hughes Faculty Research Award, and a California State University, Fullerton, Summer Stipend Award. Access to historical documents was facilitated by good-natured librarians at the Biblioteca Nacional in Rio de Janeiro (especially the Rare Books and Rare Manuscripts Sections), the Arquivo Público da Bahia in Salvador, the Biblioteca de Geografia e História in Salvador, the Bancroft Library at the University of California at Berkeley (especially the William Bascom Collection), the UCLA Main Library (Rare Book Collection), and the Library of Congress.

SACRED LEAVES OF CANDOMBLÉ

1 INTRODUCTION

The conquest and colonization of Brazil (and of most of the rest of the Americas, for that matter) found inspiration and justification in Christian religious doctrine. The New World provided hoards of pagans to be proselytized, vast new territories to be brought under the domain of the Christian cross, and a golden opportunity to cleanse the medieval church of long-entrenched decadence and corruption. It is true, of course, that this ecclesiastical agenda was decisively undermined by economic and political interests, and that conversion of the native population translated in short order to ethnic genocide of continental proportions. But however steep the price in lives and cultures, these spiritual objectives were ultimately realized on a hitherto unprecedented scale: Iberian Catholicism prospered throughout tropical Middle and South America, while Protestantism came to predominate in temperate North America.

The principal exception to New World Christian hegemony, to total spiritual monopoly by one or another of the monotheistic religions of salvation, occurs not among the descendants of the conquering Europeans, nor among the scattered remnants of the indigenous population, but rather among the least willing of the numerous waves of Old World immigrants to arrive in the Americas—African slaves and their descendants. In spite of the horrific conditions of the Middle Passage, the brutal and dehumanizing influence of plantation existence, and the imposition of an alien and oppressive social structure, Africans managed, remarkably it would seem, to transplant the roots of their native belief systems successfully to the Americas. From New York to Los Angeles, from Cuba to Uruguay, African Americans are chanting the praises of distant African deities, charting their life paths with ancient African divination methods, and healing the body and spirit with African-derived medicine and magic.

The transatlantic diffusion of African-based healing systems was fraught with obstructions. Beyond all the social, economic, and religious impediments that served to limit the implantation of African ethnomedical systems, which were grounded in a spiritual and intellectual worldview that was anathema to Western Christian beliefs, newly arrived healers were confronted with a basic material dilemma: how to continue practicing plant-based medicine and magic in an alien floristic province. For newly arrived West Africans, separated from their healing forests and fields by over two thousand miles of ocean, the bio-geographical differences between the Old and New Worlds represented more than an intellectual curiosity. They meant the difference between staking out a claim to power and influence among their people—perhaps even the ruling class—or acquiescing wholly and forever to the European social order imposed by the oppressors.

A review of those regions dominated by people of African descent suggests that, by whatever means, this ethnobotanical puzzle was solved (Fig. 1.1). African-based religious and ethnomedical systems not only arrived and survived, but much to the chagrin of those who predicted their eventual collapse, they have expanded their geographical ranges, in some cases dramatically. Haitian Vodun, known variously as "hoodoo," "juju," "root work," and "conjure" in North America, has spread from its eighteenth-century introduction in New Orleans to the northeastern and southwestern United States. Bahamian Obea men, purveyors of magic and medicine, are found throughout the Caribbean, the southeastern United States, and Panama. Cuban Santeria, a New World Yoruba belief system that is steeped in African ethnobotanical knowledge, has diffused to Florida, New York, and California, and even as far as Venezuela and Spain. Umbanda, an Afro-Brazilian religion that has incorporated considerable elements from Amerindian and spiritualist sources, is estimated to reach 30 million largely white, middle-class followers. And this list is not exhaustive.[1]

The belief systems that survived with the African diaspora, derived from disparate source regions and following independent New World trajectories, exhibit more differences than similarities. Each adapted to, borrowed from, and was ultimately reformulated by social, political, economic, and religious features that were peculiar to each region. Most neo-African religions have little in common, and some exhibit little more than an odd assortment of

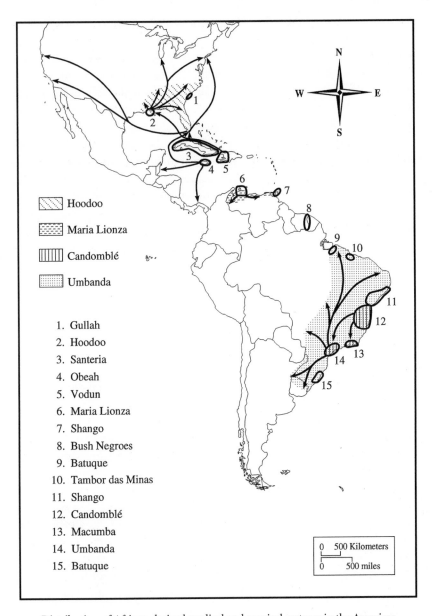

Hoodoo

Maria Lionza

Candomblé

Umbanda

1. Gullah
2. Hoodoo
3. Santeria
4. Obeah
5. Vodun
6. Maria Lionza
7. Shango
8. Bush Negroes
9. Batuque
10. Tambor das Minas
11. Shango
12. Candomblé
13. Macumba
14. Umbanda
15. Batuque

1.1 Distribution of African-derived medical and magical systems in the Americas.

African-derived cultural traits. There is, nevertheless, a thread of common purpose and practice that runs through the New World African religions. They are practical and they are hedonistic. African-derived belief systems concentrate on the resolution of earthly problems, the everyday dilemmas of the here and now, the health and prosperity of adherents and of the African American community at large. Thorny questions about the hereafter—salvation, redemption, and the like—are seldom addressed.

African American belief systems provide a culturally acceptable context within which the origin of health problems can be determined and the process of healing effected. Because illness is perceived to represent reactions to forces outside the realm of secular comprehension, African American religious leaders frequently occupy the social role of community curers, acting as spiritual brokers between the physical and material worlds. Such healing traditions include but are not limited to theories of etiology related to the spiritual realm, the capacity to associate symptoms with specific diseases, and the ability to prescribe and prepare treatments that are related to the source of the problem. Through recourse to the tools of divination, healers concentrate on *why* a patient is suffering, such as spiritual offenses or lack of respect for ancestors, rather than the emotionally unsatisfactory *how* offered by the Western medical profession.[2]

African American healing systems, to a greater or lesser extent, represent the blending of various ethnic and religious traditions. They are the end products of several centuries of New World cultural evolution, far removed from the context of the African reality within which they first developed. It seems pointless to argue for the orthodoxy of one or another African American belief system since rigidly exclusionary systems were probably never found in Africa. Elements of African cosmology and practice diffused gradually from group to group and from region to region—as did beliefs and practices from Islam and Christianity—prior to and during the length of the slave trade.[3] The success of these systems, both in the Old and New World settings, must be attributed in part to their flexibility, their ability to assimilate features that were complementary and useful and to reject those that were not. The vestiges of these native African systems in the Americas are uniquely American: not distant outposts of ancient cultures, but amalgams of African, European, Amerindian, and other traditions.[4]

African American healing systems rely heavily on the use of plants. Trained in the arts of herbalism and magical conjure prior to making the Middle Passage, African priests had developed their native healing systems with reference to a protean Old World tropical flora. Their plant pharmacopoeias were decidedly products of place. In order to continue practicing their vocation in the New World, African priests and their descendants were forced to recreate their healing pharmacopoeias in an alien landscape. By one means or another, they were obviously successful. Notwithstanding the generally low esteem afforded their healing capabilities by outsiders, African Americans managed to incorporate a vast list of plant species into their healing ceremonies and rituals.[5]

It is this process, the means and ends of an ethnobotanical reconstruction that was centuries in the making, the recreation of the Yoruba healing system within the limits imposed by an alien flora and a restrictive European civilization, that is the principal topic of this book. It is a lesson in the dynamic biogeography of culture. I begin near the beginning, before Africans were forced across the sea, when the continents and floristic assemblages of Africa and South America were beginning their separate voyages.

2 THE BAHIAN LANDSCAPE

For recently arrived African slaves, the physical landscape of the captaincy (and, later, the state) of Bahia, Brazil, must have seemed vaguely familiar. The culture and language were incomprehensible, the work regime intolerable, and the level of degradation unbearable, but the general physical setting must have struck a chord of familiarity: brick red soils; a warm, wet climate; and tall evergreen rainforests. Details differed, but the visual panorama corresponded in many respects to the landscape left behind. This similarity was more than superficial. Africans were viewing a mirror image of Mother Africa, a long-lost fraternal twin, one that had changed considerably since continental plate separation, but to the discerning eye was clearly of the same parental stock.

In the Beginning

Until about 135 million years ago, at least until the early Cretaceous period, Africa and South America were joined as the supercontinent of West Gondwana. The now distant coastlines of the South and Equatorial Atlantic represented a single Cretaceous landmass. Even without the mountain of geophysical evidence to support the theory of plate tectonics, the astonishing cartographic fit of eastern Brazil and the Gulf of Guinea point to a common origin sometime in geological history. Their lithospheric neighbors up until the continental breakup—Australia, India, Madagascar, and Antarctica—had drifted away from the supercontinent at an earlier date, leaving behind what would become

Africa and South America to solidify their shared evolutionary history. Although the details of their separation are controversial, it is clear that the southern panhandles of Africa and South America experienced rifting first, ripping apart from south to north, but for some time leaving Africa north of the Niger delta firmly attached to Brazil. Sometime later—certainly by 90 million years ago, and perhaps 5 to 10 million years earlier—Africa and South America were finally torn apart by sea-floor spreading, separated for eternity by the voracious maw of the incipient Atlantic Ocean (Fig. 2.1).[1]

West Gondwana, prior to its fragmentation into Africa and South America, was mantled by a tropical flora of considerable antiquity. Tree ferns, conifers, and palm-like cycads dominated, just as they had for over 100 million years, arborescent forage in the age of dinosaurs. It was at about the time of the plate separation, or perhaps a bit earlier, that the flowering plants first appeared. With a probable origin somewhere in Gondwanaland, the angiosperms would challenge and, in a relatively short time, supplant their more ancient rivals.[2] Early representatives included ancestors of present-day palms (Arecaceae) and custard apples (Annonaceae).[3] The tectonic division of Africa from South America thus set in motion a grand experiment in biogeography. Shared African–South American floristic associations, already in the throes of major membership change, were forced by separation to follow individual evolutionary paths: some elements radiated into myriad new forms, while others followed the well-worn trail to biological oblivion.

One hundred million years later, the flora of Africa and South America appear to have less in common than might be expected if flowering plant diversification had occurred to a great extent prior to fragmentation. All of the world's tropical regions share roughly sixty plant families, but of these, only twelve are essentially restricted to Africa and South America.[4] No families are absolutely restricted to these two continents. The distinctiveness of these two floras, at least at the regional level, is striking as well. The New World tropics have about forty-seven endemic families, including the speciose pineapple (Bromeliaceae) and cactus (Cactaceae) families.[5] So different are the two floras and, in particular, so depauperate is the flora of Africa compared to that of South America, that Africa has been termed the botanical "odd man out."[6] If the floras of these two sister continents had common origins, what happened?

Although the answer is still being unraveled, it is clear that following the early Cretaceous divorce of Africa and South America, the two continents floated off to separate destinies. Africa remained much in the same geographical position, but seems to have received more environmental abuse. Particularly during the Pleistocene ice ages, drops in temperature and precipitation over tropical Africa were dramatic. African lakes dwindled or dried up alto-

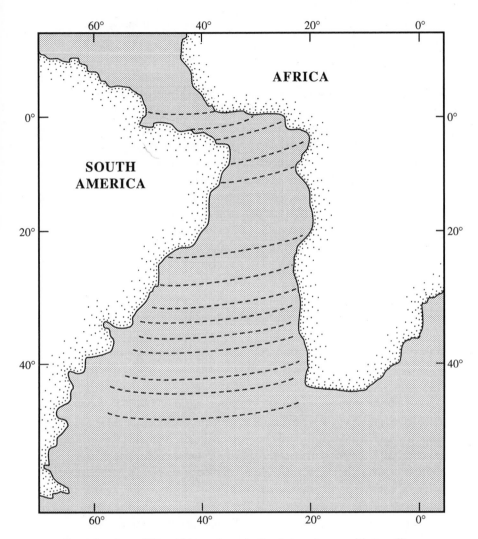

2.1   Coastal regions of West Africa and eastern South America, roughly 84 million years ago (Early Campanian period). The first rifting had begun about 50 million years earlier. (Adapted from Pitman et al. 1993)

gether, glaciers expanded, and vegetation suffered.[7] The temperature dropped by up to 10°C, and precipitation declined by as much as 50 percent. These changes coupled with the generally more active tectonic history (much of tropical Africa was uplifted after the plate division) meant that the wet equatorial climate that Africa once shared with South America went through periods of extreme spatial constriction. The result, predictably, was massive biological extinction.

South America suffered environmental changes that were similar, although apparently less severe than Africa's, and the biological outcome may have been quite different. Various lines of evidence suggest that South America experienced climatic changes during the ice ages, although the environmental evidence has never been as strong as for Africa. Jürgen Haffer, noting the mounting evidence that South America experienced a series of arid cycles during the Pleistocene, has reasoned that regions that are especially wet today would have constituted islands of Pleistocene moisture. Haffer boldly proposes that, unlike the case in Africa, where biodiversity was exterminated by climatic change, South America's climatic fluctuations in fact stimulated Amazonia's species diversity. Surrounded by a sea of savanna and dry forest, island-like Amazonian refuges provided the geographical isolation necessary for taxonomic differentiation.[8] From this point of view, the ice ages in South America were biologically creative rather than destructive.[9]

Following their protracted separation, Africa and South America traveled in different circles, making geological associations that contributed significantly to the later faunal and floral make-up of each. Africa came to be attached to Eurasia, and was thus both a recipient of and a contributor to the great Old World biotic revolutions. Angiosperms took charge, placental mammals appeared, and then, some three million years ago, hairy bipedal hominids showed up. All were major movers in shaping Africa's bioscape, and all would not arrive until much later in South America's prehistory. For its part, South America, as it drifted off toward the west, retained a sporadic relationship with a preglacial Antarctica. This contact allowed for an indirect migratory connection between the New World and such distant lands as Australia and New Zealand, with which South America still shares biotic affinity. Within the last five million years, the Americas, North and South, finally linked up via the Isthmus of Panama, creating a land bridge between these long separated landmasses. The resultant Great American Interchange—perhaps more appropriately termed the First North American Invasion of the South—led to massive marsupial extinction and, ultimately, replacement by their newly arrived placental cousins. Humans, who would go on to modify so much of the Old World's biological landscape prior to the Age of Discovery, arrived in the New World quite late, probably no more than thirty to forty thousand years ago. Clearly, the recipe for both Africa's and South America's biotic assemblages was inventive rather than deterministic. Their biogeographical patterns were the results, in large part, of a pinch of this and a measure of that.[10]

An alternative view, the one I will attempt to develop later, is that the New World that African slaves and their descendants were forced to adopt was not nearly as different from the Old World as most botanists would suggest. There are considerable floristic similarities between the continents, notwithstanding what regional lists suggest. Over two-thirds of the plant families that occur in Africa are also found in South America. At the rank of genus, Africa and South America probably share more than seven hundred different groups.[11] The level of genus (such as oak, beech, maple, or pine) represents the most basic cognitive category in folk categorization of plants, which is to say, it is the rank of plants that people seem universally able to differentiate, to remember, and to give names to, regardless of culture.[12] Some of these plant groups, as will be seen later, formed the basis of simple substitutions of South American species for their closely related African liturgical counterparts. At the same time, although regional floras underpin the "odd man out" concept, studies carried out at the community level in Africa and South America suggest that these floras are in fact remarkably similar. The lowland forests of Africa and South America are dominated by virtually the same families. They share upward of one-third of their genera and, after adjusting for soil and precipitation differences, have nearly identical levels of species richness.[13] This floristic similarity between the two continents, already considerable, was formidably enhanced about five hundred years ago as a result of European colonization.

Landforms and Climate

For Portuguese settlers and their African captives, the coast of Bahia presented something less than a dramatic visual panorama (Fig. 2.2). Characterized by gently contoured surface features—elevated terraces descending to ample sandy beaches—the entire coastline is underlain by deeply decomposed granites and gneisses, intruded when Africa and South America were one with Pangaea. Only well to the interior, removed from the moist forests and cacao plantations, do the ancient igneous rocks yield to younger sedimentary formations. The Bay of All Saints, home to Salvador and to much of the region's early colonization efforts, is a patchwork of fault-derived escarpments, testimony to earlier episodes of tectonic upheaval. Today, seismic activity is rare. And the nearly level 100,000-year-old marine deposits that line the coast suggest that geological stability has characterized the region at least since the late Pleistocene.[14]

Moving north of the Bay of All Saints, the coastal landscape is dominated by tabuleiros, or tablelands, consisting of a diverse array of clayey to sandy

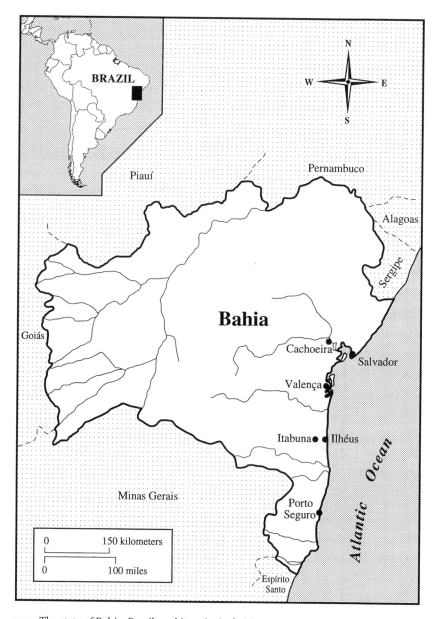

2.2   The state of Bahia, Brazil, and its principal cities.

sediments.[15] Mesa-like in appearance, these Tertiary-aged landforms suggest that the ever-wet tropical climate has yielded to the effects of intermittent arid cycles.[16] The stabilized sand dunes located on the outskirts of Salvador lend support to this arid cycle hypothesis. To the south of the Bay of All Saints, where rainfall figures increase, an excess of weathering, as compared with erosion, has softened the physical landscape. Here the sharp edges of the table mountains grade into gently rounded bluffs. These undulating landforms, responsive to the erosive action of various interglacial marine transgressions, terminate abruptly at a fifteen- to twenty-meter coastal escarpment above the beach. In places, these coastal bluffs degenerate into poorly sorted alluvial fans, providing evidence that the natural erosion control effected by the vegetation has diminished in the past, perhaps due to drier glacial climates during low sea-level stands. Superimposed on these sands and gravels are at least two barely discernible marine terraces, suggesting the occurrence of at least two minor Holocene transgressions.[17]

Most of Bahia's soils developed on the granite and gneissic shield that once was joined with West Africa. Following hundreds of millions of years of weathering under a tropical moist regime, this crystalline parent material has decomposed to such a depth that rock outcrops are fairly rare along the coast. The alternating red and yellow horizons frequently exposed by road cuts attest to the high concentrations of iron and aluminum sesquioxides; both compounds are relatively impervious to further decomposition. Technically known as oxisols, these soils have high concentrations of clay, often approaching 50 percent. Soil nutrient and pH levels are low in these coastal soils, even by tropical forest standards, for reasons that are as yet unclear. Potentially toxic aluminum ions are in abundance, especially as soil depth increases.

The red and yellow oxisols yield in places to coarsely textured, bleached white sands, reminiscent of soils occurring under boreal forests far to the north. Patchy and poorly studied, these spodosolic soils retain physical and chemical conditions even more inimical to plant growth than the more ubiquitous oxisols. Compared to oxisols, these coastal soils exhibit lower levels of magnesium, calcium, potassium, and carbon, higher soil porosity, and more elevated levels of aluminum.[18] Judged by standard agronomic criteria, the edaphic potential of Bahia's natural substrate types—oxisols and spodosols—appears to be limited.

The climate of Bahia is as benign as its landforms, seldom interrupting the flow of human activities. Hurricanes, tornadoes, and freezing temperatures are unheard-of. Trade-wind inversions guarantee that lightning storms are relatively infrequent events. Summer temperatures, from December through February, seldom exceed 30°C. The locals speak with evident discomfort of the chilly Bahian winters, but temperatures in fact seldom drop below 20°C. Even the daily rainfall fails to interfere with human actions, falling with greater frequency after the sun has set.[19]

For a region extending from 12 to 18 degrees south of the equator, coastal Bahia's annual rainfall pattern is remarkably aseasonal. From Valença south to beyond Porto Seguro, the mean annual precipitation of 1600 to 2000 mm falls with reasonable regularity from one month to the next. February usually registers the highest monthly rainfall, and August the least.[20] Summer moisture is derived from water vapor traveling from Amazonia toward Brazil's coastal regions, drawn by the southerly descent of South America's low pressure zone. Reaching as far north and east as Salvador, this moisture is the source of consistent convective rainfall that falls throughout much of the summer. During the winter, the line of tropical convergence migrates to the north, and the coast of Bahia comes under the influence of cold fronts emanating from southern South America. Cold only by equatorial standards, these winter fronts are associated with days upon days of drizzly rainfall activity.[21]

Coastal Bahia stands as an island of tropical moist climate, hemmed in to the north, east, and south by increasingly arid and seasonal conditions. Toward the north, moisture deficits occur as summer rainfall fails to match evaporation and transpiration. Summer drought is the rule. Moving toward the west, away from the marine influence and the coastal cold fronts, winter drought becomes more common. Even further toward the interior, the climate experiences year-round aridity. Below Porto Seguro, high pressure reaches landward from the South Atlantic to block the effects of incoming fronts, resulting in considerably diminished rainfall figures, particularly during Bahia's winter.[22]

Vegetation and Soils

Responsive to the moist tropical climate, Bahia's thin coastal strip, from the table mountains to the sea, is mantled with a verdant layer of evergreen rainforest (Fig. 2.3). Part of a north-south belt of forest stretching from Rio Grande do Norte to Rio Grande do Sul, the Atlantic coastal forests once covered upward of 1 million square kilometers. These tropical forests are now reduced to tiny remnants, many of which occur in southern Bahia. With less than 1 percent of its original forest intact, the Atlantic coastal biome represents one of the most endangered tropical rainforests in the world (Fig. 2.4).[23]

Homogeneously green to the undiscerning eye, Bahia's forested landscape is in fact a mosaic of structurally and floristically distinct vegetation types. Where

2.3 Old-growth rainforest located roughly 70 km south of Ilhéus, Bahia. (Photo: Robert Voeks)

2.4 Recently cut and burned old-growth forest roughly 25 km north of Ilhéus. Area was later given over to cattle pasture. (Photo: Robert Voeks)

rivers join forces with the sea, muddy estuarine environments harbor impenetrable mangrove forests. Above the beach, which is inhabited mostly by cosmopolitan creepers, a strand of heath-type vegetation, five to twenty kilometers wide, inhabits the porous spodosols of the elevated beach terraces. This poorly known vegetation, rich in Bonnetiaceae, Lauraceae, and Arecaceae, grades from low shrubs and sedges to forest thirty meters high. Where this sandy substrate yields to the dominant granite-derived oxisols, these stunted restinga formations yield to the taller forests, the once-ubiquitous broadleaf, evergreen rainforests. Moving even further inland from the coast, the precipitation becomes more and more seasonal, the forest diminishes in stature, and the plants become increasingly drought-deciduous. Finally, increasing aridity toward the west results in a transition from arboreal vegetation to the shrubby **caatinga.** Representing, as Euclides da Cunha commented, "the agonized struggles of a tortured, writhing flora," the **caatinga** is characterized by small, twisted trees, sclerophyllous shrubs, and a host of endemic cacti.[24]

The once-contiguous broadleaf forests, now reduced to isolated patches, are beginning to reveal their secrets. Seldom achieving more than twenty-five meters in height, the trees are neither tall nor massive by tropical forest standards. Although some are supported by the characteristic flaring buttresses, this feature is not as common as in the forests of Amazonia or Southeast Asia. Lianas are common, however, and epiphytes occur on eight out of ten trees encountered. Flowering trees are more likely to be discovered during the spring or summer, although some level of flowering as well as fruiting continues throughout the year.[25]

Bahia's forests are floristically unique, on both the regional and the global scale. Unlike most of the world's rainforests, which are dominated numerically by leguminous trees, the most important family in Bahia's moist forests is the myrtle family (Myrtaceae). Only the moist forests of northeastern Australia exhibit a similar floristic dominance. Tree species richness is as high or higher than that recorded for any other tropical forest. In a one-hectare plot of old-growth forest, a total of 450 tree species over five centimeters in diameter (at breast height) were recently recorded.[26] By comparison, this is more tree species crammed into an area of 100 meters by 100 meters than occur in all of North America. Moreover, the dominance of myrtles and legumes, the high number of lianas, the deficiency of palms and nutmegs (Myristicaceae), and other factors suggest that these formations "are more typical of African forests than South American forests."[27]

Most of the plants and animals that inhabit the Atlantic forests occur nowhere else. Over half of the tree species are restricted to this coastal swath of vegetation, as are 80 percent of the primates and nearly 40 percent of the mammals.[28] These curious biogeographical patterns, as well as the unusually high occurrence of plant groups with primitive characteristics, such as bamboo, led many researchers to conclude that the Atlantic forests had been carved up into island-like refuges during the ice ages, surrounded on all sides by a sea of grassland and dry forest formations. Geographically separated during these protracted arid cycles, the flora and fauna of each forest patch had the time and isolation believed necessary to differentiate into new taxa.[29] Although the validity of the refuge theory is open to question, particularly since Pleistocene arid landforms have been mapped in the middle of what are purported to have been moist forest islands,[30] the uniqueness of the life forms that exist here is not.

By most orthodox measures of biogeographical similarity, Africa and South America have little in common. The combined effects of nature's devices—continental vicariance, 100 million years of geographic isolation, climatic and geomorphic change, and taxonomic divergence—add up to relatively little evidence for a shared floristic ancestry, certainly at the rank of species. African immigrants, by this reckoning, would have been as little familiar with this floristic landscape as if they had they been transported to the Canadian tundra.

There is a serious shortcoming to this system of biological accounting, however—namely, that the botanical products of human intervention are purposely culled from the biotic ledger. As the poor and rather vulgar kin of nature's divine creation, crop plants, medicinals, potherbs, ornamentals, and weeds are routinely trimmed from the list of intercontinental relations. Five centuries of navigating the Atlantic, of advertently and accidentally homogenizing the floras of Africa and South America, are ignored by such a method. As agents of change in the distribution of plants and animals, people are generally judged to be spoilers and destroyers. Yet, however perceived, humans were perhaps the major factor that shaped the biogeography of coastal Bahia, a land that would ultimately play host to an African diaspora and their Old World ethnobotany.

Indigenous Land Use

The sylvan South American landscape that incoming African slaves were obliged to call home had long felt the effects of humans—perhaps not to the degree of the Old World, and certainly not for the same duration, but significantly nonetheless. When fortuitously encountered by Pedro Alvares Cabral on 22 April 1500, the forests of coastal Bahia were inhabited by slash-and-burn cultivators: the Tupinambá, the Tupinaquim, and, recently driven to the interior, the Aimoré.[31] Cabral's scribe, Pero Vaz de Caminha, furnished the first verbal snapshot of Bahia's land and people. Besides their shameless nudity, which he never tired of describing, Caminha was clearly impressed by the robust and healthy nature of a people that possessed no domesticated animals: no goats, cattle, chickens, or pigs. Rather, they subsisted on the products of their hunting and gathering efforts and a few domesticated crop plants.[32] Their principal crops were manioc, chili peppers, pumpkins, broad beans, sweet potatoes, and gourds, supplemented by collection of domesticated passion fruit, cashews, and guavas.[33] Their simple slash-and-burn (swidden) agricultural technique, described by a captured German gunner in the early 1500s, was to "cut down the trees and leave them to dry for one or three months and then set fire to them and burn them. Afterwards they plant the roots [of manioc] between the trunks, from which the roots take sustenance."[34]

Judging by research in contemporary tropical forest societies, the shifting cultivation carried out by Bahia's original rainforest residents was probably more involved than was obvious to early European chroniclers. The pristine landscape, in all likelihood, had been considerably altered well before Europeans arrived. Today, for example, as the plot is being cleared, forest fellers tend to leave those species perceived to be of value, especially fruit, fiber, fodder for game animals, and medicinals, rather than systematically cutting all the trees in a swidden plot. Along with the seeds and seedlings of other useful species gathered from the forest and planted in the plot, these spared individuals guarantee that the site will eventually represent an unnatural concentration of valuable plants, well after the annual plants have been harvested. The floristic effects of such small-scale horticultural practices are in some cases evident for centuries. Seeds of useful wild species are cast along forest trails, later to become collecting points for indigenous residents, and even temporary forest toilets eventually come to represent concentrations of valuable plant resources.[35]

Palms exemplify this process. Their occurrence, often in unexpected clumps and patches, suggests the fading signature of former human habitation.[36] Compared to other moist forest families, palms exhibit an unusual level of tolerance to fire, bordering on adaptation. The seeds of some species, after lying dormant in the soil for years, are stimulated to germinate by the heat of the flames.[37] Others survive burning by maintaining their seedling meristem well below the soil surface, away from the deleterious effects of heat.[38] As adults, most palms are able to withstand the effects of fire better than their dicotyledonous cousins due to the scattering of vascular tissue.[39] Their fire tolerance, considered in light of the multiplicity of uses to which they are put by forest residents, suggests that most tropical palm dispersion patterns are testimony to human rather than natural processes.

Species patterns are modified as well by culturally enforced constraints on forest manipulation. Sacred groves and geological features, the dwelling places of good or malevolent spirits, may pass centuries without feeling the effects of the harvest and the hunt.[40] Long-protected sacred trees, such as West Africa's iroko, India's ficus, or Jamaica's ceiba, attain positions of prominence in their tropical habitats that nature would never have allowed. Taboos against the killing of certain animals, wild pigs or omen birds for example, could conceivably alter plant distributions by modifying coevolved patterns of seed dispersal and pollination.[41] Thus, although there is little direct evidence from Brazil's Atlantic forests, proxy data suggest that the seemingly pristine forests viewed by Cabral and his compatriots may well have represented centuries, if not millennia, of human-induced modification.

Extractive Cycles

The biological changes effected during the pre-European period, subtle but significant, were dwarfed in scale by the tidal wave of changes introduced by the Portuguese settlers. The natives of eastern Brazil, still cutting and chopping with sharpened rock, bone, and wood, were anxious to put the stone age behind them once exposed to the miracle of metal. Entrance into the iron age came quickly, as the Portuguese had early need for the services of the "savages." Having discovered the valuable dyewood pau-brasil (*Caesalpinia echinata*) on Cabral's visit, the Portuguese began to barter iron tools for labor, eager to seduce the Tupinambá into cutting and hauling the logs to the ships. Thus was initiated Brazil's first extractive cycle, one that was from the beginning "wonderfully profitable."[42] Roughly 1,200 tons per year of pau-brasil were extracted during the first few years. In a remarkably short span of time, Bahia's littoral was being scoured clean of the tree from which the entire country would ultimately gain its name. Most importantly, the stone-age indigenous population had gained a tool of unimagined utility for landscape modification. The scope and scale of these forest changes went unrecorded, however.[43]

In 1534, so as to stimulate the colonization effort, King Manuel of Portugal divided Brazil's coastline into nine sections. These captaincies were the sites of the colony's first efforts at settlement. Most were failures. Later, in 1549, an entourage of roughly one thousand Portuguese, commanded by General Tomé de Sousa, established a permanent settlement at Salvador, the colony's first capital, on the Bay of All Saints. Counted among these early settlers were Brazil's first Jesuit missionaries—six, including their leader, Padre Manuel de Nóbrega.[44] Cane plantations and sugar mills soon surrounded the Bay of All Saints and trickled down the coast of Bahia.[45] Sugar represented the highest return on agricultural investment and became the agronomic activity of choice for the status-minded Bahian planter. Settlers were loath to use any land with cane potential for the cultivation of less valuable foodstuffs for their laborers.[46] Bahia's tall forests were cut and cleared for cane production, while the cultivation of manioc, the region's staple food, was directed toward the nutrient-poor soils under <u>restinga</u> vegetation.[47] As most of these tropical podzols occur in southern Bahia, this region became a focus of manioc production for markets around the Bay of All Saints. The area about Ilhéus bore the brunt of manioc cultivation during the early decades of settlement, and by the early 1600's <u>farinha</u> (manioc meal) was produced in sufficient quantities to permit occasional export to Africa and, later, to Europe and to other Brazilian captaincies.[48] During the seventeenth and eighteenth centuries, the region about Valença and Cairú was heavily planted with manioc as well, to feed the burgeoning population of slaves, both indigenous and African, in and around Salvador.[49]

Bahia's second major extractive cycle involved the collection of *piassava* fiber (*Attalea funifera*) from an endemic coastal palm. Able to withstand long periods of immersion in sea water, *piassava* was employed on local ships as a cable material and by the seventeenth century was the cordage material of choice for Atlantic shipping.[50] Later, fashioned into brooms and brushes, the fiber became Bahia's principal export during the nineteenth century. In response to growing international demand, the palm was exploited on a massive and destructive basis. A municipal judge complained in 1881 that exporters were "causing total destruction because . . . they cut the whole tree in order to collect the fiber." [51] Within a few years, *piassava* was economically extinct in the region.[52]

Plantations and Gardens

However destructive and long-lasting Brazil's early cycles of boom and bust, the most enduring biogeographical changes the region would witness were not the outcome of its extractive enterprises. Rather, the Age of Discovery was about to provide transatlantic passage for scores of domesticated plants and untold numbers of their regional varieties. Developed in isolation for nearly ten thousand years, cultivars from all over the world were suddenly able to

bridge the ocean barriers that had long separated them. The effects were star-
tling and without biogeographical precedent. Within a century, most major
crop plants and medicinal species—not to mention livestock, fowl, and beasts
of burden—had been transplanted to the far corners of the tropical world.
Although all the maritime powers would ultimately get involved in the botanical exchange, many of the first introductions were made by the Portuguese.
Aside from their South American holding, they pioneered and for a time dominated the trade routes from Asia and Africa to Europe and South America.
Their trading posts included Mozambique, Mombasa, Goa, Malacca, and Ma-
cao, where for a period they were able to control the international trade in
pepper, cloves, nutmeg, mace, ginger, and other highly sought-after spices.[53]
Intercontinental transfers of cultivated plants were successful in part because
so many of the Portuguese outposts were in tropical latitudes with similarly
warm and ever-wet climates. Moreover, long-distance transfer away from their
place of domestication allowed cultivars to escape many of their coevolved
predators and pests. The botanical similarity of West Africa and eastern Brazil
was about to increase dramatically.

Judged by the glacial momentum of most biogeographical processes, the
pace of floristic exchange between Brazil and the Old World can be reasonably
described as frenetic. Only the rejoining of the South American and African
plates could have more effectively neutralized the floristic differences than the
changes that were set in motion by the European efforts at exploration and
colonization. In his first view of Bahia's vegetation, Padre Nóbrega found the
flora strange and alien; the plants he encountered were "many and different
from those in Hispana. . . ."[54] In 1557, Frenchman John de Léry offered a similar opinion, noting that "there are no trees, or herbs and lastly no fruits, which
are not unlike to ours, except these three plants, purslane, basil royall, and
fearne."[55] But this situation changed quickly. By the end of the sixteenth century, the abundance of newly arrived domesticated plants and animals of Old
World origin moved Padre Fernão Cardim to state that, at least in terms of its
biota, "This Brazil is already another Portugal."[56]

The first wave of introductions were destined for the kitchen gardens and
plantations of the sugar barons and the Jesuits. Judging by the tone of their
correspondence, the Portuguese were bent on replicating their Iberian agrosystem in Bahia, however impractical the goal. Soon Padre Nóbrega could boast
that several species of fruit were acclimatizing well, including grapes, citron,
oranges, lemons, and figs, and that there were plenty of cattle, sheep, and
chickens.[57] Friar Vicente de Salvador in the 1560s could speak of the abundance
of European food in Bahia, including wheat, rice, and yams.[58] Gabriel Soares
de Sousa, who owned a sugar mill south of Salvador, noted the successful cul-

tivation of English plantain (*Plantago major*), basil (*Ocimum canum*), and pennyroyal, all Old World imports.[59] Padre Fernão Cardim reported later that lettuce, cabbage, turnips, mustard, mints, cilantro, peas, onions, and garlic were all doing well in Bahia.[60] In the late 1500s, Father Francisco Soares could add peppermint, quince, fennel, carnations, and roses to the list of European imports.[61] Anthony Knivet reports that many plants were "brought from Portugal, and grow well in the country," including mints, dill, peas, and leeks.[62] Africa was contributing to Bahia's floral facelift as well, according to Padre Joseph de Anchieta, who recorded that "from Guiné there are many squashes and beans, that are better than those from Portugal."[63] By the middle of the next century, Dutch physician Guilherme Piso recorded the growing number of plants common to Brazil and Europe, including sorrel, aloe, lily, thistle, cucumber, calamus, mallow, marsh mallow, purslane, polypody, snakeroot, licorice, sage, smartweed, tamarind, and squash.[64]

On the commercial side, there were concerted efforts on the part of the crown, first to limit the introduction of Asian species to Brazil, and later to encourage it. During the sixteenth century, Portugal's wealth and power rested on its control of the Asian spice trade. In order to preserve his country's mercantile superiority, King Manuel ordered that cultivation of commercially important Asian plants—save ginger—be halted in South America. Within a few decades, however, as the Dutch and English increasingly threatened their control of the spice trade, Portugal's royalty hatched an entirely new strategy. Rather than challenge the interlopers directly, Portugal would facilitate the transplant of Asian crop plants to Brazil, thus providing a home-grown and hopefully cheaper source of these much sought-after commodities. Although the plan ultimately came to nothing, considerable numbers of seeds and seedlings of valuable Asian species were brought to Brazil.[65]

The Portuguese did not limit their botanical transplants to esculent crops. Medicinal plants were being discovered throughout the Portuguese possessions and transferred from colony to colony. A sixteenth-century physician in Goa could claim that "The medicines were never better known than at present, especially by the Portuguese . . . as a result of having transplanted them from one land to another."[66] There was considerable financial incentive to introduce exotic pharmacopoeias, as imported medicines in colonial South American apothecaries were extremely expensive.[67] Anthony Knivet noted, for example, a host of Old World medicinal species that had successfully diffused to Brazil, including thistle, purslane, beets, endive, and basil.[68] Pineapples, native to Northeast Brazil, were introduced by the sixteenth century into West Africa,[69] probably for medicinal as opposed to consumptive reasons, as they were well known to be good "for them that are troubled with the stone."[70] The Reverend

William Bosman reported from the Guinea coast during the seventeenth century that maize, papayas, capsicum peppers, and pineapples—all New World species with medicinal properties—were being cultivated by the Africans.[71] The cashew nut tree, another native of Northeast Brazil, had been introduced by the Portuguese to India and probably to Africa by the sixteenth century. Although the usual explanation for its transport to these distant lands was its value in erosion control, the cashew may well have been introduced for its medicinal properties, as it was employed in colonial Brazil to treat fevers.[72]

Tobacco (*Nicotiana tabacum*) was widely regarded as a medicinal species and probably owes its dispersal throughout the world to this early use. Native to the Americas, tobacco was integral to indigenous healing ceremonies. According to the early Jesuit accounts, swallowing the smoke "greatly aids digestion and other problems."[73] It was being cultivated in Europe by the late sixteenth century, and in Africa by at least the seventeenth century. Early eighteenth-century West Africans were fond of "this devilish weed" which "stinks so abominably."[74] Its reputation for healing properties soon gave way to the notion that this foul-smelling smoke was the invention of the devil, and Popes Urban VIII and Innocent XI sought to discourage its use by excommunication. Although smoking tobacco in Europe was eventually punished by cutting off the offender's nose, by the seventeenth century this New World weed had become too widely dispersed and accepted as a chemically addictive social custom to be effectively prohibited.[75]

One of the European imports that clearly owes its distribution to its medicinal and magical properties is rue (*Ruta graveolens*). This small cultivated shrub has a long history of ethnomedical use, extending back to the Greek and Roman empires, where it served as a panacea for all ailments.[76] Roman ladies are said to have hidden cuttings from rue in their clothing to fend off evil eye. It was popular enough to merit mention in the Bible (Luke 11:42).[77] Although it is not clear when rue was brought to Brazil, it must have arrived early, as physician Luis Ferreyra was able to recommend its medicinal use by the early 1700s.[78] French traveler Jean Baptiste Debret reported its use among Rio de Janeiro's Afro-Brazilian population in the 1830s. He noted that they hid it inside their turbans or behind their ears as protection from bad luck. They also prepared it as an infusion to induce abortion.[79] Now dispersed widely throughout the New World, rue continues to be employed for magical and medical properties. In Cuba, it is used by Lucumí followers against witches and bad spirits.[80] Afro-Brazilians continue to wear it behind the ear or hidden on their body as a form of protection against evil eye, as well as preparing it for myriad medicinal ailments (Fig. 2.5).

2.5   Rue (*Ruta graveolens*) being worn by a Bahian street vendor in Salvador to ward off evil eye. (Photo: Janira Voeks)

In West Africa, crop plants traditionally served both food and medicinal purposes. Grains, fruits, and tubers served to sustain the body, while leaves, bark, and roots from the same plants were employed to heal it. Because so many crop plants retained medicinal properties, the introduction of Old World food plants to feed a burgeoning African slave population inadvertently supplied bondsmen with an array of familiar medicinals. The South American peanut is a good example. Naturalized by the Portuguese in West Africa, peanuts were incorporated into various African ethnomedical systems. Later, it made its way to the Caribbean, where it continued its dual function as food and medicine for captive African slaves.[81] Likewise the lemon, originally brought from Southeast Asia, ultimately found its way to Africa and South America, where it served more as a medicinal than as a food product.[82] Okra, an African domesticate introduced as a staple food for the slave population, was employed as an abortifacient by African slaves in eighteenth-century Guyana.[83] Other early introductions of medicinal food crops included winged yam, pigeon pea, sorghum, oil palm, watermelon, akee, and black-eyed pea, all of which were exploited for both medicinal and consumptive ends.[84]

Species were also introduced purely for their medicinal and liturgical value.[85] Imported spice plants from Africa and Asia, such as cinnamon, ginger, pepper, and cloves, were common constituents of early European pharmacopoeias. Their use in medicinal recipes is traced at least to the ninth century.[86] The African kola nut (**obí**) is a case in point. Belonging to two tree species, *Cola acuminata* and *C. nitida*, kola nuts have long been prized as stimulants. Native to West Africa, the kola nut formed the mainstay of the twelfth- to sixteenth-century Arab trade route from the Gulf of Guinea across the Sahara to North Africa.[87] These kola caravans, moving their product by camel from the orchards of Ghana to the markets on the Mediterranean, were controlled by the Muslim Hausa in the seventeenth through nineteenth centuries.[88] Sucking the juice out of the nuts, seventeenth-century Africans and Europeans used kola as a type of "African betel," according to William Bosman.[89] Kola was used extensively by West Africans in the early nineteenth century,[90] and this demand stretched across the Atlantic to the New World African population. Frederic Welwitsch reported from Angola in the mid-1800s that the nuts represented a lucrative item of export to South America, being "much sought out by the slaves there imported from Africa."[91] This enterprise was also pursued by slaves who had bought their own freedom, such as José Francisco do Santos. Returning to Whyda, Dahomey, from Brazil, he carried on a successful business from the 1840s to the 1870s shipping slaves and later palm oil and kola nuts to Bahia.[92] Seeds were undoubtedly planted during the latter part of the

nineteenth century: by the early part of this century, there were several recorded kola groves in Bahia.[93] Employed in African divination and initiation
ceremonies in the Old and New Worlds, kola continued as an item of trade to
Brazil and Cuba throughout this century, and can still be found in the street
markets of Salvador, Bahia.[94]

The flora of colonial Bahia was enriched by an endless assortment of Old
World cultivars. But in spite of these successes, Bahia's weak tropical soils
proved a disappointment for those attempting to transplant their Portuguese
agrosystem. Padre Ambrosio Pires lamented early in Bahia's settlement that
once the land had been cleared, after two or three years of harvest, the soil
"becomes sterile and unable to produce anything."[95] The dark massapês were
best for cane, but the ubiquitous latosols, according to Padre André Antonil,
"weaken quickly."[96] Forest clearance and soil exhaustion, combined with the
introduction of so many exotic cultivars and domesticated livestock, translated
to a landscape ripe for the invasion of Old World weeds. Although their arrival
was not recorded with the fanfare afforded the useful cultivars, weeds had undoubtedly slipped into Bahia with the first Europeans, and have continued
their transatlantic intrusion to the present.[97]

Weeds

Some of the earliest weeds to invade the increasingly disturbed Bahian landscape must have been exotic grasses. Having persevered through thousands of
years of treading and chewing by sheep, cattle, goats, and horses, Old World
grasses had developed a tenacity and dispersibility that far outstripped that of
their New World rivals. Their diffusion to the Americas, according to James
Parsons, "may be one of the most rapid and significant ecologic invasions in
the earth's history."[98] As the Portuguese imported domesticated grains such as
wheat, rice, and oats for their nascent horticultural experiments, copycat weed
seeds undoubtedly slipped in as well. Slave ships coming from Africa dumped
their soiled straw bedding on the shore, providing another direct means of
weed immigration. Some weeds were purposely imported as ornamentals and
curiosities for botanical gardens, while others were introduced for livestock
forage value. By whatever means, the "Africanization" of Brazil's disturbed
areas resulted in the spread of forty-four species of African grasses alone.[99]

The castor bean plant (*Ricinus communis*) is another African weed with a
lengthy ethnomedical history. Readily dispersed by means of its barbed and
occasionally explosive fruits, the castor bean is considered a noxious weed of
cosmopolitan distribution. Castor bean seeds have been excavated from six-

thousand-year-old Egyptian tombs, suggesting an early appreciation of its purgative properties. The Bible suggests that its broad palmate leaves provided shade for Jonah.[100] The castor bean had arrived and been exploited medicinally in Cuba by at least the early nineteenth century,[101] and botanist Karl von Martius listed the species as a common Brazilian medicinal in the early 1800s.[102] It may have been introduced into California during the Spanish colonial period as a medicinal.[103] Widely dispersed in Africa and the Americas, the castor bean has retained its notorious reputation as an unpleasant purgative.[104] Adopted by West Africans and their Brazilian diaspora, castor bean is known by its Yoruba name, **ewe lara,** on both sides of the Atlantic and continues to be employed by both groups for similar ritual purposes.[105]

English plantain (*Plantago major*) ranks as one of the world's worst weeds.[106] It also ranks as one of the world's most widely employed medicinals. Native to western Europe, this tap-rooted perennial herb has colonized at least fifty countries, trying the patience of gardeners on six of the seven continents. Long before its close association with humans, plantain was a tenacious pioneer plant, quickly colonizing ground made bare as the Pleistocene ice masses relaxed their grip on Europe. Accustomed to a life of chance and opportunism, plantain was supremely preadapted to occupy a disturbance regime when humans began, a few millennia later, seriously modifying the natural landscape.[107] Although it does exhibit temperature and soil limitations and apparently does not compete well in moist tropical forests, plantain can survive and compete in almost every physiographic province, from tundra to tropical savanna, provided it finds a sufficiently disturbed location. It grows best where disturbance is most severe and treading is most intense. Because individuals produce upward of fourteen thousand sticky seeds per year, dispersal is not a major impediment to diffusion.[108]

Before the Age of Discovery, plantain was widely used as a medicinal in medieval Europe, where it was considered to be "a plant with extraordinary virtues." [109] In spite of its amazing ability to diffuse, plantain was apparently introduced to Brazil purposely in the sixteenth century, probably for its medicinal properties. Gabriel Soares de Sousa, in his commentary on the successful cultivation of European spices and medicinals in Bahia, noted that plantain (transagem) was "already well distributed." [110] This species is still recognized as a medicinal in West Africa and Brazil, although at least in Bahia it is cultivated rather than appearing spontaneously.[111]

Originally native to India, **dandá,** or **dandá**-da-costa (*Cyperus rotundus*), can rightfully be called the king of weeds. An herbal imperialist of global proportions, this wetland sedge is perhaps more effective than any other species in colonizing and occupying space. It is able to persevere through extremes of floods, drought, and whatever nature chooses to dish out. At last count this species had achieved noxious weed status in ninety-two countries.[112] Although its arrival in Brazil went unnoticed, **dandá** was undoubtedly recognized as an Old World native by early African immigrants. It retained most of its African magical uses and, in Bahia, is known only by its Yoruba vernacular name (Fig. 2.6).

Folha-da-costa (*Kalanchoe integra*) and folha-da-fortuna (*Kalanchoe pinnata*) are two morphologically similar species that are employed for similar medicinal purposes almost everywhere they occur. The former is native to the Americas; the latter, to the Old World tropics. Both have become pantropical weeds and garden cultivars in Africa, Asia, and the Americas. In locations as geographically distant as Ghana, peninsular Malaysia, Borneo, Colombia, the Caribbean, and Brazil, the afflicted secure a leaf compress of one or both species on their foreheads in the hope of relieving migraine headaches.[113] West Africans arriving in Brazil must have recognized folha-da-costa, as it serves similar purposes in both regions and is known in Bahia by its Yoruba cognate, **ewe dudu.**[114]

Afro-Brazilians recognize that elements of their local ethnoflora also inhabit their West African homeland. While discussing one or another plant with a priest, I was often informed with assurance that "they [Africans] also have it." The vernacular name is in some cases a giveaway. The Bahian name for *Kalanchoe integra*, folha-da-costa, translates in Portuguese to 'leaf of the coast,' telling the user that this species, or one very similar, occurs on the west coast of Africa. **Obí**-da-costa (*Cola acuminata*) is the domesticated kola nut, which, as mentioned earlier, is a West African native used by Candomblé adherents in divination ceremonies and initiation. The names **dandá**-da-costa (*Cyperus rotundus*) and pimenta-da-costa (*Aframomum melegueta*) transmit similar messages to the user. Likewise, taxa that refer to the Yoruba pantheon are usually present on both shores. For example, tapete-de-Oxalá 'Oxalá's carpet' (*Plectranthus amboinicus*), espada-de-Ogun 'Ogun's lance' (*Sansevieria* cf. *aethiopica*), and **tiririca**-de-Exu 'Exu's **tiririca**' (*Scleria* sp.) inhabit both sides of the Atlantic and serve similar liturgical functions.

Whether the product of advertent importation or chance arrival, most species that inhabit the coasts of Africa and South America owe their pantropical distribution to the actions of humans. Very few species made the transatlantic journey on their own. Those that did, such as beach morning-glory (*Ipomoea pes-caprae*), attained their cosmopolitan ranges by means of their inherent dispersal capabilities. Well-adapted to long-range sea dispersal, this tenacious

2.6 **Dandá** (*Cyperus rotundus*) for sale in Salvador herb stand. Magical powers are associated with chewing the rhizome. (Photo: Janira Voeks)

beach vine is one of the first species to appear on shorelines after hurricanes. It was also one of the first plants to colonize Krakatau after the 1883 cataclysm.[115] It was recognized in early seventeenth-century Bahia by Friar Vicente do Salvador, who noted that it retained the same medicinal use as it did in Portugal.[116] Beach morning-glory must have arrived in Brazil prior to colonization by Europeans, as it was known by an indigenous name—***tetigcucú***—by the Tupinambá in the sixteenth century.[117] Today, it retains the vernacular name, **aboro aibá,** and similar liturgical uses among both the African Yoruba and their descendants in Brazil.[118]

The bottle gourd (*Lagenaria siceraria*), or cabaça as it is known in Brazil, arrived in the Americas and was being cultivated several millennia before the Iberian conquest. Perhaps native to West Africa, its cultural history stretches back at least twelve thousand years in the Old World, and some seven to fifteen thousand years in the New World.[119] Whether cultivated or a spontaneous trash-heap plant, the cabaça is supremely adapted to long-distance oceanic transport. Its seeds retain viability for long periods of time in its water-resistant containers, time enough to navigate the currents of the Atlantic.[120] The presence of cabaça in Brazil may have been of more than material interest to newly arrived Africans. For the Yoruba and their American diaspora, a cabaça that is cut into halves symbolizes the division of the two worlds—the spiritual and the material—which are separate but equal, like the hemispheres of a cabaça. A more forceful message that the African deities were already present in the New World is difficult to conjure.

The process of floristic reconciliation between Africa and its estranged South American partner, initiated by the arrival of Europeans, continues to this day. The exchange of taxa between the continents, intentional and accidental, continues to blur botanical distinctions set in motion 100 million years ago. Fully twenty percent of the flora recorded for the Outer Leeward Islands is alien.[121] In the 1940s, even a cursory botanical survey turned up over one hundred exotic species in Bahia, many of which had been introduced only recently.[122] Plant introduction can be a quirky process, subject to human caprices. A maid in Aruba, for example, noted that she had personally brought oregano (*Lippia alba*) from Curaçao to treat stomach ailments, and that it is now widespread in the neighborhood.[123] A Santeria adherent I met in Miami, unable to find a local source of plantain (*Plantago major*), showed me the plant she had grown from seed sent by her sister in Cuba.

Akokô (*Newbouldia laevis*) is a case in point. Endemic to West Africa, this tree is known in Bahia only by its Yoruba lexeme. Easily propagated by stem cuttings, **akokô** in West Africa is used as a living fence and serves as a treatment for a multitude of medical complaints, from epilepsy to earache, heart disease to hemorrhoids.[124] As the species is held in spiritual regard by the Yoruba, it is often cultivated as a hedge around shrines. Cutting or burning of this sacred tree is avoided.[125] Although the **akokô** was held in considerable esteem by Candomblé adherents in Bahia, apparently only one jealously guarded individual existed in the 1940s. To satisfy the demand, anthropologist Pierre Verger carried some cuttings back from Nigeria and gave them to several Candomblé houses in Salvador. African **akokô** is now a relatively common liturgical species in Salvador.[126] I took some cuttings from Salvador to Ruy Póvoas's Candomblé temple in Itabuna in 1991, and at last report they were doing well.

In the centuries since Cabral's landfall, Bahia's flora has come to resemble that of many other tropical forest regions: an ocean of homogeneous agricultural crop plants and their associated weeds, punctuated by the occasional island-like stand of pre-Columbian flora. The divisive forces that yanked apart the Cretaceous African–South American biome have been counteracted by five centuries of human-induced floristic reconciliation, as close to a continental reunion as Africa and South America will ever witness. Thus, the floristic landscape that Africans encountered in Brazil, dominated by sugar, cacao, oil palm, coffee, and a host of pasture grasses, was pretty much what they had left behind in Africa. The major botanical differences, found mainly in the old-growth forests, dwindled as deforestation progressed. Afro-Brazilian ethnobotany would never be based on knowledge of the jungle. Their understanding of plants, particularly the healing flora, would be assimilated from indigenous sources, picked up from their European masters, and, ultimately, blended with the traditional knowledge of their ancestors.

3 INDIANS AND AFRICANS

"It is very healthy," proclaimed Manuel Nóbrega about Bahia soon after his arrival in 1549, and he boasted that those few who do fall ill, "we cure quickly." [1] Flushed with the optimism of youth and spiritual conviction, the good brother prematurely envisioned the new land to be a refuge from the disease and pestilence that had long plagued Europe. The native Tupinambá, robust, healthy, and estimated to survive 150 years or more, reinforced this initial perception.[2] Elderly and diseased Portuguese who wished to restore their youth and vigor were soon being advised to visit the distant colony and take advantage of the healthy air and "good winds." [3] For those very few who take sick, proclaimed Vicente do Salvador, "there are not illnesses in this land against which there are not herbs." [4]

Virgin Soil Epidemics

Unfortunately for Bahia's native inhabitants, the disease-free paradise described by Padre Nóbrega was short-lived. In Brazil and throughout the New World, the arrival of missionaries, adventurers, and colonists signaled the introduction of a flotilla of Old World viruses, bacteria, protozoa, and parasites. "The European colonizer," according to medical historian Lopes Rodrigues, "was the vehicle of disease that was unknown to the virgin bosom of the Brazilian jungle." [5]

Native Americans certainly suffered from illness prior to the arrival of Europeans. Syphilis, for example, was clearly endemic to the Americas, and its unintentional transference to the European interlopers represented a vengeful gift of considerable significance. And, judging from present-day indigenous pharmacopoeias, tropical forest dwellers must have suffered a host of common maladies—skin disorders, snake bites, fevers, and sundry fungal infections. But by most estimates, the New World was relatively contagion-free. This favorable situation must have been fostered by the dispersed nature of many New World populations. In the Atlantic forests of Brazil, the pre-Portuguese population density was only 0.3–0.4 persons per square kilometer, hindering the spread of infectious disease. For the local Tupinambá and Tupinaquim, incessant warfare and cannibalism were probably more decisive implements of population regulation.[6] In any case, the arrival of the Portuguese changed this situation forever.

Ten thousand years of blissful quarantine had left native Americans immunologically unprepared for European-style germ warfare. As the first of many biological invasions swept through the long-isolated and poorly protected Americas, romantic visions of a salubrious American Eden, free of illness and aging, yielded to the brutal reality of epidemics and premature death. Indigenous people succumbed in droves to exotic diseases; Mediterranean colonists battled hitherto unknown tropical maladies; and soon, imported African slave laborers, overworked and underfed, would fall prey to both.[7]

There was a vague understanding among the Tupinambá, even in the beginning, that the presence of the foreign fathers was somehow at the root of the growing health crisis. When the first of their numbers to be baptized suddenly fell ill, the *pajés* (native shamans) claimed with some intuition that the Jesuits were poisoning them "with the baptismal water and with the doctrine of death."[8] In some areas, when the natives saw Jesuits approaching, they burned salt and pepper to drive off the anticipated impending illness.[9] But these initial contacts were of relatively minor medical significance. The complete demographic collapse of the indigenous population would begin in earnest shortly, driven by the plantation masters' hunger for slaves and the padres' desire for souls.

Sugar plantation owners initially bartered beads and metal tools to meet their labor needs. But indigenous workers proved to be unreliable and easily distracted. Several thousand years of a simple shifting-cultivation mode of subsistence had left the Tupinambá ill-prepared for the dawn-till-dusk drudgery of plantation existence. With few Indians willing or able to tolerate plantation life, the owners quickly resorted to slavery of the Tupinambá to meet their growing labor needs. Although enslavement of the native population was officially banned from the outset of the colonization effort, slaves were often acquired during "just wars" with intransigent indigenous groups who refused to acquiesce to Portuguese control.[10] Others were ransomed legally after having been taken prisoner by another indigenous group, since slavery under Christian planters was viewed by the crown and the church as preferable to ending up in the stomachs of their cannibalistic captors. Working conditions in the sugar mills were as close to hell as the pagan Tupinambá would ever experience, and mortality figures were, not surprisingly, astronomical.

The Jesuits, often portrayed as the saviors of the natives, were in their own way perhaps more efficient Indian exterminators than their rivals on the plantations. After initially carrying their message of salvation directly into the forest, the padres discovered that such a conversion strategy was both ineffective and ephemeral. As a result, they revised their proselytization policy: they rounded up thousands of Indians and crowded them into mission villages. Within only a few years of arriving in Bahia, the Jesuits could boast of thirty-four thousand Indians living in eleven villages.[11] The consequences were devastating. Overwork, cramped living quarters, and a lack of natural resistance made native Brazilians particularly susceptible to the impact of Old World microbes. Smallpox and other contagious diseases raced through the population within a few short years of European arrival. Some thirty thousand mission Indians perished during the smallpox epidemic of 1562–1563.[12] This was only the first of a long list of pandemics, mostly of African origin, that would decimate the indigenous and later the Afro-Brazilian population.[13] Being "obsessed with their personal soul-count," the Jesuits apparently believed it was better for the native peoples to be baptized and buried than pagan and alive.[14] By the end of the century, less than seventy years into the colonization effort—an imperialist action justified on the grounds of bringing the one true god to the gentle heathens—roughly 95 percent of the Atlantic forest's indigenous population had disappeared.[15]

Colonial Medicine

The epidemics that raged through the new colony encountered little qualified resistance from the nascent medical community. Colonial doctors, few in number and often self-trained, offered the best medical care that medieval and Renaissance Europe was prepared to offer. Physicians, surgeons, bleeders, and priests, whose views on causation ranged from astrological imbalances to the effects of malevolent spirits and bad air, responded to the best of their abilities to the ensuing epidemics.[16] Besides cutting hair and shaving beards, barbers pitched in with "a little surgery . . . blood letting, [and] scarification."[17] So that the disease would find only "healthy" blood (which, in theory, was less easily infected), Indians stood in long lines waiting for the musicians and smiths employed to open their veins, reddening the streets with the result of their treatment.[18] Colonial medicine was characterized by "the lowest level of ignorance and incompetence, arising from that alarming decadence of Portuguese medicine."[19]

The Jesuits represented the first and usually last Western medical attention that the indigenous population would experience. Initially ill-prepared for this role, the padres gradually assimilated what medicinal knowledge they could: a little bloodletting here, some imported powders there, always mixed with a heavy dose of praying to the appropriate saint. Most importantly, they learned the properties of the local medicinal herbs from the indigenous folk and ultimately became the instruments through which elements of the native Brazilian plant pharmacopoeia would become naturalized throughout the Portuguese empire.[20] If the Age of Discovery represented a harbinger of genocide for many isolated indigenous societies, it at least served to break up some of the regional monopolies on the earth's medicinal plant wealth. Sixteenth-century Spanish physician Nicholas Monardes was sanguine on the topic: the medicinal "Trees, Plants, Hearbes, Rootes . . . exceed much in value and price" all the gold and silver from the new lands, he wrote. The New World discoveries had revealed "new medicines, and new remedies, which, if we did lack them, [the new diseases] would be incurable."[21] The Portuguese physician Garcia Orta made a similar observation from his post in Goa, noting that "each day brings new diseases . . . and God is so merciful that in each land He gives us medicines to cure us. He who causes the illness provides the medicine for it."[22] Such optimism ignored the plight of Brazil's indigenous populations, however, who did not find much mercy in the god of the whites or in his medicines.

The Bahian Jesuits recognized that the jungle flora harbored a cornucopia of covert plant medicines. Colonists such as plantation owner Gabriel Soares de Sousa came to understood the value of the native pharmacopoeia, "the effectiveness [of which] is great compared to that of Portugal."[23] The padres also realized that the key to unlocking these secrets was kept by the Tupinambá shamans, who were focal points of indigenous collective knowledge. The shamans were "barbarous," to be sure, but at the same time many were privy to "herbs and other medicines" that were sorely needed in the colony.[24] Although eager to exploit some of this native intellectual property, the Jesuits nevertheless faced a serious moral and practical dilemma in doing so. Because they were recognized by the tribal people as influential leaders, healers, and purveyors of witchcraft and sorcery, shamans represented the principal impediments to wholesale catechism.[25] They were instruments of the devil who spread their evil influence by their barbaric healing ceremonies.[26] If the Jesuit spiritual quest were to be successful, the tribal religious leaders needed to be humiliated and degraded in front of their vassals. The process was outlined in a letter by Padre Nóbrega, who related the story of a famous Tupinambá shaman who claimed to be a god. After being verbally browbeaten by the good brothers, he begged to be baptized into the Christian faith "and now is one of the converted."[27] Only after being thoroughly demoralized were the shamans encouraged to divulge their medicinal secrets.[28]

Indigenous Medicine and Magic

At the time of European contact, the coastal indigenous people had a well-developed ethnomedical system, one strikingly similar in form and function to that which was arriving on the African slave ships. Shamanistic duties were roughly divided between the **pajés,** who tended to physical illness, and the **caraibes,** who acted as diviners and intermediaries with the spiritual realm.[29] Although Jean Léry believed that, aside from the devil, the natives "neither acknowledge nor worship any false gods,"[30] it is clear from various sixteenth-century narratives that the coastal Tupi speakers retained a rich pantheon to which they directly connected medical and spiritual problems. Their deities included a high god, Monan, who introduced mankind to horticulture, as well as a host of lesser animistic entities associated with the secrets of fire, water, forest, and health.[31] Coastal people also recognized and feared "a prophet called Toupan," the god of lightning, thunder, and rain, who "revealeth secrets to their Caraibes."[32] Celestial bodies such as the sun, moon, and stars, blocked out by the verdant forest canopy, appear not to have rated deification. The cosmology of the coastal Indians was perhaps as rich as that of the bearded invaders who were attempting to convert them.

Important ceremonies drew **caraibes** from distant territories.[33] Central to these group encounters was the possession trance of religious adherents, an opportunity for the deities to manifest on earth in the bodies of mortals. Hans Staden described how "They go first to a hut and take all the women . . . and fumigate them. After this, the women have to jump and yell and run about until they become so exhausted that they fall down as if they were dead . . . [after which the women] are able to foretell future things."[34] After dancing and singing in a circle, according to Jean Léry, the women would begin to foam at the mouth and "suddenly become possessed with the devil."[35] The women were initiated into witchcraft "by such ceremonies as smoke, dancing, etc . . . and make her able to foretell things to come . . . and pretend conference with spirits."[36] Women clearly represented the principal vehicle of communication between the material and spiritual realms.

Tobacco (*Nicotiana tabacum*) was widely employed by the traveling shamans. Jean Léry observed that "with a very long cane, wherein they put the herbe Petem [tobacco] set on fire, they . . . blew out the fume of that herbe upon them that stood round about them with these words: Receive the spirit of fortitude, whereby you may all overcome your enemies."[37] The Portuguese community also came to appreciate the effects of tobacco, perhaps to a fault, for its ability to stave off the effects of hunger and thirst.[38] Anthony Knivet describes the European addiction to this "holy herb," noting that they are "all day and all night laid in their nets [hammocks], to drink this smoke, and are drunk with it as if it were wine. . . ."[39] While acknowledging the reputed medicinal benefits of tobacco, the Jesuits nevertheless refrained from its use, so as not to "conform with the unfaithful, that appreciate it greatly."[40] By the end of the century, tobacco was being cultivated in the hills of Portugal, and Europeans throughout the Old World had acquired the habit of swallowing the sacred smoke.[41] The slave population in the New World appears to have picked up the practice early, as Monardes could observe in the 1570s that "The black people that have gone . . . to the Indias, have practiced the same manner and use of the tobacco."[42] Most importantly, tobacco was in the process of being introduced to West Africa, where its medicinal and liturgical properties would be incorporated into local ethnomedical traditions and would eventually make the return journey via slave ships to Brazil and other points in the African American landscape.[43]

The most sacred object of the Tupinambá was the rattle gourd, fashioned from the pantropical cabaça (*Lagenaria siceraria*). Padre Nóbrega stated that they placed human figures inside the gourd so as to effect their magic.[44] Hans Staden reported, "They put their faith in a thing shaped like a pumpkin . . . filling it with small stones so that it rattles. They shake it about when they sing and dance, and call it Tammaraka, and each man has one of his own." The power of the sacred gourd was reinforced by the traveling shamans, who fumigated it "with a herb called Bittin [tobacco]."[45] The bottle gourd, as noted earlier, was one of the few species common to South America and Africa prior to the fifteenth century. Its presence in Brazil, like that of tobacco, allowed African slaves and their descendants to carry on their own ceremonies and to adopt some of those of the soon-to-be-extinct Tupinambá.[46]

With a host of novel tropical maladies to contend with, the burgeoning Portuguese community experimented with and ultimately assimilated many elements of the native plant pharmacopoeia. They prepared lengthy descriptions of the native medicinals, including species identifications, methods of preparation, and purported health benefits.[47] They learned what modern pharmacologists would understand later, that certain species should be picked at a certain point in the plant's life cycle in order to guarantee the presence of the active properties.[48] Over time, a few of these local medicinals were discovered to be so effective that they were incorporated into Western medicine. The roots of *Cephaelis ipecacuanha*, known in colonial times by the Tupi name *ipecacuanha,* was employed medicinally for its antihemorrhage properties. It later became the source of pharmaceutical *ipecac.* Pilocarpine, the major treatment for glaucoma, was derived from the local medicinal shrub *jaborandi* (*Pilocarpus jaborandi*). The enzyme papain was extracted from papaya and used as a digestive aid as well as a meat tenderizer. Pineapple lost its value as a folk remedy in Bahia but was developed by Western medicine into the anti-inflammatory drug bromelain.[49]

The Portuguese came to understand the healing properties of other native plants. Most, unfortunately, were inadequately described in early documents, and their identities have faded with the centuries. A few, however, have retained their original names and continue to be employed for their perceived medicinal properties. These include *capeba* (*Pothomorphe umbellata*) (Fig. 3.1), fedegoso (*Senna occidentalis*), *embaúba* (*Cecropia pachystachya*), alfavaquinha-de-cobra (*Peperomia pellucida*), and *jurubeba* (*Solanum* sp.).[50]

However profound the medicinal knowledge of the Tupinambá, and whatever value their ultimate contribution to medicine—folk and, later, Western—their healing flora and magical medicine proved no match for plantation slavers, religious zealots, and alien diseases. Given the often small size and isolated nature of indigenous settlements, contagious disease was probably never a serious problem among South America's pre-Columbian swidden societies. Their plant pharmacopoeias, no doubt oriented toward treating simple infections, parasites, and the like, would have little prepared them for the likes of such a microbial onslaught, particularly by so virulent a killer as smallpox.[51] The Tupinambá treated smallpox by digging a hole, lining it with burning coals, pouring on special herbs, and laying the patient in the steaming mass.[52] If smallpox didn't kill the patient, the herbal heat treatment probably did. They also practiced bloodletting, which was undoubtedly picked up from the Portuguese, and employed hot and cold herbal baths.[53] Fumigation and sucking the skin of the patient were also common treatments.[54] Infusions were

3.1 **Capeba** (*Pothomorphe umbellata*) growing in second-growth forest. The use of this plant to treat kidney and liver ailments, dating as far back as the sixteenth century, appears to have been learned from the indigenous population. (Photo: Robert Voeks)

employed for various medicinal ends, including as abortifacients.[55] The Tupinambá must have marshaled all of their time-tested therapies and watched them fail. Few of their numbers survived into the seventeenth century.

The population vacuum created by the extirpation of the Tupinambá and other coastal societies forced the Jesuits to seek ever-more-distant sources of indigenous souls. The plantation masters mined the interior for their workforce as well, but soon shifted the source region for their ever-expanding labor needs to the west coast of Africa. The role of the indigenous healers, the *pajés* and the *caraibes*, vanished within a few short decades of colonization, to be replaced by European physicians, priests, and charlatans, soon followed by the ethnomedical traditions of newly arriving Africans.

African Immigration

African slaves had reached the shores of Brazil by the 1530s, first as supplements and later as substitutes for the dwindling aboriginal workforce. When the first Africans arrived in Bahia is unknown, but they were certainly present by the 1550s. Padre Nóbrega requested some African laborers to work in his College of Bahia orphanage, and in 1552 he acknowledged having accepted three Guinea slaves.[56] By the 1580s, Bahia could claim a black population of some three to four thousand, and by the early seventeenth century, sugar mills throughout the colony were numerically dominated by African as opposed to indigenous chattel slaves.[57]

From the perspective of the Portuguese crown, the establishment and expansion of the African slave trade found justification on several fronts. The success of the highly profitable Brazilian sugar economy, and by default of the colonies themselves, depended on access to a skilled and readily available force. However, enslavement of the native population for this purpose, at least in the early years of colonization, was irreconcilable with ecclesiastical doctrine. Conquest and colonization had been undertaken principally to bring the word of God to the heathens, not to enslave them. Africans, on the other hand, who had long been perceived as somehow beyond Christian redemption, rarely found protection under this theological umbrella. If nothing else, slavery appeared to provide passage from the hell of Africa to the salvation of Brazil. The dominant Catholic orders—the Jesuits, Carmelites, and Benedictines—while providing some degree of succor to the indigenous population, were themselves major African slaveholders. With few exceptions, slaves found no defense of their interests within the church.

In any case, because Indian slavery represented an activity that could not easily be controlled or taxed by the crown authorities, its existence contributed in no way to the Portuguese coffers. African slaves, on the other hand, had to be transported across the Atlantic. Packed on ships like so many head of livestock, African slaves were accountable, taxable, and thus more likely to generate a profit for the Crown.[58]

The success of the Bahian sugar economy quickly came to depend on the technical skill and physical endurance brought by African laborers. Unlike their Native American counterparts, whose stone age technology, shifting cultivation, lack of domesticated animals, immunological vulnerability, and generally easygoing life style left them ill-prepared for the technical specialization and sustained drudgery of plantation labor, Africans had long been familiar with the lifeways of settled agrarian existence. They had also proved their ability to tolerate plantation conditions on the first sugar estates on the Atlantic islands of Madeira and São Tomé almost a century before. These perceived differences in ability to work were early recognized by Brazilian planters, who were willing to pay roughly three times more for an African than for an Amerindian slave.[59]

It is important to remember that in the areas of agriculture, animal husbandry, and metallurgy, African slaves were drawn from societies every bit as advanced as their European captors. Cattle-raising as well as equestrian skills were well-developed in African societies and were recognized by New World slaveholders.[60] Significant elements of the Iberian agrosystem, including many of the crop plants introduced to the Americas, in fact had their origins among African societies, or had diffused through Northern Africa to Southern Europe during the Islamic occupation of Iberia.[61] Monoculture would not have represented an innovation for the newly arrived Africans; nor would raising domesticated cattle, pigs, goats, or sheep. In the early stages of the Atlantic slave trade, metallurgy was as well developed in Africa as it was in Europe. Iron, which had been smelted in Nigeria since at least 500 B.C.E., was perhaps of better quality than that being produced in Europe.[62] Although most Africans were drawn from societies whose knowledge was preserved and passed on as oral rather than written text, a fair number of literate Africans also arrived in Bahia. The incongruity of literate slave and illiterate planter, particularly in the case of Hausa Muslim slaves, was by no means uncommon. Nor would the existence of populous towns necessarily come as a shock to slaves, especially those from Yorubaland, whose civilization was characterized as perhaps the most urban in Africa.[63] In terms of technological and intellectual adjustment, the incoming African was clearly better prepared than the local indigenous population to take a place in a reformulating European civilization.

Slave Medicine

Resistance to illness represented another motivation for importing African laborers. From the perspective of Europeans, Africans were viewed as adapted by nature to toiling long hours in the tropical sun without succumbing to the effects of exhaustion and illness. They were accustomed to the tedious regimen of agrarian existence and, most importantly, had established a measure of resistance to the panoply of Old World contagions that were decimating the indigenous population. Although recent arrivals suffered high rates of mortality, those Africans that survived were thought to be "seasoned" against disease. As time passed and Brazilian slaveholders acquired more experience, they were able to classify different African ethnic groups in terms of their intelligence, ability to work, and vulnerability to illness.[64] According to Father André Antonil, "The ardas and minas are robust. Those from Cabo Verde and São Tomé are weaker. Those from Angola, born in Luanda, are more capable of learning mechanical professions. . . . Among the Congos, there are also some quite industrious and good not only to work in the sugar mills, but for the shops and for maintenance of the house."[65] Twenty years of caring for slaves in the gold-mining region taught physician Luis Ferreyra that "among slaves from the Cobus nation, and the Angolans, sickness is quite gentle, and those from the Minas nation are very difficult."[66]

Because African slaves represented "the hands and the feet of the plantation master," their owners had, at least in principle, a vested interest in maintaining the physical well-being of their workers. Most slaves, however, were given free rein to tend to their own health needs.[67] Colonial physicians, expensive and of questionable competence, were infrequently called upon to see to the health problems of the slave population. Given the quality of European medical care, this situation was perhaps a blessing for the Africans. Not much is known about the role of African slaves and freedmen in the practice of medicine. Most would have passed unnoticed in the slave huts of the sugar plantations and gold mines. The few descriptions that do exist suggest that slave medicine could be divided roughly between the treatment of organic illness, on the one hand, and problems resulting from magic and sorcery, on the other. Because it was shrouded in "deep mystery,"[68] magical medicine received more attention from contemporary writers than the treatment of everyday illness.

African physicians apparently administered only to other Africans.[69] One of the few descriptions of an African doctor was provided by Robert Walsh in Rio de Janeiro in the 1830s. He reported seeing a doctor treat a woman suffering from rheumatism: "I saw a negro doctor administering to some patients, who were sitting on the steps of a church. He bound the arm and shoulder of a woman, who seemed in great pain; and making slight scarifications in several places with the broken blade of a razor, he patted the parts with the flat, till the blood began to ooze out, he then placed small cow horns over them, and applying his mouth to a perforation at the tip, he dexterously exhausted the air, and then stopping it with clay, it remained firmly attached to the skin . . . when removed, the arm was covered with blood; and the woman said she was greatly relieved." [70]

The practice of herbalism must have had a long history in West Africa, and it would be surprising if leaf doctors were not counted among the throngs of incoming slaves. [71] Native healers from Africa's Gold Coast, according to a Dutch observer in 1600, "make use of green leaves" to cure what ails them. [72] From late seventeenth-century Guinea, William Bosman expressed mixed feelings about African herbalism. On a decidedly negative note, he reported that "The natives are very much to be pitied, that being shot, cut, or otherwise wounded in their wars, they neither know nor have any other way of cure than by green plants." Later, setting aside his prejudices, he noted that "The green herbs, the principal remedy in use amongst the Negroes, are of such wonderful efficacy, that it is much to be deplored that no European physician has yet applied himself to the discovery of their nature and virtue." [73] If recent accounts of West African herbalism are at all suggestive of former patterns, it would appear that African healers may have brought to Brazil a theory of etiology and system of therapy that rivaled the complexity and, in all probability, the success rate of Portuguese colonial medicine. [74]

However advanced their herbalism arts in the Old World, African healers in Brazil were greeted with skepticism. Their ethnobotanical skills were, according to one writer, "quite inferior to the indigenous medicine." [75] The logic of this conclusion is inescapable. Brazil's floristic landscape was as alien to Africans as it was to the Europeans, and it stretches the imagination to believe that they could have assimilated in a short time the herbal skills acquired over millennia by the native people. A Yoruba slave who spent twenty years in Brazil in the early 1800s, Osifekunde, related that he was unable to treat fevers as he had in Africa with **ewe eloukeze** because he was unable to locate "an analogy" of the species in Brazil. [76] During the course of the slave trade, Africans and their descendants must have assimilated at least the rudiments of ethnobotanical knowledge from their Portuguese captors and Amerindian coworkers. It is also likely that they went through a period of trial-and-error experimentation with the local flora, although this is purely speculative. [77] By whatever means, as shown later, Afro-Brazilians in time came to know the healing flora of their New World homes as well as any other group did.

Africans were not willing participants in their diaspora, and their ability to transplant their native healing flora was consequently limited. There is the belief maintained among many Afro-Brazilians that somehow their slave ancestors cleverly smuggled the seeds of liturgical species, hidden in their hair, clothing, or magical pouch, and were thus able to introduce important elements of their native African pharmacopoeia. It is also conceivable that crewmen on the slave vessels, which often employed African slaves as deckhands, transported liturgically important species to the Americas.[78] A limited number of African species with commercial or liturgical value were imported during the slave trade—**obí** (*Cola acuminata*), **orobô** (*Garcinia kola*), **dendê** (*Elaeis guineensis*), and **atarê** (*Aframomum melegueta*)—some of which are now naturalized in Brazil. There seems little question that during the course of slavery the flora of Brazil did come to resemble more and more that of the humanized Old World, and this undoubtedly enhanced the incoming Africans' ability to recognize and utilize familiar taxa.[79]

But the romanticized view that the increasingly exotic flora depended even to a limited degree on the clandestine efforts of incoming slaves seems remote. The horrendous conditions experienced during slave capture and transport to the African coast, the weeks to months of imprisonment prior to the voyage, and the subhuman conditions of the Middle Passage militate against any floristic conspiracies. The vegetation of the New World slave coasts did become increasingly Africanized as the slave trade progressed, but this was the result of the steady stream of weeds and cultivated plants that crossed the Atlantic, as both advertent and accidental outcomes of European enterprise, and not of the wishful thinking of homesick bondsmen.

African Magic in the Americas

The widely held conviction among Europeans and their descendants that African American herbal medicine was somehow inferior to its Amerindian counterpart was not a question simply of ethnobotanical expertise. Spanish and Portuguese colonists and their descendants were equally ignorant of the New World flora, and yet their folk medicinal skills were seldom alluded to with the same level of contempt as that leveled at African healers. African-based medicine was and is cognitively codified as a form of "deviant science."[80] The source of this attitude, I believe, was a visceral fear of the Africans' mastery of magic and sorcery. If the indigenous American cosmology was early perceived as a blank slate upon which Europeans could fill in their own evangelical message, the worldview held by Africans, on the contrary, was seen as so thoroughly steeped in idolatry, superstition, and allegiance to the occult powers that an army of priests could not erase it. Magic represented one of the few weapons of resistance in the African's arsenal, and the anxiety it created in the Portuguese community played a key role in the evolution of Afro-Brazilian ethnomedicine.

The notion that minority ethnic and racial groups possess enhanced powers of magic and sorcery is widespread,[81] and the New World slave-owning class was no exception. The progressive development of this belief is nicely illustrated by the early colonial history of Guadeloupe. During the initial decades of settlement, incoming French colonists took advantage of their slaves' knowledge of plant medicine. Africans seemed to recognize the medicinal properties of many of the local species—some naturally native to the island, and others that were recent arrivals from Africa and elsewhere—and the French initially encouraged their medical efforts. This attitude changed, however, as the slave-owners came increasingly to fear slave uprisings in the late 1700s. Père Labat noted that "Almost all negroes who leave their country are sorcerers or at least they are able to use magic, witchcraft and poison with success." By 1767, growing European paranoia had found expression in a series of ordinances outlawing the use of plants for medicine or surgery by African slaves. Even to consult a slave on medicinal matters was banned.[82]

African magic, or at least the fear it spawned, represented a potent force wherever sizable numbers of slaves were found. The high priest Boukman carried out voodoo chants and rituals during the Haitian rebellion in order to immunize his followers against the white man's magic.[83] In South Carolina, African-born priest and doctor Gullah Jack was a principal conspirator in the Vessey Rebellion of 1822.[84] Henry Bibb, a North American slave, described how conjured powders and roots were used, albeit unsuccessfully, to control the plantation master.[85] African sorcerers in eighteenth-century Surinam entered trances and encouraged slaves to murder their owners.[86] White Roman Catholics in colonial Venezuela called on African witches to exorcise the devil from parishioners.[87] It was, according to anthropologist Alfred Métraux, "the witchcraft of remote and mysterious Africa which troubled the sleep of the people in the big house."[88]

African magic was to become equally worrisome to Brazilians. In the early centuries of colonization, while the African population was still small, recourse to the occult forces was limited to the dwindling indigenous population and to Portuguese colonists. During the first visits of the officials of the Inquisition to sixteenth-century Brazil, Africans were not even mentioned among those denounced for heretical activities.[89] This situation must have changed by the eighteenth century, however, when reports of African magical ceremonies became rather common. Discussing an African cult house discovered in the 1760s, the governor of Pernambuco reported that adherents made "an altar of live goats . . . anointing their bodies . . . with the blood of a rooster."⁹⁰ A police raid on another African temple in 1775 turned up a hoard of magical paraphernalia, including "various gourds with ingredients for their black magic."⁹¹ An Inquisition visitation to Belém in 1773 led to denunciation of a Mandingo slave named Pedro, who effected cures of other slaves with magical herbs. Consuming his own magical medicine caused him to speak "in a manner that no one could understand."⁹²

The growing perception that African bondsmen were versed in the black arts had its practical implications. Padre Antonil observed, for example, that legal union between slaves was often prohibited by the masters as it was believed that, "getting bored with the marriage, they kill each other soon with poison or with fetishes, not lacking among them celebrated masters in this art."⁹³ Mysterious or otherwise inexplicable illness was frequently attributed to magical potions administered by their slaves or to the evil eye. Robert Walsh observed in nineteenth-century Rio de Janeiro that "The people labor under various symptoms of undefined illness, which are frequently attributed to the effects of poison, administered by their slaves." Among their "secret means of destroying life," according to Walsh, was the use of "human hair, cut into very minute portions, which attach themselves to the coats of the stomach and intestines, and produce their effect by slow erosion."⁹⁴ And João Rugendas reported that there were African feiticeiros, purveyors of black magic, who prepared talismans from herbs, roots, and animal parts, for the purpose of killing, influencing, and other nefarious purposes.⁹⁵

Africans' dominion over the occult powers extended into prevention and removal of spells, as well as white magic. African feiticeiros were widely sought out to administer magical cures for victims of snakebite.⁹⁶ Sexual magic, in particular, was the exclusive province of the Afro-Brazilian. Aged white clientele depended on the philters and aphrodisiacs supplied by their black sorcerers to bolster their last forays into carnal pleasure.⁹⁷ Rams' horns, figas (carved wooden fists), and pieces of rue (*Ruta graveolens*) were dispensed to fend off the effects of mau-olhado (evil eye), a superstition entertained by members of all Brazilian races and classes (Fig. 3.2).⁹⁸

The influence that magic and sorcery held over white Brazilians can be traced not only to the African's perceived aptitude in this area—although that was and continues to be formidable—but also to the precolonial Portuguese worldview, a vision that accepted the existence of the occult forces without question. Belief in magic was widespread among the Portuguese prior to the

3.2   Pieces of rue (*Ruta graveolens*) being sold on the streets of Rio de Janeiro in the early nineteenth century. (Source: Debret 1978 [1834–1839])

Iberian conquest, and manipulating the powers of the spiritual realm was regarded as part and parcel of the everyday world. European witchcraft prior to the fifteenth century was directed toward specific ends—love potions, spells, amulets, and predictions. As far as the church was concerned, such mundane activities were morally neutral, neither good nor evil.[99] It was only in the centuries that followed that Christianity redefined magic and witchcraft as the handiwork of Satan. While the bonfires of the Holy Inquisition burned across Europe, colonial Brazil was for the most part spared the conflagration.[100] Belief in the supernatural, in the ability of humans to summon forth the occult forces of nature, found refuge in the distant land beyond the sea. To Brazil's early colonists, many of whom hailed from northern Portugal—a region known to be particularly rich in pagan practice and superstition[101]—were added souls who had been convicted of witchcraft and other crimes against the church and exiled to the colonies, who buttressed the belief in magic and sorcery among the evolving neo-European population.[102]

The power of magic is measured by its performance as well as by its reputation and pedigree. Africans capitalized on the superstitious beliefs of their European captors, but they must also have perceived that European magic was, in many respects, considerably more effective than their own.[103] That Africans were the slaves and Europeans the masters was proof enough that European control of the occult forces was considerable. Rather than acquiesce to the white man's magic, Africans took action to incorporate the European repertoire of superstition and witchcraft into their own.[104] This enriched New World mysticism, neither completely African nor European but rather a syncretic amalgam of the two traditions, pushed the Afro-Brazilian practitioner of the black arts into a position of considerable power and prestige among his own people as well as among the ruling class.

The African's command of magic and sorcery constituted one of the few areas in which blacks held sway over their white masters. On one level, feiticeiros occupied a culturally accepted role that was in considerable demand among the Portuguese, a service-sector job like any other. At the same time, their elevated status represented an ongoing threat to the personal safety of the ruling elite and to the stability of the social order. The history of Brazilian slavery is punctuated by individual as well as orchestrated acts of resistance. The existence throughout the slave period of **quilombos,** communities of escaped slaves, underscored the precarious hold that Europeans exerted over their African captives. During the nineteenth century, Bahia witnessed almost constant slave rebellions, the most famous of which was the 1835 uprising in Salvador. Specifically directed at driving the whites from power, this insurrection was organized and carried out by African Muslims (**Malês**), who were widely perceived as masters of the occult powers. Had it not been revealed to the authorities by a few traitors, the rebellion may well have changed the course of Brazilian history.[105]

The diffuse threat posed by African feiticeiros came into sharp focus in the early nineteenth century with the formation of temples dedicated to the Yoruba pantheon. From the perspective of white Brazilians, these fetish houses stood in direct opposition to four centuries of Eurocentric social order. The role of herbalist, folk healer, diviner, and shaman—long vacated by the demise of the Tupinambá—as well as that of magician and sorcerer, would come to be occupied by pais and mães-de-santo, Afro-Brazilian priests and priestesses of the Yoruba religion known as Candomblé.

4 RELIGION OF THE ORIXÁS

The Candomblé religion, a set of beliefs, practices, and cosmology introduced by Yoruba slaves and freedmen, has a fairly brief history in Brazil. The first houses of Candomblé—temples of worship dedicated to the Yoruba gods and goddesses—were established in early nineteenth-century Bahia. Founded by three freed African women, Iyá Dêtá, Iyá Kalá, and Iyá Nassô, the Engenho Velho was the mother of Bahian candomblés. It was clearly established by 1830, and some accounts trace its existence to the mid-1700s. To ensure the orthodoxy of this early terreiro (temple), several founding members returned to Nigeria, spent some years in the city of Ketu studying the fundamentals of Yoruba religion, and then returned to take their place at Engenho Velho. Later, a fractious dispute over the leadership of the Engenho Velho resulted in the establishment of a second house of worship—the Gantois—another of Bahia's pedigreed terreiros. This was followed by another power struggle and the founding of still another house of Candomblé, this by the famous mãe-de-santo Aninha, at Axé Opó Afonjá. These three candomblés, Engenho Velho, Gantois, and Axé Opó Afonjá, which were founded by women and which rigidly maintained the ritual and ceremony of the Yoruba, served as models as well as progenitors for many of the terreiros presently encountered in Bahia,[1] the majority of which are still led by women.

Other houses of Candomblé undoubtedly came and went, leaving little or no hint of their existence. One such terreiro operating in 1785 is known only from court records of arrested participants.[2] Having received reports of African magical ceremonies being carried out in a house on the outskirts of Cachoeira, the authorities raided the house, arrested the occupants, and confiscated considerable religious paraphernalia. The nature of the materials confiscated and the ethnicity of the occupants suggest that the house was dedicated to the **vodun**, a religious pantheon with its origins in ancient Dahomey (currently Benin). The spiritual leader of the house, a freedman named Sebastião, appears to have established a reputation as a curandeiro (healer) and magician. Although the ultimate fate of Sebastião's nascent religious center is lost to history, Cachoeira continues as a regional center for Vodun practice, known in Bahia as Candomblé de Jeje.

However ephemeral these early efforts, Africans were clearly on the spiritual offensive. Empowered perhaps by manumission, Africans and their descendants were actively sowing the seeds of religious rebellion, a collective resistance to the spiritual and cultural hegemony imposed by the ruling class. These early houses of African worship offered perhaps the only viable alternative to the European social and religious order, to which slaves and freedmen had little or no access. Humble shacks with red dirt floors became islands of sacred space, structured communities in which Africans were able to occupy all levels of the hierarchy, refuges within which African beliefs and practices could survive and prosper. Just as importantly, Candomblé terreiros came to represent houses of healing, fertile habitats where African medical and magical traditions could take root and, in time, hybridize with complementary Amerindian and European traditions.

The Atlantic slave trade drew on many sub-Saharan lands and peoples during its four centuries of existence,[3] and this ethnic and linguistic diversity is reflected among the cultural survivals of its descendants. But in spite of the wide variety of religious traditions brought to Bahia, it was the cosmology of the Yoruba, a spiritual universe circumscribed by the **orixás**, that had the greatest impact on Afro-Brazilian religion. For the most part, the other African ethnic groups abandoned their own spiritual vision in favor of the one transported in the hearts and minds of the Yoruba. Although the reasons for the dominance of the Yoruba have not been fully explored, it stems in part from the geographic movements of the slave trade. The last wave of African immigrants, from the late eighteenth century to the final slave shipment in 1851, were predominantly from the Bight of Benin: the Dahomeans and the Yoruba (Fig. 4.1). Their religious dominance thus resulted in part simply from their numerical superiority. The Yoruba also provided a rich and complex cosmology, a rigidly defined social structure, and a highly portable animism, one

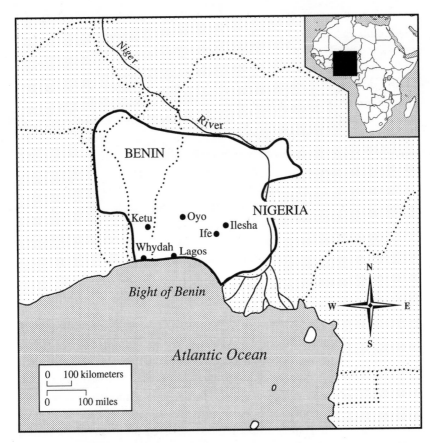

4.1 The Yoruba-Dahomey region, source area for the last phase of Bahia's African slaves. Area encompasses much of the present Republic of Benin and western Nigeria. (Adapted from Akinjogbin 1967)

that was tied less to object and place than were the beliefs of the other African groups.[4]

Bahia's major ethnic groups reconstituted their own native beliefs and practices within the religious framework provided by the Yoruba. The Yoruba provided the central structural text within which various ethnic and cultural messages could be retained. Candomblé is thus represented by a variety of religious types, each founded with a unique set of cultural elements, and each following its own individual trajectory. The Candomblé types encountered today, known as <u>nacões</u>, or nations, include Candomblé de Ketu, Candomblé de

Angola, Candomblé de Jeje, Candomblé de Congo, Candomblé de Ijexá, and Candomblé de Caboclo. Each nation maintains a lexicon, chants, deities, offerings, sacred plants and animals, and other traditional knowledge linking them to the source from which they were originally derived.[5] Adherents to Candomblé de Jeje, for example, which can be traced to the Fon people of Dahomey, invoke the **vodun**, their original pantheon—most of which correspond to one or another of the Yoruba **orixás**. The Candomblé de Caboclo has blended the religion of the **orixás** with Amerindian and Catholic beliefs and rituals, such as the manifestation of indigenous and even foreign entities during possession trance and the use of tobacco and alcohol.[6] Over the years, as mixing and miscegenation erased the boundaries between the different ethnic groups, emotional and linguistic associations with particular African societies faded. Members of one or another of the Candomblé terreiros began to be drawn more by the charisma of the priest or priestess, the prestige of the terreiro, or a hundred other sundry features than by ethnicity.[7]

The Orixás

Candomblé is the religion of the **orixás**. Adherents recognize the existence of a supreme god, Olórun, the unknowable creator of all things, but he is perceived to be distant and unapproachable by humans. Olórun does not manifest during possession trance, has no **peji** (shrines) or terreiros dedicated to his name, and is not specifically worshipped by devotees. Although he enters into Yoruba mythology, Olórun may be alien to the original Yoruba cosmology, a product of early Christian or Moslem influences.[8] It is the **orixás** of the Yoruba pantheon, serving as the earthly ambassadors of Olórun, who are directly linked to the everyday world of mortals.

The pantheon of Yoruba deities in Africa may have been enormous (some accounts range from four hundred to over three thousand)[9] but only a fraction of this number direct the lives of New World African descendants. Although there is considerable variation from one house of worship to the next and from one nation to the next, roughly a dozen **orixás** are well developed and find devotees in nearly all Candomblé terreiros. This figure, however, can multiply quickly when one considers the different forms or qualities attributed to each deity. Exu, for example, manifests in twenty-one different forms; Oxum, in sixteen. Each of these forms represents a variation on a central, archetypal theme whereas some, such as the Odudua quality of Oxalá, are perceived as entirely different genders. The twelve principal **orixás** include Xangô, Ogun, Oxalá, Oxóssi, Omolu, Ossâim, Iroko, Yemanjá, Oxum, Iansã, Nanã, and Oxumarê. A few <u>terreiros</u> worship a much larger pantheon than this, while others, particularly those of the Jeje nation, possess much the same list of deities, but under Fon labels.[10]

Not all the immigrant gods that landed in Brazil found fertile spiritual ground. Some took root and proliferated, while the memory of others withered and died. Although various factors influenced the content of the Yoruba pantheon that would ultimately survive in Brazil, the historical idiosyncrasies of African slave operations stand out. Xangô, the warrior god of thunder and lightning—one of the most geographically successful African gods in the Americas—is a good example. Xangô is traced by oral tradition to the early monarchy of the Oyo kingdom. A magician as well as a great warrior, Xangô is said to have controlled the powers of lightning and thunder. Following his death from suicide, Xangô entered the sacred ranks of the Yoruba pantheon.[11] Xangô is still summoned forth during coronation ceremonies in Nigeria.[12] His ubiquitous presence in Brazil and other New World locales is explained in part by the early nineteenth-century fall of Oyo, ravaged by internal treachery and defeated by the armies of the Muslim Fulani and the Dahomean Fon.[13] Counted among the defeated must have been leaders and priests of Oyo, loyal followers of Xangô, now war booty to be auctioned off to eager European slavers. The **orixá** Oxóssi, deity of the hunt, followed a similar path to the Americas. Eradicated from Africa during the Yoruba wars, Oxóssi arrived and prospered in the New World, finding refuge among the slaves and free blacks of Cuba and Brazil.

The success or failure of the African deities in their New World milieus was also determined by their cultural relevance. The spiritual survivors were those who empowered the captive population—who employed their powers to further the cause of their believers, not of their oppressors. Ogun, **orixá** of iron, war, and revolution, is such a god. Hot-tempered and merciless, his role is to open doors, clear paths, and vanquish the enemy. An obvious symbol of strength and resistance, Ogun found a receptive following among oppressed Brazilian and other New World African slaves and their descendants.[14] Ogun continues to wield his power in Candomblé and throughout the neo-Yoruba landscape: his geographic sphere of influence stretches from New York to Buenos Aires. Xangô's archetype also found relevance in the Americas. The tempestuous god of lightning and thunder, Xangô personifies the indefatigable strength and aggression of his mortal followers. So great was his influence that in Trinidad and Recife, Brazil, the religion of the Yoruba came to bear his name.[15]

The **orixá** Okô was not so successful. One of the Yoruba gods of agriculture,

Okô is acknowledged in a few Bahian terreiros, but she has few followers. For rural slaves, planting and harvesting were times of misery, not causes for celebration. The spiritual cultivation of Okô would have symbolized nothing less than endorsement of the source of their oppression. Not surprisingly, Okô failed to generate much of a New World following, and few devotees sing her praises.

The **orixás** are nature gods. They are associated with distinct provinces of the natural world—water, air, forest, and earth—and it is from these primary sources that they gather and impart their **axé**, or vital energy. Each physical domain, in turn, corresponds to an array of perceived personality traits. The **orixás** are archetypes for the range of behaviors exhibited by their mortal followers.[16] They embody the strength and foresight of their adherents as well as their weaknesses. Oxóssi, for example, is the masculine god of the hunt. Wandering in the forest primeval, he is the consummate naturalist, forever studying and analyzing his surroundings. His temperament, as well as that of his adepts, is characterized by keen intelligence and curiosity. An itinerant seeker, discoverer, and traveler, Oxóssi is never fully satisfied—materially, romantically, or geographically. The female deity Yemanjá, on the other hand, is cool and calm. The Yoruba **orixá** of the river Ogun in Nigeria, she was transformed in Bahia into the goddess of the sea, the patron saint of fishermen. Warm, maternal, and stable, with thick bones and ample breasts, Yemanjá is the 'milk **orixá**,' the archetypal symbol of fertility and motherhood. Because of the Brazilian obsession with the beach and the sea, the image of Yemanjá found a huge following both inside and outside of Candomblé. Her annual public ceremonies, held around the New Year, have become institutionalized into popular Brazilian society (Fig. 4.2). Iansã is another female deity, although her temperament breaks rank with the stability and temperance exhibited by the other feminine goddesses. In Nigeria, she is the **orixá** of the Niger River.[17] In Brazil, where her physical domain became the wind and storms, her personality is characterized by impatience and a short temper. An emotional tornado and a sexual dynamo, Iansã is hot-tempered, is easily excited, and has a penchant for creating trouble. She is, according to Ruy Póvoas, "**dendê** boiling on the fire."

The physical provinces of the **orixás**, and their corresponding temperaments, are clearly divisible between those that are hot- and those that are cool-tempered. This primary opposition—hot versus cool, fire versus water, masculine versus feminine—is a fundamental feature of the religion of the **orixás**, as it is practiced in Bahia, and of its attendant health and healing functions. The hot deities, the gods of fire, are short-tempered, volatile, and reactive. The role of these bellicose and unpredictable gods is to clear obstructions,

4.2　Candomblé adherents making offerings to Yemanjá, **orixá** of the seas, near Ilhéus. (Photo: Janira Voeks)

win battles, and wreak havoc on their enemies. Their ranks include the male deities Exu, Xangô, Ogun, Oxóssi, and Omolu and the female goddess Iansã. These battle gods find their antitheses in the goddesses of peace and tranquillity, the calming and stabilizing influences in the spiritual realm. Cool and earth-bound, the feminine deities Yemanjá, Oxum, and Nanã and the masculine gods Oxalá and Ossâim serve as spiritual counterweights to their volatile peers. In addition to these there are some gods, such as Oxumarê, that are less easily codified. The personality of this elusive deity, half-male and half-female, varies in accordance with his/her gender. The same is true of Logunedé, the mythological offspring of Oxóssi and Oxum, who for six months is the masculine hunter, and for the other six months, the feminine water goddess.

The archetype of each **orixá** is complemented by appropriate preferences and prohibitions. These features take the form of taboos, offerings, sacred foods, preferred time of worship, icons, and geographical locations. Oxalá, for example, is the masculine god of creation, peace, and love. Considered by some as the son of Olórun, Oxalá is the supreme god of the pantheon, father to all the **orixás**. He is clothed in white, head to foot, and assiduously avoids wearing

4.3 Elderly Candomblé priestess in Itabuna. Her gold-colored clothing and jewelry show that her principal **orixá** is Oxum, goddess of vanity. (Photo: Robert Voeks)

anything black. He prefers lofty locations, and his consecrated day is Friday. He requires the sacrifice of chickens, doves, and female goats, and his **euó**, or taboos, are horse meat, crabs, and salt. Oxum is the female goddess of sweet water. Originally associated with the River Niger in Africa, she emerged as the protector of all rivers and streams in Brazil. She is the **orixá** of riches, of vanity, and of material excess (Fig. 4.3). Oxum adores gold and perfume. She is most comfortable in the cool shade provided by riparian forest. Narcissistic, jealous, and inclined toward hypochondria, Oxum and her adepts often possess striking physical beauty. Her sacred day is Saturday. The beads of her necklace, like most of her clothes, are golden yellow. Oxumarê is the deity of rainbows and good weather. She is symbolized by the serpent. A Dahomean deity adopted by the Yoruba, Oxumarê is one of the meta-**orixás**, alternating between male and female. Consistent with this hermaphroditic gender division, Oxumarê emotes two energies, two faces, two personalities. Like the rainbow, Oxumarê is ever-changing. The colors of Oxumarê are yellowish green, and his/her material icon is an iron snake.

One of the striking processes that occurred in Candomblé, as well as throughout the New World African religious landscape, was the intellectual integration of the Yoruba **orixás** and the Dahomean **vodun** with the deified saints of the Catholic Church. In Brazil, Cuba, Trinidad, and Haiti, each of the African spiritual entities in the local pantheon came to correspond to one or more of the Catholic saints.[18] Oxalá merged with Jesus Christ, Omolu with Saint Sebastian; and Iansã with Saint Barbara. On the one hand, this blending and blurring of divinities was a natural and fluid process, an anticipated cultural product of extended, if one-sided, interaction between Africans and Europeans. Because Christian conversion had begun long ago in West Africa, well before the major waves of Yoruba and Dahomean arrivals, there is every reason to believe that the concept of Catholic saint–Yoruba **orixá** correspondence was familiar, if not already accepted, by incoming Africans. Catechisms taught in seventeenth-century Dahomey, for example, allowed the name of the Fon deity Lisa to replace Jesus Christ.[19]

In the New World, the ubiquity of this correspondence in geographically remote regions has been attributed to the structural similarity of folk Catholicism to the Yoruba religion. The cosmologies of both religions are essentially pantheistic; both recognize a high god, distant and largely inaccessible to mortals, as well as a pantheon of lesser divinities, to whom direct appeal can be made during periods of adversity. Like the Yoruba gods and goddesses, who are viewed as deified heroes of African antiquity, the Catholic saints once were mortal beings, whose exceptional deeds are immortalized in myth. And, like their West African counterparts, the saints took on certain "pagan" qualities: dominion over nature, control of fertility, and influence over health.[20]

The parallel orientations of the Catholic hagiology and the Yoruba pantheon toward resolution of practical problems gave direction to these paths of correspondence. In medieval Europe and later in colonial Latin America, Catholics adjured God, Jesus, Mary, and, above all, the saints to cure what ailed them. Prayers and blessings were directed at saints who exercised influence over specified diseases or particular body parts. Saint Rocco received prayers and votive offerings during epidemics; Saint Nicholas was consulted by those suffering from ailments of the throat; Saint John was greeted with "sexual songs and practices" to enhance fertility.[21] For Africans in the process of forced religious conversion, the sometimes uncanny functional correspondence between the white man's gods and their own must have suggested that there were multiple religious labels for what appeared to be identical spiritual entities.

Candomblé tradition offers an alternative view of this apparent syncretism. According to pais- and mães-de-santo, the substitution of the names of Catholic saints for Yoruba deities was purely superficial, an intentional strategy on the part of early religious practitioners to deceive the whites. By chanting the names of Catholic saints during their ceremonies and by hanging their pictures in their meeting areas, Africans duped their white observers into believing that they were in the process of adopting the Christian faith. Given the constant legal harassment endured by early terreiros, such a strategy had obvious merits. But, however appealing, this notion implies a level of gullibility on the part of the ruling class that is difficult to accept. More likely, this apparent deception constituted a calculated tolerance on the part of the authorities, a feigned ignorance meant to lull Africans into conversion. In fact, this process of gradually substituting the images of Catholic saints for pagan deities had long been a cornerstone of conversion policy.[22]

By whatever means and for whatever motives, these correspondences are now deeply ingrained in African American cosmologies. Omolu, the feared Yoruba god of smallpox and contagious disease, became known in many parts of the neo-Yoruba landscape as Saint Lazarus, the disabled Catholic saint honored for his healing ability. In some Candomblé terreiros, this ancient and diseased deity is associated with Saint Sebastian; the correspondence in this case emanates from the image of the saint, who is often portrayed as covered with arrow wounds, which are reminiscent of the smallpox scars said to cover Omolu's body.[23] Iansã, the mercurial **orixá** of wind and storms, is referred to as Saint Barbara, the divinity known as the protector against lightning. Ogun, the war god of iron and the foundry, is associated with Saint Anthony, whom

Portuguese Catholics often depict as a conquering military hero, sitting astride his horse while slaying a dragon.[24] But in spite of their behavioral similarities, African deities are not Catholic saints, and the fit between the pairs was never perfect. The predictable outcome is variation in correspondences from region to region and from temple to temple.[25]

The degree to which saint and **orixá** have actually merged in the minds of the faithful varies as well. Among most Candomblé priests, well-educated adherents, and intellectuals, the juxtaposition of similar religious images represented nothing more than a historically necessary inconvenience. Catholic and African deities are separated by a wide gulf of culture and history, and archetypal similarities are interesting but purely coincidental. The saints and the **orixás** are, according to Pai Balbino, "like oil and water." Such followers contend that, for political motives as well as to maintain religious orthodoxy, the black gods and white saints must be maintained in a state of spiritual segregation.

For many adherents, however, this long association has led to a color-blind blending of African and Christian icons. This is especially true for those followers—the vast majority—who frequent the myriad proletarian terreiros and whose understanding of the Yoruba pantheon and of the Catholic hagiology is more emotional than intellectual. For them, Oxalá is Jesus Christ; Iansã is Saint Barbara. That this syncretism is more than a veil of deception is vividly evidenced by the fact that nearly all Candomblé adherents consider themselves to be good Catholics. In many terreiros, baptism into the Catholic faith is a prerequisite of initiation into Candomblé. Adherents see no contradiction whatsoever in attending a Sunday morning mass after a night of animal sacrifice and spiritual possession by African deities.[26] For most of the faithful, the images and the legends of the African **orixás** and the European saints have become hopelessly tangled. A dreamy depiction of a voluptuous and porcelain white Virgin Mary passes without notice for the maternal African goddess Yemanjá (Fig. 4.4). A radiant Christ preaching to his flock from a hill is Oxalá, the Yoruba deity of love and peace, who prefers elevated locations. For those who subscribe to Candomblé religious and ethnic orthodoxy, these couplings represent a continuing and unacceptable whitening of African expression in its purest form, a spiritual cancer in need of excision. For most of the faithful, however, for whom Candomblé provides so many practical and spiritual benefits, the issue is unnecessarily divisive and uselessly intellectual.

If Catholics and Yoruba exhibit a degree of shared vision in terms of spiritual actors, they nevertheless place their respective deities in distinct cosmological kingdoms. The Yoruba and their New World descendants have retained much

4.4 Ceramic figure, showing the Virgin Mary–Yemanjá correspondence, being carried to the sea during festival of Yemanjá. (Photo: Janira Voeks)

of their original view of the spiritual universe and the hereafter, and it has little in common with the Christian concepts of heaven and hell. The Candomblé cosmos is characterized by a simple opposition between the realm of the spirits, **orun**, and the realm of the material, **aiê**. **Orun** is the celestial dwelling place of the divinities—the **orixás**, the high god Olórun, the Irumalé (spiritual entities closely associated with Olórun and with primordial existence),[27] and **eguns**, the souls of the dead. Divided into nine levels, or spaces, **orun** is depicted as a series of energy levels, concentric rings of ever-increasing power surrounding the world of mortals, **aiê**. Although all of the spirits reside in **orun**, those that exist at the highest levels, Olórun and the Irumalé, are too distant, geographically and energetically, to return to the land of the living. They occupy the end of space: infinity. The **eguns** are dispersed in all the nine spaces, with their level of ascent (perhaps) dependent upon the level of spiritual growth achieved during their mortal existence. The **orixá** Iansã is said to have special migratory powers, as she is the only spiritual entity capable of moving freely among the nine spaces.

The **orixás** inhabit the primary levels of **orun**, where the energy intensity is believed to be similar to that on Earth. This balanced energy status translates to a highly permeable membrane separating the parallel worlds of the spiritual and the material. The deities who occupy this intermediate zone are provided free passage to **aiê** when summoned forth by their supplicants. Incarnated in the bodies of their devotees during possession trance, the **orixás** can once again savor the precious fruit of material existence. Humans are more limited, able to enter even the lowest layers of **orun** only through death.

Candomblé Terreiros

The social hierarchy of the Candomblé terreiro is rigidly defined and maintained. Each is directed by the pai- or mãe-de-santo, infrequently referred to by the Yoruba terms **babalorixá** or **ialorixá**. Literally translated as the 'father-' or 'mother-of-saints,' the Candomblé pai- or mãe-de-santo represents the principal line of communication between the material world of mortals and the spiritual world of the deities. Although either a woman or a man can direct the terreiro, there is a general gender division between the dominant Candomblé nations. Candomblé de Ketu is generally a matriarchy, with all of the high offices, including the priest position, occupied by women. The hierarchies of Candomblé de Angola and Candomblé de Jeje, on the other hand, are generally dominated by men, although elevated stations may be occupied by women (Fig. 4.5).[28] In any case, the authority of the pai- or mãe-de-santo is absolute.

4.5 <u>Pai-de-santo</u> of a Candomblé de Angola <u>terreiro</u> in Itabuna. Having been possessed by his female deity, Nanã, he is dressed in a dark blue dress and petticoat. (Photo: Robert Voeks)

He or she takes responsibility for all the important functions, administrative and spiritual, and adjudicates all disputes, internal and external. The pai- or mãe-de-santo is the administrator of the central precepts of Candomblé—maintaining respect, carrying out obligations, and protecting the secrets.[29] He or she is the living repository of the "fundamentals" of the terreiro, the guardian of the sacred knowledge, and the principal educator of novices.

Pais- and mães-de-santo also serve as community curandeiros, divining the sources of medical and spiritual problems and prescribing culturally acceptable solutions. They may also work with magic, manipulating the occult forces for their own ends and those of their clients, although this activity is downplayed in the more prosperous terreiros. The primary objective of the pai- or mãe-de-santo, however—the one that overrides all others in importance—is the maintenance and cultivation of **axé**, the vital force of existence. **Axé** is the fulcrum upon which the success of the terreiro turns. Nurtured and properly tended, **axé** grows like a sacred flame, imparting spiritual strength, prosperity, and health to its mortal attendants.

There are numerous other established roles in the temple. Most are occupied by filhos- and filhas-de-santo, the **iaô**—literally, 'sons-' and 'daughters-of-the-saints.' These roles are most often occupied by women. Having passed through at least the early stages of initiation,[30] the filhas-de-santo are ritually and symbolically linked to the past and future of the terreiro (Fig. 4.6). Their ability to incarnate the deities during possession trance—an obligation for all, but also a pleasure for many—serves to impregnate the individual as well as the terreiro with the elevated **axé** of the **orixás**. The filhas-de-santo represent the peasant work force of the terreiro, the cooks, the cleaners, and the gardeners. Among the filhas-de-santo, one serves as second in command, the mãe pequena, literally 'little mother.' The function of the mãe pequena is to see that the wishes of the pai- or mãe-de-santo are enforced and generally to manage the day-to-day functioning of the terreiro. The **ogã** are male members of the temple whose role is more honorific than functional. They normally do not pass through initiation, nor do they manifest the deities. Often of high social or political status outside the terreiro, the **ogã** contribute financially and politically to the terreiro and generally enhance its prestige among the secular public. The faca (knife) or **axogun** is in charge of the animal sacrifices. He carries out the matanças (killings) and separates the various offerings to the deities along rigidly prescribed lines. Finally, the mão-de-ofá serves as the terreiro leaf specialist. He or she knows the identities of all the sacred leaves, how and when to collect them, and the appropriate offering to leave for the forest deities, Ossâim and Oxóssi.

4.6 <u>Filha-de-santo</u> and her daughter at a Candomblé ceremony. (Photo: Janira Voeks)

Candomblé temples vary enormously in their physical appearance and aesthetic attributes. The prosperous terreiros—those with pedigrees stretching back to the era of slavery—receive financial support from wealthy and well-respected sponsors, both black and white. Famous performers, government officials, and intellectuals are counted among the patrons of these illustrious and much-publicized terreiros. With substantial resources, a few of these terreiros have been modeled to resemble tiny African communities. These usually include a spacious meeting room, or barracão, where public ceremonies are held. Small shrines, or **peji**, dedicated to the indoor **orixás** (Xangô, Oxalá, or Oxum) are located around the perimeter of the barracão, whereas the shrines to the **orixás** of the forest or outdoors (Ossâim, Omolu, Oxóssi, and Exu) are hidden away in the adjacent garden and forest. The barracão is also joined to several tiny rooms, the **roncó**, where novices pass their months of initiation sleeping on beds of sacred leaves and learning the fundamentals of their religion. There is also often a separate reception area where the stream of clients seeking council with the pai-or mãe-de-santo wait, often on separate benches for males and females. Finally, all the illustrious terreiros are surrounded by both natural and cultivated vegetation, symbolizing the forest and the farm, the habitats of the outdoor **orixás** and the sources of the sacred leaves.

But Candomblé is not a religion of celebrities. Although a few temples and their famous priests receive ample attention from the media (not to mention a retinue of researchers), Candomblé is very much a religion of common folk.[31] Its rank and file are dominated by washerwomen, domestics, street hawkers and rubbish collectors, denizens of the favelas (poor neighborhoods) that represent the Afro-Brazilians' heritage from slavery. For the majority of Afro-Brazilians, emancipation meant little in the way of material improvement, and the shrines and meeting places dedicated to their gods reflect this economic reality. The proletarian terreiro is usually the personal residence of the pai- or mãe-de-santo, perhaps with a spartan barracão erected for public ceremonies. Clients wait patiently in the living room while consultations take place in a cramped closet or bedroom, frequently in competition with the din of television and crying children. Sacrificial chickens await their fate, tethered to the legs of the kitchen table. Corpulent filhas-de-santo sweat over a small stove cooking the favorite food offerings of the gods. The forest deities may be crammed into a tiny backyard plot or may have no designated space whatsoever. The collection of liturgical and medicinal leaves may require a bus journey out of town or a morning ride to the nearest casa de folhas, or herb stand.

Wealthy or modest, the terreiro always imparts a sense of calm to clients and members. There is an indescribable sense of having entered a different world, a reality out of phase in time and space with the bustle and blare on the street. It is a mutually supportive environment, a parallel society where people of color give respect and expect it in return. Often conversing in hushed tones, filhas-de-santo nevertheless walk with heads high, confident of their position, humble but not degraded. The economic division that governs much of Brazilian society loses its meaning as you enter the terreiro. To cross the frontier of a house of Candomblé, whether small and nondescript or rich and illustrious, is to exit the European world and enter a space that is ideologically and culturally African.[32]

Candomblé is a practical, here-and-now belief system, dedicated to the realities of life rather than the uncertainties of death. It is, as Pierre Verger aptly describes, an "exaltation turned toward life and its continuance,"[33] as opposed to a religion of salvation directed toward the hereafter. Hell, heaven, and purgatory are alien concepts to the Candomblé way. Rather than chain the body and soul to an unknowable European paradise, Candomblé resonates with the power to improve the lives of people during their brief passage through **aiê**. Dedicated to the liberation of mortals during this as opposed to the next life, Candomblé has a powerful appeal for the descendants of Africans as well as for an increasing number of Brazilians of European ancestry.

5 CANDOMBLÉ MEDICINE

To say that the majority of white Brazilians reject the legitimacy of Candomblé healing practices is an understatement. Reactions generally range from visceral repulsion to mild amusement. At the extreme, Candomblé is seen as impregnated with devil worship and **macumba**, and its practitioners as embracing the lowest form of heathenism. Those with a milder reaction see it as a jumbled compendium of European superstition and African hocus-pocus, a benign blending of rituals meant to attract the simple-minded and the desperate. The notion that Africans and their descendants could be masters of a serious and relevant intellectual tradition seems beyond the pale of most neo-Europeans.

The religion of the Yoruba and their New World descendants is centered on practical issues. Unapologetically hedonistic, it revolves around the resolution of the everyday trials and tribulations of human existence. Unlike the religions of salvation, which are obsessed with the day of reckoning, the Yoruba belief system seems wholly unconcerned with preparing its flock for the afterlife.[1] Their cosmology clearly distinguishes the world of mortals (**aiê**) from the world of spirits (**orun**), and transcendental communication is a means to an end, as it is in most religious ceremony and ritual. But the Yoruba conception of the hereafter is "relatively imprecise and unelaborated."[2] In Africa and Brazil, the focus is on the here-and-now, on real-world problems—prosperity, fecundity, physical health, and spiritual well-being.[3]

According to the Yoruba worldview, the human condition is largely a product of interrelations with the spirit world. It is, of course, recognized that accidents "just happen," with no attendant spiritual meaning or causation. But most difficulties can be traced to disequilibrium with the spirit world. Thus, the sources of problems as diverse as headaches and heartaches, bankruptcy and boils can be traced to disharmony between mortals and their spiritual guardians. Candomblé priests are thus called upon to administer to a list of sundry, seemingly unrelated phenomena. In addition to issues of health and wealth, pais- and mães-de-santo are trained in the arts of sorcery and conjure. They can negate the nefarious effects of black magic and, if the situation warrants, employ the occult arts for their own ends or those of their clients.

Despite its formidable scope, Candomblé medicine represents a cohesive medical system. It is characterized by a well-developed theory of causation, and its priests are able to associate symptoms with specific illness, defined in the broadest possible sense, as well as to prescribe culturally acceptable treatments. Also, because health problems have a definable origin, they can, in principle, be avoided. Prevention is considered preferable to cure. The problems that beset humankind, in terms of health, the material world, and other matters, can be avoided, provided that the appropriate prophylactic measures have been implemented.

Preventive Medicine

Preventive medicine is dominated by the concept of establishing and maintaining a state of equilibrium with the spiritual universe. This transcendental balance between gods and mortals is achieved by adhering to the strictures of Candomblé, by avoiding material and spiritual excesses, and by understanding as well as putting into practice the lessons contained in Candomblé mythology. In West Africa, **babalaô** priests nurture a rich oral history of the origins and actions of the Yoruba pantheon, and this wisdom has survived as part of the fundamental knowledge of Candomblé. Although the role of the babalaô priest did not persist in Brazil, their unwritten scriptures have survived, albeit fragmented and modified, as part of the knowledge of the Candomblé pai- or mãe-de-santo. The most significant myths, or **odu**—those that priests and their followers have found most relevant to their New World setting—are passed on to Candomblé adherents during long years of initiation. Apprehending the message of the **odu**, and thereby understanding the basics of Yoruba cosmology, represents one of the means through which supplicants maintain spiritual equilibrium. Knowledge is power; ignorance is dangerous. Many of the physical, emotional, and material problems experienced by Afro-Brazilians are traced to a lack of understanding of the text of the **odu**.

Consider the following two examples of well-known **odu**. The first addresses the origin of mortals and of the material world in the actions of Oxalá, god of creation.

Olórun decided to create the universe. And he gave the bag of existence to Oxalá and ordered him to scatter its contents. But on the journey, Oxalá became thirsty, and stopped to drink palm wine. But this trip was not in the material world, it was in the **orun** world, because everything that exists here exists there as well. This world [aiê] is a copy of **orun**. So Oxalá drank the palm wine and became intoxicated. And Odudua [wife of Oxalá] came to see how the job was going and found Oxalá fast asleep. She picked up the bag of living things and returned it to Olórun. So Olórun ordered her to return to create the world. And Odudua created the world. When Oxalá woke up, he looked for the bag of living things, but couldn't find it. So he returned to Olórun to relate what happened. And Olórun said, "It's too late, the world is already created. You will retain the power to create the human beings." And so Oxalá went and created humankind. But who created the world was Odudua.[4]

This story contains several necessary messages. First, by describing the origin of the material world and its human inhabitants, it supplies an important piece of the creation puzzle. Oxalá created humans; his wife Odudua created the material world. Second, it underlines the supremacy of Olórun as the high god, he who has power over all aspects of creation and the other deities. Olórun is seen to be distant and unapproachable, so much so that he assigns the tasks of creation to his spiritual ambassadors. Third, the myth reveals a fundamental dimension of Yoruba cosmology, that the material and spiritual worlds are exact duplicates, parallel expressions of the same reality. All material objects and beings—plant, animal, mineral, and human—find their copy in **orun**, the spiritual universe. Fourth, by means of allegory, the story addresses the issue of obligation and opportunity. By indulging in excesses and neglecting his spiritual mandate, Oxalá squanders his chance to be the creator of the material world. The message for mortals is clear. Finally, the story gives spiritual justification for one of the **euó**, or taboos, of Oxalá and his followers: palm wine.

This next **odu** illustrates the mortal origin of Oxóssi, Yoruba deity of the hunt.

Odé [mortal forebear of Oxóssi] was a stubborn hunter. Beyond being a great seeker, a procurer, Odé was stubborn in the sense that he was stuck in his paradigm. He couldn't understand explanations of the world beyond his own paradigm. Odé went together with Oxum in a perfect pair. And one day he went hunting, and he encountered an enormous serpent. A serpent so large that it was the size of the world. But because he was a man who did not know fear, he loaded his bow to kill the serpent. And the serpent sang out, "Don't kill me, because I'm an enchanted serpent." But Odé became frightened and killed the serpent anyway, because he couldn't understand that the serpent was enchanted. Then he took a knife out of his belt to cut off a piece of the snake. And the snake sang, "Don't cut me in pieces, because I'm an enchanted serpent." And Odé said, "A serpent, even an enchanted one, doesn't talk after it's dead." So he cut off a piece of the serpent. He carried the piece to a river to clean it, and the serpent sang, "Don't clean a piece of me in the river, because I'm an enchanted serpent." Odé said, "A piece of enchanted serpent can't sing." So he began to cook it, and the piece of serpent in the pan sang, "Don't cook me, because I'm an enchanted serpent." And Odé said, "A piece of cooked serpent can't talk." He began to eat the cooked snake, and the serpent sang, "Don't eat me, because I'm an enchanted serpent." And Odé responded, "A dead serpent can't sing." He continued to eat the serpent, and the serpent continued to sing inside of his belly. And the belly of Odé began to grow, and grow, and grow, filled up completely, and finally exploded. When his stomach exploded, Odé left **aiê**, the land of life, and Oxum, the mother of **agô** [entreaty], poured onto him the tears of **agô**. And the tears caused a miraculous return, and when he returned he was enchanted. And when he became enchanted, he was no longer Odé; he was Oxóssi.[5]

The members of the Yoruba pantheon were, according to myth, living entities who were transformed into gods or goddesses by virtue of their exemplary lives and heroic deeds. In this story, the mortal Odé becomes the god Oxóssi, confirming the material ancestry of one important deity. The myth also sheds considerable light on the archetype of Oxóssi, one of the principal Candomblé deities, and in particular on the weaknesses to which he and his mortal followers are prone. Oxóssi is a skilled hunter. But his ceaseless search for knowledge, his insatiable curiosity, can be his undoing. In many aspects of his life, such as in personal relationships and material endeavors, the chase takes precedence over the kill. Solitary, self-reliant, and obstinate in his opinions, Oxóssi and his disciples are unable to accept the views of others. He is hardheaded. His intellectual myopia is symbolized by his habitat, the closed tropical forest, where the visual field is severely constricted by the density of the vegetation. Curiosity and stubbornness, Oxóssi's primary survival mechanisms, can be either assets or liabilities—for even virtue, if carried to excess, can be hazardous. The health and prosperity of Oxóssi and his followers depend upon using their considerable talents. At the same time, if they transgress the frontier of acceptable behavior—if they fail to respect the limits of their archetype—they are vulnerable to spiritual disequilibrium and all of its attendant problems.

In the course of reciting the **odu** and deciphering their meanings, priests and priestesses of Candomblé spiritually reinforce the importance of respecting material prohibitions and preferences. These myths yield necessary insights into the personalities of the deities, piecing together the archetypes of the gods to which each adherent belongs. Myths elaborate the activities of the deities and yield theological insights into Yoruba cosmology. The fact that many of the **odu** have changed since arriving in Brazil, having been redefined and reformulated in the context of a new social and physical environment, is irrelevant to their function. Their role is not only to impart the rich oral tradition that successfully traversed the Atlantic, but also to legitimize a worldview that is decidedly at variance with that of the religion of whites. Rather than an atavistic relic of a primitive and pagan past, the religion of the **orixás** emerges as a powerful and persuasive competitor to Christian hegemony and European dominance.

Axé

While knowledge of the Yoruba myths plays a necessary role in Candomblé preventive medicine, equilibrium with the spiritual realm is achieved by maximizing **axé**, the vital force. **Axé** is a concept central to Yoruba-derived belief. As the life-giving nutrient of the material and spiritual realms, **axé** represents power, energy, and strength. Without it, "existence would be paralyzed, deprived of possibility and action."[6] All that is material and spiritual—divinities, humans, plants, animals, or rocks—is endowed with its own innate level and quality of **axé**. This source of energy is concentrated in specific organs or materials. In humans and other animals, **axé** is abundant in the lungs, heart, liver, and especially the blood. In plants, it is located in the leaves or roots—any part that yields liquid. **Axé** is a fluid and dynamic force, transferable between objects and entities by which it is possessed. It can be assimilated and accumulated by the individual and the <u>terreiro</u>, or it can be eroded and lost, depending on the level of sincerity and adherence to the strictures of Candomblé. Meticulously planted and nourished, **axé** grows in strength, towers over the <u>terreiro</u>, and succors its loyal servants from adversity and calamity. Failure to cultivate this vital force, or straying from the natural equilibrium it instills, threatens not only the individual, but all those associated with the terreiro. Preventive medicine, with its materials, rituals, and obligations, is about following the path that maintains and enhances the magical energy of **axé**.[7]

Guardian Deities

Adherents balance their personal **axé** by respecting the behavioral limits and material preferences established by their guardian deities, the 'owners of the head' (donos da cabeça). Two deities dominate each person.[8] They represent dichotomous forces, opposing energies, hot and cool, apparent and transparent. One is masculine; the other feminine. They are temperaments constantly in conflict: one revealed, the other hidden; one dominant, the other recessive. This dichotomy is similar to the division of the Candomblé universe into **aiê** and **orun**, symbolized perfectly by the two halves of the sacred bottle gourd (*Lagenaria siceraria*), separate but equal. For example, someone who is outwardly calm and accepting is, on rare occasions, subject to flashes of anger and intolerance. Someone who is normally shy and reticent becomes, under unusual circumstances, gregarious and talkative. These behavioral aberrations are not faults or perversions. Rather, they constitute natural manifestations of a deep-seated psychological dualism, an opposition that is codified by association with two different gods and which is successfully maintained by respecting the limits of each.

The dominant or revealed **orixá** is the one that is most apparent. The archetype of the deity—whether fiery, curious, sensual, or otherwise—corresponds to the outward behavior of his or her mortal follower.[9] Because the suite of characteristics of each principal **orixá** is known by everyone, it is usually abundantly clear which deity dominates each person. A hot-tempered, outgoing, sensuous woman, incapable of forming permanent relationships, is clearly associated with Iansã, the hot-blooded goddess of storms and wind. A serious, obdurate, scholarly person, especially if he or she has a skin problem (lots of moles or blemishes, for example), will be dominated by Omolu, god of smallpox and disease. Someone who is aggressive, jealous, and corpulent, with evident leadership abilities, is likely connected with Xangô, masculine god of thunder and lightning. The gender of the adherent is not a factor in determining the gender of his or her revealed deity. Aggressive and rotund female Xangôs abound, as do svelte and high-strung male Iansãs.

The elusive nature of the second governing deity is seldom revealed. It shows itself infrequently, and then possibly only to intimates. For example, a person may be dominated by the masculine deity Oxóssi, the hunter, and may normally manifest his behavioral qualities. The opposite dimension of this restless personality, the hidden side, could be under the influence of Oxum, the narcissistic goddess of fresh waters, an archetype characterized by warmth, personal hygiene, vanity, and jealousy. Or someone lacking physical beauty and disinterested in sexual relationships, with a distinct intolerance of dishonesty, would likely be dominated by Nanã, the aged goddess of rain, swamp, and mud. This feminine side, the known personality, would be counterbalanced by a masculine deity, infrequently revealed, but present and occasionally apparent. Not surprisingly, these two opposing psychologies create considerable internal struggles and crises, and reconciling the inherent conflicts of these forces constitutes one of the goals of preventive medicine.

The difficulty of establishing a balance between the forces of opposing **orixás** is compounded by the fact that each deity retains his or her individual state of equilibrium. Xangô is aggressive, Oxalá is peaceful, and Iroko is plodding. These are the inherent dispositions of the gods and goddesses. Neutral forces, neither good nor evil, these personality traits become problems only when taken to extremes. For the Candomblé believer, behavioral excesses translate to disequilibrium with the spiritual realm. Oxum, for example, is on the one hand fraternal and communicative, and on the other vain and materialistic. This is the natural state of Oxum and her followers, and it is useless to attempt to correct one or another of her ways. Nevertheless, like all the **orixás**, Oxum is tempted by excesses. Personal hygiene can develop into compulsive washing; hours can be spent deciding on the proper clothes; all her money can be spent on perfume. Under these circumstances, Oxum has fallen out of balance. Oxalá, the god of creation, is naturally loving, patient, and sensitive. Greatly admired, he is a gifted arbitrator and peacemaker. At the same time, Oxalá's patience can be his failure, and if it is taken to an extreme, he is prone to fritter away opportunities by being too cautious and thorough. In both of these examples, the **orixá**—and, correspondingly, the spiritual condition of his or her supplicant—has strayed from the center of the path, from the salubrious and beneficial region of controlled **axé** to the risky and unpredictable region of chaos. This hazardous place, beyond the zone of acceptable behavior, is personified by the most dangerous of the deities: Exu.

The concept of Exu is integral to Candomblé health and healing. On the one hand, he is a problematic **orixá**, as enigmatic as he is unpredictable. As the owner of streets and crossroads—the arteries of communication—Exu symbolically directs traffic between **aiê** and **orun**. He facilitates horizontal contact between the different **orixás** as well as vertical communication between the **orixás** and humans. During divination via the <u>jogo-de-búzios</u>, it is Exu who transmits the messages of the divinities to the pai- or mãe-de-santo, who in turn translates them for the client. During terreiro celebrations, Exu receives the first offerings, the **padê**. This is done to encourage Exu to transmit the further offerings to the appropriate gods, as well as to discourage him from disrupting the proceedings. Nothing is done in Candomblé without first placating the spirit of Exu. It is his malicious side, his penchant for introducing calamity and chaos into the lives of humans, that makes him such an object of fear in the Afro-Brazilian community, and that has led many to associate him with the Christian devil. Capricious and enormously powerful, Exu is a catalyst of change, for both good and evil. He delivers divine protection to those who propitiate him and disaster to those who do not.[10] Exu is never taken lightly.

But Exu is more than just a messenger and trickster. He symbolizes the wild and unbalanced side of human nature. According to Candomblé tradition, each person retains, in addition to a revealed and transparent guardian deity, an inherited form of Exu. Twenty-one varieties of Exu are believed to exist. All mortals are associated with one or another of them, which is often referred to as an adherent's escravo, or slave. Exu reveals his presence only when mortals indulge in the excesses and compulsions of their guardian deities' temperaments, when the bounds of spiritual equilibrium established by the archetype of the **orixá** have been trespassed. It is at the frontier that separates order and balance, where acceptable idiosyncrasy grades to hopeless obsession, that the trickster lies in wait. Exu is disequilibrium.

Prohibitions and Preferences

Spiritual equilibrium is maintained partially by avoiding the excesses of Exu. In the first instance, this follows from adhering strictly to the behavioral limits set by the **orixás**. Harmony is also nourished when adherents observe their guardian deities' specific preferences and **euó**, or prohibitions, concerning food, drink, color of clothing, necklaces, hazardous places, herbs, and other matters. Candomblé novices learn the likes and dislikes of their deities during initiation. Most are presented by the pai- or mãe-de-santo. Others are learned by chance, just as one might discover a food allergy. For example, followers of Abaluaiê, the youthful manifestation of Omolu, are prohibited from eating fish with skin, such as shark and dolphin. Devotees of Iansã must not consume squash or lamb, whereas those of Ossâim, god of the leaves, should avoid contact with dogs. Oxalá and his followers refrain from eating crabs and hot peppers, and they always dress entirely in white. Black clothing is strictly taboo for Oxalá. Devotees are spiritually renewed by visiting the geographical province of their guardian deities: for Oxum, the riparian zone; Yemanjá, the seashore; Oxalá, a hilltop; Nanã, a valley. Xangô lives in fear of cemeteries, so his supplicants avoid them.

These **euó** represent points of weakness for the individual and for the group. As a rule, Candomblé followers are hesitant to discuss them in detail. Because there are believed to be rival priests who are bent on threatening the **axé** of other <u>terreiros</u>, nothing is to be gained by broadcasting an adherent's personal **euó**. Thus, personal taboos enter into the closely watched cache of <u>terreiro</u> secrets.

Candomblé adherents wear necklaces made of colored glass, crystal, or ceramic beads. Consecrated to the individual's guardian **orixás**, these symbolic rings of protection and obeisance underscore the unity of the spiritual and material worlds. Before being worn, the beads are washed by the <u>pai-</u> or <u>mãe-de-santo</u> in an herbal bath while he or she recites the incantation necessary to invoke the magical power of the leaves. The color of the beads represents the color preference of the deity.[11] The beads of Oxalá are always white, symbolizing the peaceful side of his nature. Those of Exu are red and black, suggesting his hot temper and dark powers. Oxum's necklace is golden yellow, reflecting her love of wealth. The beads of Yemanjá are transparent crystal, suggestive of her aqueous environment. Candomblé adherents wear one necklace for their dominant **orixá** and another for the deity to which the <u>terreiro</u> is dedicated. As a sign of respect, the necklaces are placed in an appropriate place when not being worn, not dangled from a hook or tossed on a table. Also, they should never be worn while engaging in sexual relations.

Adherents further honor the deities by respecting their individual food preferences. Ritual food offerings are placed on the **peji**, or altar, of each **orixá** on the day of the week dedicated to that deity. During this **ossé** ceremony, the **otá** (sacred stones), and other consecrated objects located in each **peji** are cleaned, and previous offerings are removed. For Omolu, food offerings are likely to include rice, black beans, black-eyed peas, and roasted corn. More elaborate functions might involve sacrifices of his favorite animals, male goats and pigs. Yemanjá receives white corn, rice, mush, and hominy. Her sacrificial animals include female goats, female sheep, and chickens. The offerings to Exu include black beans, honey, <u>farofa</u> (a mixture of toasted ground manioc, onions, and shrimp cooked in **dendê** oil), and, true to his nature, wine and <u>cachaça</u> (sugarcane rum).

The days of the week dedicated to each **orixá** represent periods of heightened **axé**. These are the most effective times to make offerings and carry out other functions. Monday is the day of Exu, Iroko, and Omolu. Saturday is the day of most of the female **orixás**, Nanã, Yemanjá, and Oxum. Thursday is the day of the forest, and is dedicated to Ossâim, god of sacred leaves, and Oxóssi, the hunter. Friday is reserved for Oxalá, the god of creation, and no actions that are seen as harming the fruit of his creation, such as sacrificing animals or collecting sacred leaves, are carried out on his day. Sunday is known as the day of all the **orixás**, and no specific deities claim this day.

Aside from ritual offerings to the deities, the consecrated foods are also hawked on the streets of most Bahian cities. Filhas-de-santo tend to their small food stalls attired in the traditional clothing of the terreiro: voluminous skirts and petticoats, white turbans, and necklaces dedicated to the **orixás** (Fig. 5.1). The ubiquitous street corner presence of Baianas, as they are popularly known, represents the strongest visual signal of the continued strength of African traditions among the Brazilian population. Long an important source of income and independence for Bahian women,[12] food stalls serve as a traditional form of obligation for filhas-de-santo inasmuch as they are preparing and dispersing the material preferences of the **orixás**. Besides homemade confections and fried fish, Baianas dispense a host of West African delights, including **acarajé** (black-eyed pea dumpling fried in **dendê** and filled with shrimp), **vatapá** (manioc paste cooked with **dendê**, shrimp, and hot peppers), and **abará**

5.1   Baiana selling consecrated foods of Candomblé on a Salvador street corner. (Photo: Janira Voeks)

(steamed black-eyed pea meal wrapped in banana leaf). In the process of savoring these exotic delicacies, unwitting locals and pink-skinned tourists make offerings to one or another of the African gods or goddesses.

Omolu

In addition to fastidiously adhering to the preferences and **euó** of the guardian **orixás** and of Exu, Candomblé followers pay particular attention to cultivating the goodwill of an especially dangerous deity, Omolu, the god of smallpox and infectious disease. Known among the Yoruba in Africa as Shopona, this hot-tempered deity is so feared that even mentioning his name aloud is avoided, lest it incite his wrath. The image of Omolu is ancient, bent, and twisted, with limbs horribly gnarled by arthritis. The archetype of Omolu and of his followers is extremely serious, uncompromising, and tactless, with an inherent inability to entertain the ideas of others. Normally quiet and reserved, Omolu is dynamite waiting to be ignited. Those who fail to propitiate this god of illness and suffering risk an outpouring of vengeance and misery.[13]

Omolu should not, however, be perceived as the harbinger of medical calamity. He is not only the source of disease and death. Rather, as the following myth describes, he has learned through personal experience how to keep these malevolent forces at bay.

> Omolu and Oxumarê are both descended from Nanã. The first born was Omolu. Soon after he was born, he contracted the famous disease smallpox. Since his mother Nanã could not cure him, she left him in a basket at the seashore. And when Yemanjá, the **orixá** of the ocean, was passing by, she encountered him covered with crabs. The crabs were devouring him. So, even though Omolu was so diseased, she picked up the baby and carried him away to be raised in the sea. But he remained with horribly deformed skin, profound pox scars, so Yemanjá sewed a hood for him made out of palha da costa [raffia fiber] so that his deformities wouldn't be seen. And so he was raised by Yemanjá. But very soon, because he was raised sequestered away, he became very studious and demonstrated himself immediately to have great knowledge. When Yemanjá perceived that he had become extremely knowledgeable about human nature and human diseases, Yemanjá proposed to him that he overcome the differences that he had with [his] true mother Nanã. So Yemanjá leaves the waters with Omolu, and goes to the land to present Omolu to Nanã, to overcome the impasse between the mother and son. And as a result of Yemanjá's actions, there is a reconciliation between Nanã and Omolu. Because he

had by inheritance from Nanã this great knowledge of the soil, the principal generator of human life, he became known as the master of the land, the owner of the land. By the **axé** that he had received from Yemanjá, the owner of the ocean, and the **axé** of Nanã, owner of the soil, and the knowledge that he had personally acquired, he became the counseling doctor: the one who knows how to avoid evil, how to avoid disequilibrium.[14]

Omolu embodies the dual energies of humankind, both creative and destructive. Feared by his followers for the misery he is capable of releasing, Omolu is nevertheless the owner of the land, by virtue of his birthright by Nanã, as well as "the doctor of the poor" (as he is frequently called), by virtue of his period of isolation and research. With the aid of his emblematic **xaxará**—a whisk broom fashioned of raffia, *piassava*, or oil palm and adorned with divination shells—he can either unleash the full power of epidemic or sweep up the ills of the world.[15] Omolu's actions, good or evil, depend on the level of devotion of his followers. A deity uneasy in the presence of others, Omolu has his **peji** located outdoors, in a natural setting, away from human settlement. His **ossé** is made on Monday, his consecrated day, in order that good health may follow during the balance of the week.[16] His favorite food offerings are black beans, black-eyed peas, popcorn, rice, and roasted corn.

Omolu has acquired the knowledge necessary to contain or release disease, but he is not a healer. His understanding of medicine, of the curative energy of the sacred leaves, is limited. It is Ossâim, guardian of the leaves, who knows all the plants and how to invoke their magical properties. But this deity of medicine is even less sociable and communicative than Omolu. He hides behind his wall of vegetation and receives no one, whereas Omolu hides behind his suit of straw and receives all who will listen. The medicine of Ossâim is curative, while that of Omolu is preventive.

Collective Axé

Candomblé followers seek health and prosperity by establishing spiritual equilibrium with their own guardian deities, as well as with Exu, Omolu, and the god to whom the terreiro is dedicated. But the Candomblé temple is more than an odd assortment of individuals, each with his or her own personal goals and aspirations. It is an integrated community of like-minded members, a religious organism that assimilates as well as imparts the salubrious benefits of controlled **axé**. In this way, the terreiro generates a collective energy, a group **axé** whose value is greater than the sum of the individual energies. This interdependence can function in either direction. Members who are balanced contribute to the power and collective **axé** of the group, which, in turn, imparts this collective energy to the individuals. Mutualism prevails, with both the group and the individual feeding on the **axé** that each contributes. It necessarily follows, however, that failure on the part of a single adherent to tend his or her own field, to dutifully worship the gods, or to scrupulously observe his or her personal **euó** ultimately places not only the individual but the entire terreiro at risk of a spiritual backslide. Preventive medicine thus depends in part on nourishing the **axé** of the terreiro.

The terreiro maintains and increases its **axé** through adherence to the fundamentals and obligations of the religious community. The primary set of obligations—those that attract the interest and curiosity of outsiders—are the public ceremonies dedicated to the worship of the **orixás**. These annual events provide the opportunity for the terreiro to heap adulation on individual deities. It also allows the gods and goddesses to return to earth, to taste once again the fruits of mortal existence by reincarnating for a brief time in the bodies of their supplicants.

Public ceremonies are held on a special day of the year consecrated to the deity. The precise date varies with the terreiro and the nation. Some celebrations, such as those for Yemanjá and Oxalá, have been adopted by the greater Brazilian population and thus take the form of enormous public ceremonies. The public celebration for Yemanjá, goddess of the sea and adopted patron saint of fishermen, is held near the arrival of the New Year on the beach. Attended by hundreds of thousands in the principal cities of Brazil, especially Rio de Janeiro, the festival ends with the scattering of flower offerings in the tide, to be carried away to Yemanjá's watery depths. In Salvador, the largest outpouring of public participation takes place during the lavagem do Bonfim, or washing of the Church of Bonfim, realized in mid-January (Fig. 5.2). This celebration, dating at least from the nineteenth century, takes mães-de-santo, members of their terreiros, and several hundred thousand tourists and locals on an eleven-kilometer procession to the church. There, following the directives contained in a Yoruba myth, the mães-de-santo ritually wash the steps of the church.[17] Accompanied by samba bands and thousands of beer stands, the lavagem has become classically Bahian.

Most celebrations, however, are more modest in scope, limited to the terreiro membership and a few interested onlookers. Activities begin with the matança, or ritual killing, of the preferred animals of the deity. These are usually goats, chickens, Guinea fowl, and white doves. The killing is carried out

5.2 Mães-de-santo and spectators preparing for the lavagem do Bonfim in Salvador.
(Photo: Robert Voeks)

by the faca ('knife'), the filho-de-santo responsible for delivering the appropriate incantation, dispatching the animal properly, and dismembering the
body parts that are employed as offerings to the gods. These include the vis-
cera, such as the heart, lungs, and liver, as well as those body parts thought to
impart special qualities (**exés**)—the wings for flight, the feet for locomotion,
the head for vision and thought. As blood is the transporter of animal **axé**, it
is carefully drained from the body, and a portion is poured on the sacred stones
retained in the **peji**. After being doused with oil of **dendê** (Fig. 5.3), the body
parts are also stored in the shrine. The remainder of the carcass is not wasted,
but rather finds its way to the ceremonial meal served to members and visitors
at the midpoint in the celebration.

Previous to the celebration, the barracão, or central meeting place, is ritually
prepared with liturgical leaves. The main entrance and windows are festooned
with **mariuô**, shredded and woven leaves from the **dendê** palm (*Elaeis guineensis*). Collected prior to the celebration, the leaves are cut from the olho, or 'eye'
of the palm, the pliant young fronds that have yet to separate from the stem.
Mariuô functions as a line of defense against the negative energies and forces
that invariably enter with visitors. In some terreiros, **mariuô** is believed to

5.3 **Dendê** oil for sale in open market in Salvador. Besides its use in Candomblé, **dendê** is a staple in Bahian cooking. (Photo: Robert Voeks)

guard against the entrance of **eguns**, ancestral spirits of the dead, which are considered to be disruptive influences. Some houses of Candomblé hang the long, lanceolate leaves of **peregun** (*Dracaena fragrans*) on the wall in the shape of an *X* or simply place them in a vase. In its native West Africa, **peregun** is planted around the outdoor shrines of the **orixás**.[18] In Bahian terreiros, this introduced treelet is believed to repel the spirits of the **eguns**.[19] The floor of the barracão, in the past made of hard red soil but now usually cement, is littered with leaves dedicated to the deity of the celebration. Gathered in the forest, the folhas de pisar (leaves to be stepped on during public functions and celebrations) serve to neutralize bad energies and fluids tracked in with visitors. Later the leaves are discarded, their spiritual energy spent. Flowers consecrated to the deity being honored—white for Oxalá, red for Xangô or Iansã, purple for Nanã, or yellow for Oxum—are often placed near the center of the barracão.

The ceremony begins with the **padê**, also known as the despacho for Exu. To placate his capricious nature, the filhas-de-santo sing the verses of Exu's songs and place his favorite foods outside of the barracão. The dancing and singing that follow are accompanied by three drummers, each an **ogã** (Fig. 5.4). The drums, or atabaques, which come in three sizes and are covered with stretched leather, are beaten with sticks or bare hands. One of the filhos- or filhas-de-santo or else the pai- or mãe-de-santo rings an **agogô**, constructed of two metal bells of different sizes joined at the ends. Each of the **orixás** are serenaded in their proper order, the **xirê**, beginning with Exu and ending with Oxalá. The filhas-de-santo gather in a roda (circle) and begin dancing in a clockwise direction to the rhythm of one deity after another (Fig. 5.5). Male members as well as females dance in Angolan candomblés, but less commonly in Ketu and Ijexá. The filhas trace out the choreographed movements of each deity, movements learned during the long months of initiation. For Iansã, dancers push the front parts of their palms in the air, stirring up the wind and storms of this tumultuous deity. Oxóssi dances with fingers linked in the form of a weapon, the hunter tracking down his game. Ossâim, one-legged and maimed, stoops as he moves to the music, collecting his healing leaves.

It is during the dancing, at first slow and methodical but later bordering on frenetic, that the deities penetrate the translucent field separating the parallel worlds. Descending to earth, summoned by the salutary music and chants, the gods arrive to occupy the bodies of their disciples. Although possession can appear at any time during the evening's proceedings, each **orixá** tends to manifest late in the dance to him or her, when the tempo is at its maximum. As one or more participants appear close to being mounted by their deity, one of the

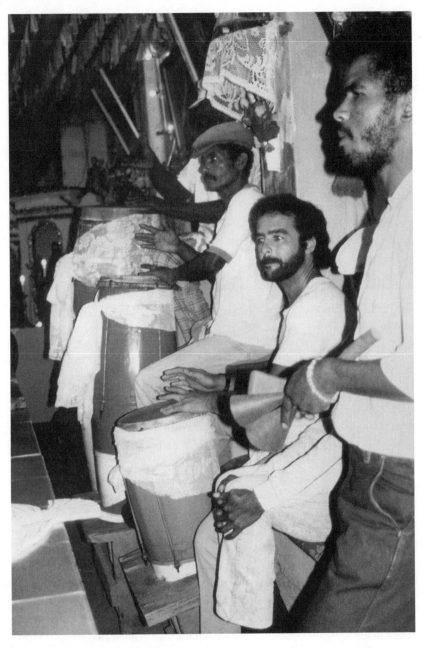

5.4 Candomblé drummers during a Candomblé evening ceremony. (Photo: Janira Voeks)

5.5   Filhas- and filhos-de-santo dancing in the roda during Candomblé ceremony.
(Photo: Robert Voeks)

drummers changes the beat, hammering out a discordant message that pushes
the filha over the edge. With muscles twitching at the first shock of the deity's
entrance, the possessed is immediately attended to by an **ogã** and the mãe
pequena, who removes glasses, watches, and other material encumbrances. The
orixá, once firmly seated in the body of the supplicant, is free to wander about
the barracão, dance, and sporadically announce his or her presence. Omolu
greets the material world by shouting "**Atotô**." Oxóssi announces his presence
with "**Okê**" (Fig. 5.6). Eventually the possessed are led to a separate anteroom
where they are attired in the ritual clothes and icons of their mounted deity.

After each deity has been serenaded three times and a light refreshment of
the **orixá**'s preferred foods have been served to the guests and members, the
dance sequence begins again. The possessed filhas are brought back to the barracão, many now adorned in the traditional costumes of their mounted deities.
For both female and male deities, this is usually a brightly colored dress un-
derlaid by layers of starched petticoats. Filhas of Ogun, god of iron, wear a
metal helmet and bracelets and carry a war ax. Oxum dons a crown and bracelets, wields a sword, and adores herself in her **abebé**, her combination fan and
mirror. Iansã wears a crown and carries a sword and an **eruquerê**, the tip of a

5.6 <u>Filha-de-santo</u> possessed by Oxóssi, god of the hunt. (Photo: Janira Voeks)

cow's tail used to battle **eguns**. Some terreiros are also frequented by an indigenous spirit, the Caboclo, who wears a feathered headdress. Eyes glazed and
heads lowered in respect, the filhas assimilate the **axé** of the earth and of the
orixás as their bare feet trace out the movements introduced by their African
ancestors.

Towards the end of the festivities, in the early hours of the morning, filhas
often enter a secondary trance. In this infantile state, **erê**, the deity manifests
in the form of a child, three or four years of age.[20] Usually led off to finish **erê**,
these baby gods and goddesses are sometimes allowed to stay and frolic in the
barracão (Fig. 5.7). They chase each other, cry, argue, have food fights, play
with imaginary toys, and generally assume the roles of capricious children. The
public celebration usually ends on this note.

The combined forces of individual and group **axé** serve to immunize those
who have given themselves to the deities against ill health and the other mis-
fortunes of life. A balanced Candomblé adherent—one who has fulfilled his or
her personal and community obligations, has respected the limits of his or her
guardian deities and the deities of others, and has followed Yoruba strictures
that were first established in a distant time and place—takes an active role in
controlling his or her own destiny. But mortals are frail creatures. They are

5.7   Having been in a possession trance earlier in the evening, a filha-de-santo dances
and sucks on a pacifier while in the **erê** state. (Photo: Robert Voeks)

drawn by instinct, peer pressure, and circumstances beyond their control to be less than fastidious in carrying out their obligations, or to neglect them altogether. With notable exceptions, the average Candomblé follower is poor, overworked, and underpaid. Thus, the expenses and material eccentricities associated with maintaining a well-balanced existence—proper food and drink, appropriate clothing, sacrificial animals, and a host of votive paraphernalia—are beyond the means of most Bahians. Life is short, and the temptation to indulge in excesses is considerable. Rapid descent into disequilibrium, into the territory controlled by Exu, represents an invitation to physical, emotional, and material problems. Reestablishing spiritual harmony may be a simple process or may require the employment of the full arsenal of spiritual medicine available to the pai- or mãe-de-santo.

Spiritual Medicine

As we have seen, Candomblé etiology ascribes illness to a state of disequilibrium with the spiritual realm. Adherents or clients who fail to make timely offerings to their guardian deities, indulge in excesses, or neglect the preferences and prohibitions of the gods chart a spiritual course that is fraught with hazard. The medical effects of risky behavior can range from temporary illness episodes to chronic, even life-threatening health disorders. Although illness can occur for other reasons, it is when health problems become chronic, when families confront one disaster after another, or when Western medical assistance fails that suspicion falls on failure to tratar os santos 'treat the **orixás**.' Among those who believe that African spiritual entities intervene in the lives of humans, the source of the distress can be determined only through reference to the Yoruba pantheon. Once a deity has chosen to punish his or her negligent child, and this displeasure has been manifested in physical or emotional symptoms, the consultation of a pai- or mãe-de-santo becomes necessary.

Divination

For secular patients not initiated into Candomblé, the healing process begins by identifying the client's two guardian deities, the apparent one and the concealed one. This is done by means of the jogo de búzios, or shell toss, the most enduring of the various methods of divination introduced by West Africans.[21] Carried out by both male and female Candomblé priests, this means of communication between **aiê** and **orun**, with the pai or mãe-de-santo serving as intermediary between deity and client, represents one of the principal duties (as well as sources of income) of each priest.[22] Deep in concentration, the pai- or māe-de-santo begins by murmuring salutary phrases, in what appears to be a mix of Yoruba and Portuguese, to summon the appropriate deities. He or she tosses sixteen African cowry shells on a small wooden board circumscribed by a ring of sacred necklaces (Fig. 5.8). The resultant numbers of "open" and "closed" cowries (that is, the number that land with the shell aperture facing up and facing down) and the geometric configuration of the shells transmit one or more sacred messages. The accuracy of the message is tested by a second toss, this time using only four shells.

Each shell configuration is associated with several **odu**, or Yoruba myths. It is up to the diviner to determine which of these sacred oral messages is most relevant to the problem under consideration, and how to interpret its meaning. Anthropologist Julio Braga lists examples of the **orixás** and **odu** associated with many of the possible cowry combinations, as well as the significance for the client of these oral messages. He records, for example, that three open and thirteen closed shells point to a message being transmitted by Oxóssi, deity of the hunt, by means of five different **odu**. In this case, one of the allegories describes the life of a wealthy man, a man who loses his fortune and decides to take his own life. Preparing to hang himself, the man observes the great suffering of a leper. Reflecting on the courage of the leper, the man abandons his

5.8   A pai-de-santo using the jogo-de-búzios divination method. (Photo: Janira Voeks)

suicidal plan. Later, he is called to take the throne upon his father's death. The protagonist resolves to take care of the leper who earlier saved his life.

The message of this particular **odu** is clear. The client should persevere with his current difficulties, knowing that improvement is in his future. To realize this favorable outcome, the client is advised to make an **ebó**, or offering, to Oxóssi of two doves, one land snail, and a length of rope, the implement of suicide alluded to in the story. Although the means to an end are fairly clearly stated in this particular **odu**, this is not always the case. The interpretation and the **ebó** can vary considerably from one pai- or mãe-de-santo to another.[23]

Spiritual Therapy

The therapeutic prescription contained in the message of the shell toss can take various directions. In most cases, however, a limpeza, or spiritual cleansing, is a necessary first step. The objective is to eliminate negative fluids and energies that have accumulated in the body. A limpeza will usually involve some combination of **ebó**, animal sacrifice and material offerings, a sacudimento, or leaf whipping, and an **abô**, or leaf bath. A simple cleansing may include passing consecrated leaves, raw eggs, and animals over the body of the afflicted to extract the offending energies. It is a private ceremony. The client stands on a mat in the barracão, wearing old, disposable clothing. Bowls of food precious to the deities are poured over the client's head and shoulders—for example, popcorn for Omolu, or **acarajé** for Iansã—and allowed to fall onto the mat. The sacrificial animal, usually a white dove or a chicken, is passed over the body beginning at the person's head. The client may be asked to whisper a wish to the animal before it is killed. Before dispatching the bird, its head may be rubbed with a leaf of folha-da-fortuna (*Kalanchoe pinnata*). After the pai- or mãe-de-santo, or the terreiro faca, has slit the throat of the bird, he or she removes the head and allows its blood, the conductor of animal **axé**, to drain into a ceramic bowl. The wings, head, and feet are carefully arranged on a plate, and the **ebó** is sprinkled with a mixture of the fowl's blood and the oil of **dendê** (*Elaeis guineensis*).

Later, around midnight, the spiritually contaminated food that was poured over the client's head and the prepared **ebó** are placed in an appropriate location. In Salvador, this can be the Dique, an artificial lake that has long constituted sacred African space.[24] A boatman carries the offering to the middle of the lake, where it is deposited. **Ebó** may also be placed at a crossroads, the locational domain of Exu, messenger of the gods. Often found littering the streets after Candomblé ceremonies, the rotting remains of sacrificed chickens

5.9 A <u>pai-de-santo</u> administering a leaf <u>sacudimento</u> to a client. (Photo: Janira Voeks)

are constant reminders of the ubiquity of African-derived beliefs. They also create a perceived hazard, as these decomposing offerings are believed to be charged with Exu's unstable negative energy. Unfortunate passersby may well attribute future problems to spiritual contagion accidentally picked up on a street corner.

A sacudimento, or leaf whipping, is employed to neutralize negative energies and to restore spiritual equilibrium (Fig. 5.9). One to three plant species usually enter into the sacudimento, each consecrated to the **orixás** of the client or those of the offending deity. The leaves and twigs are gathered into a bundle and either brushed lightly over the body or briskly whipped, depending on the severity of the problem and, perhaps, the temperament of the pai- or mãe-de-santo.

Healing Baths

The principal purification ritual performed on devotees and secular patients alike is the **abô**, or leaf bath. Known as the **amaci** in many terreiros, especially in Candomblé de Angola, the leaf bath is nearly always prescribed during the shell toss. It is prescribed for health problems as well as difficulties related to finance and personal relationships. The banho de descarga 'discharge bath' serves to eliminate negative energies that may be constraining the client. The banho de desenvolvimento 'development bath' is meant to attract good fortune. Depending on the nature of the problem, the **abô** may be carried out, using the specified leaves, either in the privacy of the home or at the terreiro. A simple **abô** can be prepared at home and taken immediately after the consultation. Recipes usually include the leaves of three species that "belong" to the deity of the client, although seven or more taxa are employed in complicated cases. An odd number of species appears to be the rule for **abô** prescriptions. The leaves are macerated in a basin of cool water (preferably drawn from a stream or well) and poured over the body. The head is left dry if the leaves of the **abô** are considered 'hot'—that is, pertaining to a particularly hot-tempered deity.

If the **abô** is to treat a complicated problem or is to be employed in initiation, more preparations and precautions are taken. Just as the perceived properties of the plants used in the **abô** vary, so too do the processes of plant collection and preparation. With few exceptions, a sacred species that has been improperly harvested becomes 'just a plant,' devoid of spiritual energy. This is perfectly acceptable if the plant is being employed in simple medicina caseira 'home herbalism,' where the therapeutic properties are of a chemical as opposed to a spiritual nature. But if its intended use is for spiritual medicine—if the occult powers of the plant need to be awakened—then specific collection and preparation procedures need to be observed.[25] These precepts include gathering the plant at the proper time.[26] The preferred collection time is usually late at night or early in the morning, when the leaf sap is most abundant. The liquid exudate from the leaves symbolizes the blood of the plant, the vegetal **axé**, the principal source of foliar energy. Dried leaves, which have lost their liquid energy, are not employed in Candomblé ritual. If the leaves are collected outside the grounds of the terreiro, such as in the forest, it is necessary to seek the **agô**, or permission, of the appropriate deities: Ossâim, god of leaves and medicine, and Oxóssi, god of the forest and hunt. This permission is obtained by begging the forgiveness of the deities and also paying a small offering for the leaves. The gift often consists of a few coins, a chunk of black tobacco, and some honey.

The pai- or mãe-de-santo prepares the **abô** by placing the leaves in a basin of cool water and slowly kneading them with his or her hands (Fig. 5.10). This physical manipulation of the leaves serves to augment the inherent **axé** of the leaves with that being transferred by the priest. An incantation is often whispered over the leaves in order to awaken their spiritual energy.[27] In order to marshal even more spiritual energy, the developing **abô** may be placed inside

5.10   Preparation of an **abô** by a pai-de-santo. (Photo: Janira Voeks)

the **peji** (shrine) of the appropriate **orixá** for a period of time. The final result is medicine charged with the spiritual energy of the leaves, of the priest, and of the offended deity. The client washes with the leaf bath in privacy, standing naked and pouring the greenish liquid over his or her head. A split bottle gourd (*Lagenaria siceraria*)—the sacred vessel that, according to mythology, holds Ossâim's medicinal secrets—may be used to pour the **abô**. The client lets the water and leaves dry naturally on his or her body, usually without toweling off. The aroma of sacred leaves, whether sweet or pungent, constantly follows adherents to Candomblé.

Another **abô**, known as the **abô** de casa 'house leaf bath,' is fundamental to Candomblé worship. This bath includes a complicated array of foliar elements as well as other sacred materials, including, for initiates, the blood of sacrificed animals. Also known as the purification bath, the house **abô** is administered to members of the terreiro before all major ceremonies and to **iaô**, Candomblé novices, during the months or years of initiation (Fig. 5.11). Depending on the terreiro, the initiates are usually brought out of their **roncó** (quarters) late at night or early in the morning and administered a cold **abô** by the mãe pequena. Most **iaô** are required to drink periodically from the leaf bath so as to purify both the inside and the outside of the body. While most **iaô** describe these nocturnal purges in disparaging terms, the leaf bath apparently has a profound psychological impact. Years after initiation has been completed, just the aroma of this leaf combination can induce possession trance.

Unlike the medicinal baths prescribed during consultations, the elements of the house **abô** are not modified to fit the occasion. Rather, the specific foliar composition is a characteristic of the terreiro, one that in principal never changes and that represents one of the terreiro's most closely guarded secrets. Ranging in composition from seven to sixteen to twenty-one species, each house **abô** is learned by the priest during his or her years of initiation.

Determining whether a problem is of a spiritual rather than an organic origin is not necessarily easy. Despite fastidiously attending to the wishes of the **orixás**, followers experience illness, lose loved ones, and face financial difficulties. Acts of spiritual prophylaxis serve to diminish the probability of becoming ill, but do not eliminate it. Moreover, spiritual imbalance is not the source of every predicament. There are problems that "just happen." A respiratory ailment may be nothing more than a viral infection. A broken arm may result from simple carelessness. A family member may die because it was his or her time. If a health problem is deemed to be of organic origin, the client is often referred to a physician. A few Western doctors maintain reciprocal relationships with pais- or mães-de-santo, in which one sends clients to the other if

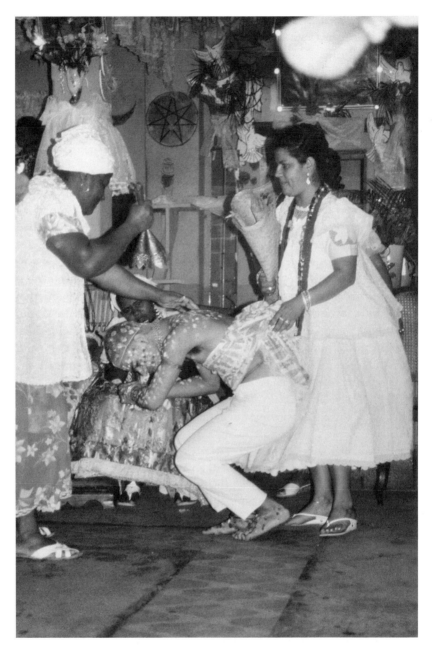

5.11 Male **iaô** during **orunkô** ceremony. While possessed by his principal deity, the initiate shouts his new Candomblé name three times to the assembled audience. (Photo: Robert Voeks)

the problem appears to be within the other's purview.[28] In those cases in which the pai- or mãe-de-santo is well versed in the practice of herbalism (which is often), he or she may prescribe a medicinal plant therapy.

Curandeiros

The distinction between organically and spiritually derived illness is fuzzy for Bahians in general, and even more so for those who are serious followers of Candomblé. In principle, all illness is believed to be derived from imbalance with the other world and, hence, within the purview of spiritual divination and treatment. According to Nina Rodrigues, most Bahians at the end of the nineteenth century attributed all disease and mortality, with the exception of violent death, to the actions of the spirits and of living magicians.[29] Contemporary Afro-Brazilians both within and outside of Candomblé are well acquainted with the causes and consequences of microbial and parasitic infections, and the European conception of germ theory has been injected with little resistance into the regional ethnomedical belief system. African slaves may have imported their own notions of disease cause and effect, such as the elaborate system retained by present-day Nigerian Yoruba, but there is little or no evidence that such a system survived in, or even arrived at, Brazil.[30] Thus, although subject to individual interpretation, illness is believed to be generally separable into that which is treatable via divination and work with the deities, and that which is treatable by Western doctors or herbalists.

Many pais- and mães-de-santo are adept at identifying and treating organic illness, and thus have come to occupy the role of community curandeiros. Others steadfastly avoid "practicing medicine."[31] For this latter group of priests, organic medicine is viewed as a negócio do médico "doctor's business,' and well outside the scope of sacred medicine. When symptoms suggest an organic cause, such as a virus, bacterial infection, or muscle pain, the client is simply referred to a physician trained in the Western tradition.

Whether the priest does or does not choose to work with herbalism follows from several considerations. First, because many pais- and mães-de-santo believe that all illness, accidents, and calamities have spiritual or magical causes—resulting, for example, from failure to observe euó or carry out obligations, or from an inadvertent evil eye—treatment of the other-worldly source of the illness may well cause the symptoms to disappear. This is particularly the case when the client has already visited a Western-style doctor without resolution of the problem. The wealth and prestige of the terreiro is another factor. With the exception of the few well-appointed temples in Salvador, the majority of

Bahian candomblés are poor and underfinanced, forever struggling to provide not only a service for the community but also subsistence for the pai- or mãe-de-santo. In these myriad proletarian terreiros (more common in some Bahian neighborhoods than the ubiquitous corner pharmacy), the pai- or mãe-de-santo may well survive on the revenue generated by fee-paying clients. The success of many terreiros is thus underpinned by the ability of the priest to be a jack-of-all-healing-trades: spiritual, magical, and organic.

It is also true that whereas mastery of liturgical and medicinal plants lies at the fulcrum of Candomblé knowledge, most pais- and mães-de-santo are nevertheless increasingly drawn from the ranks of an urban population with limited familiarity with either local or exotic flora. Open space in burgeoning cities such as Salvador, Cachoeira, Ilhéus, and Itabuna is becoming rare, and traditional knowledge of all but the most common medicinal taxa is disappearing rapidly. For most urban dwellers, including the majority of Candomblé followers, the healing forest has largely been supplanted by the ever-present, if unaffordable, corner pharmacy. Even where cognitive skills in herbalism are being preserved, decreasing access to native vegetation often forces the pai- or mãe-de-santo to travel long distances to gather sacred herbs, an expenditure that few terreiros can afford, or else to patronize a casa de folhas, or herb stand. A Salvador filho-de-santo once complained, for example, that someone had chopped down the last bico-de-papagaio (*Centropogon cornutus*) in the neighborhood, a small tree used both in initiation ceremonies and to treat stomach ulcers. Thus, while the art of herbalism survives in the Candomblé terreiro, kept alive by custom, demand, and financial reward, its continued existence is uncertain.

Herbalism

Dispensing medicinal advice and herbal remedies is part and parcel of the role of pai- or mãe-de-santo as neighborhood curandeiro. The priest's familiarity with the healing properties of leaves stems in part from his or her daily employment of plants for other purposes, especially preventive medicine and spiritual healing. Nearly thirty percent of the Candomblé species collected in this study (see Appendix 1) retain more than one use, serving the function of spiritual treatment as part of one therapy, and of organic healing in another. The aromatic leaves of leopoldina (*Alpinia zerumbet*), for example, are common constituents of a healing **abô**. In other situations, the plant serves as a leaf infusion for the treatment of anxiety and shortness of breath. The fern samambaia (*Lygodium volubile*)[32] is used in baths to dissipate negative energies as well as baths to treat rheumatism. This dual nature of the healing flora leads to conflicts, however, such as with carrapicho (*Bidens pilosa*). Representing one of Candomblé's most powerful magical plants, this innocuous little weed frequently finds its way into malevolent recipes involving animal parts and fresh grave dirt. Thus, although an infusion made from this herb is well known to be an excellent treatment for kidney problems, its association with black magic and Exu precludes its medicinal use in most terreiros.

Organic Medicine

A total of 76 taxa out of the 140 species collected in this study are employed as treatments for organic health problems. The majority are applied in the form of the characteristic chá, or leaf tea, the tried-and-true treatment of Brazilian home medicine. There is nothing sacred or uniquely African about these prescriptions, as most Brazilians can recite at least a few home remedies using infusions. They are the first line of offense against pathogens, and when you call on a doctor in Bahia, it is not unusual for him to ask if you have tried um chazinho 'a little tea' yet. If Africans have influenced the nature of these infusions, it would probably be in the unusually high incidence of leaves used in their preparation, as opposed to roots. For the Yoruba and their diaspora, leaves are the major repository of vegetal **axé**.

Herbal baths represent the next most common form of treatment. Although leaf baths are the dominant form of spiritual therapy employed among the Yoruba, their widespread use as treatments for physical maladies, both inside and outside of Candomblé, owes much to early indigenous habits. The Portuguese marveled from the first days of discovery at the frequency with which the natives bathed, especially given the notorious lack of hygiene exhibited by most Europeans of the time.[33] But by the mid-1600s, according to Dutch physician Guilherme Piso, the practice of using aromatic herb baths "against afflictions of the body as well as for pleasure" was common among the Portuguese.[34] The banho das folhas, or aromatic leaf bath, is firmly entrenched in Brazilian folk medicine.

The other medicinal preparations are as varied as the uses to which they are applied. Leaves are chewed in a raw state, dried and smoked, boiled in water until attaining a thick syrupy consistency, or steeped in hot water for vapor inhalation. Leaf juice is squeezed from raw leaves and either taken internally or rubbed on the place of affliction. Hot leaves are applied directly above the point of pain or discomfort, as is the oily extract of certain seeds. Several leaves and stems are prepared as garrafadas, or bottled medicines—meaning the leaf is soaked for a period of time in a bottle of sterilized water, white wine, or cachaça for eventual internal consumption.

Medicinal Plant Origins

The Candomblé herbal pharmacopoeia, like its spiritual healing counterpart, owes its origin to the idiosyncratic history of biogeography as well as several millennia of accumulation and diffusion of medicinal knowledge. Some species have medicinal histories predating even the Greek and Roman eras, such as castor oil, the powerful purgative made from the Old World castor bean (*Ricinus communis*). Relieving constipation since the time of the Egyptian pharaohs, the castor bean was introduced and has been employed as a medicinal in Brazil at least since the early nineteenth century.[35] The first century of Brazilian colonization witnessed the arrival of a host of Old World medicinals. Plantation owner Gabriel Soares de Sousa noted that poejo (*Mentha pulegium*), transagem (*Plantago major*), and manjericão (*Ocimum canum*) were all doing well in late sixteenth-century Bahian gardens.[36] Von Martius reported the medicinal use of **quiôiô** (*Ocimum gratissimum*), melão-de-São Caetano (*Momordica charantia*), and laranja-da-terra (*Citrus aurantium*), all familiar elements in Europe's food pharmacy, during his passage through Brazil in the early 1800s.[37]

The medicinal value of some of these species was probably divined from their perceived morphological similarity to the problem or disease to be treated. In this way, heart-shaped leaves seemed inclined by nature to cure coronary problems; pubescent leaves, to treat baldness. Dating back at least two thousand years in India and China, this Doctrine of the Signatures spread to various parts of the New World and held sway in medical theory until the seventeenth century.[38] At least until recently, the concept was commonly applied by the African Yoruba as well.[39] Plants in the Candomblé pharmacopoeia that appear to subscribe to this law include escada-de-macaco (*Bauhinia* cf. *smilacina*), a native primary forest liana. Its woody stem is cut into phallic-sized segments, soaked in white wine or cachaça, and drunk as an aphrodisiac. The rounded reproductive structures under the stem of the tiny herb quebra-pedra (*Phyllanthus amarus*), whose vernacular name means 'break stones,' hints at this plant's natural affinity for ridding the patient of kidney stones.

The degree to which the Candomblé organic pharmacopoeia reflects assimilation of indigenous knowledge is difficult to determine. Most colonial medicinal descriptions were fragmentary and, I suspect, biased toward species immediately at hand. Although practical concerns about the deteriorating health of the natives stimulated interest in the local healing flora, it is doubtful that early settlers and missionaries journeyed far beyond their villages and plantations to tap the primary forest pharmacopoeia. Moreover, like most immigrants from distant lands, colonial observers tended to emphasize familiar features of the new land, the places and things that reminded them of home. These topophylic tendencies appear to have biased their perceptions of the healing flora toward plants they remembered from Portugal. Sixteenth-century colonists Padre Fernão Cardim, Friar Vicente do Salvador, and planter Gabriel Sousa all marveled at how many medicinals were common to the shores of both continents, as did Guilherme Piso a century later.[40] In any case, because the majority of the medicinals listed in historical treatments have no lexical equivalents to today's flora, the usefulness of these lists in determining quantitative changes in medicinal plant knowledge is limited.

Perusal of Bahia's early pharmacopoeias nevertheless reveals a few native plants and remedies that have managed to persevere. Aroeira (*Schinus terebinthifolius*), a Brazilian native now of pantropical distribution, was and still is employed in healing baths to treat skin infections and external injuries.[41] Common fedegoso (*Senna occidentalis*) was used by the padres to treat kidney stones as well as to cure Indians "so they don't die." Native healers employed the plant against a parasitic flea. Fedegoso is now prepared by Candomblé priests as a febrifuge.[42] In the early 1700s, Portuguese surgeon Luis Ferreyra noted the medicinal use of the perennial forest herb capeba (*Pothomorphe umbellata*), a species currently used by Candomblé practitioners to treat liver disease.[43] Jurubeba (*Solanum* sp.), whose current uses range from treatment of liver and stomach ailments to the cure of general weakness and chronic coughs, was employed in sixteenth-century Bahia to "heal skin sores."[44] Parts of the second-growth shrub cambara (*Lantana camara*), which in the past were boiled in water and used as a wash for cuts and skin injuries, are now boiled down into a syrup to treat chest colds.[45] The addictive "Holy herbe" tobacco, whose smoke was used therapeutically by Indians and colonists to aid digestion, remedy shortness of breath, and kill worms in open wounds,[46] became a staple in the colonial diet of the African slave, who "prefers his tobacco to food."[47] Tobacco is still employed in Afro-Brazilian healing ceremonies, albeit for problems of a more spiritual nature, and particularly among groups such as the Umbanda, who encourage syncretism with Amerindian traditions.[48]

The collective knowledge of many other medicinals either was never transferred to the Europeans and Africans or was simply lost over the centuries. For example, several early writers mention the medicinal benefits of naná, a native bromeliad that much impressed early explorers and missionaries. One of these was shipwrecked Englishman Anthony Knivet, who described this relative of the pineapple as a treatment for kidney stones.[49] Today, this domesticated species is used infrequently as food and as an ornamental, but never, to my knowledge, as a medicinal. Another local medicinal plant of importance during the sixteenth century was *ipecac* (*Cephaelis ipecacuanha*), recorded by colonial observers as a treatment for ailments of the blood and for dysentery.[50] Centuries later, research showed the plant to contain a powerful emetic and amebicide, and the bioactive compound emetine is now extracted from the plant roots and marketed as a Western drug.[51] Among Candomblé healers, however, the species either never entered the plant pharmacopoeia or failed to persist as a medicinal.

In the course of interviews, it became apparent that Candomblé curandeiros often disagree over the identity and medicinal value of certain taxa. The tiny pepper alfavaquinha-de-cobra (*Peperomia pellucida*), for example, is prescribed by one healer for heart ailments, by another for high blood pressure, and by still another for prostate swelling (Fig. 5.12). Infusions from the leaves of **mu-lungú** (*Erythrina poeppigiana*) are used to treat toothache, sore throat, and anxiety. This diversity of uses does not necessarily invalidate either the efficacy of the medicinal or the competence of the healer. Single species often contain a range of different bioactive compounds, and each could conceivably target a different malady. Moreover, a single compound can manifest as a treatment for more than one problem. In any case, although all of the informants in this survey are considered to be competent healers and have a considerable following of trusted clients, they nevertheless acquired their knowledge from different sources and continue to maintain this knowledge as an oral rather than a written tradition. It should come as no surprise, then, that healers differ in what they use and how they use it.

There is, on the other hand, surprisingly little lexical disagreement between healers. Medicinals are generally known by the same name, and misidentification is rare. In a few cases, species with similar appearance in the same genus are lumped into one or another folk taxon. The fleshy-leaved rock plants *Kalanchoe integra* and *K. pinnata*, for example, may be called folha-da-costa, folha-da-fortuna, milagre-de–São Joaquim, or saião, depending on who makes the identification, or they may be called by their Yoruba equivalents, **oju orô** and **ewe dudu**. Alumã, a common medicine for stomach and liver complaints, includes both *Vernonia condensata* and *V. schoenanthus*.

The range of illness treated by Candomblé healers is substantial, ranging from cancer, diabetes, and pneumonia at one extreme to blemishes, obesity, and hair loss at the other. There are few physical maladies that one or another

5.12 The pantropical weed <u>alfavaquinha-de-cobra</u> (*Peperomia pellucida*). (Photo: Robert Voeks)

Candomblé priest or priestess healer does not claim confidence in treating. There are a total of 153 maladies that are treated by the Candomblé pharmacopoeia, or roughly twice the number of medicinal plants. Thus, each species on average has two different medicinal applications. But while the diversity of treatments is impressive, most of the prescriptions are in fact used to treat ordinary, everyday health complaints. Of the total medicinal flora, 26 percent are used as infusions for flu and stomach ailments, 20 percent for general stomach problems, and 18 percent for relief of rheumatism. Thus, although some of these medicinal plants are prescribed for life-threatening illness, much of this pharmacopoeia is best characterized as equivalent to "over-the-counter" Western medicines.

Magical Medicine

The people of Northeastern Brazil labor under an array of magically derived health problems that often defy diagnosis and prescription within the sweep of Western medicine. These culturally defined illness episodes, often viewed by Western doctors as psychological in origin and hence outside their expertise, can nevertheless lead to serious physical and emotional suffering. Although some of these perceived maladies and their cures arrived with Africans, most trace their ancestry to European magical beliefs and superstitions.[52] In their general-purpose role as neighborhood curandeiros, Candomblé practitioners inherited by default the responsibility to deal with the sundry magically derived afflictions that harass the population, including even those that traditionally require treatment by means of folk Christian rituals.

At the same time, Candomblé priests have traditionally been called upon not only to resolve the problems associated with magic, but to dispense it as well. The use of magical formulas to improve the health, personal relations, and financial status of clients has long been part of the stock and trade of Yoruba priests and their Brazilian descendants. It is inevitable, however, that the process of improving the lives of some necessarily translates into introducing pain and disorder into the lives of others. Among the African Yoruba, for example, Pierre Verger notes that recipes serving to make rain fall from the skies are "good for some people, but can be awful for others."[53] Thus, even where priests are not directly acting against others, their attempts to tip the balance of fortune inevitably create winners and losers, victors and victims.

As noted earlier, the perceived ability of New World Africans to do harm, both to their owners during the period of slavery and to enemies within the African American community, is one of the principal reasons for the survival of this and other neo-African religions. For the majority of Brazilians, in fact, Candomblé connotes **macumba**, the summoning forth of dark forces to do injury to others. Thus, while subscribing to the central tenets of Candomblé is anathema to many Bahians, most nevertheless admit to maintaining a healthy respect for the malevolent powers of its practitioners. Respect in these cases is best translated as fear. Thus, Candomblé priests to some degree maintain the dual role of purveyor of and protector from magic.

The role of magic in many terreiros, I suspect, is nevertheless slowly eroding. Candomblé and other African-based belief systems are emerging from their dubious past to become legitimate means of religious expression in Brazil. No longer persecuted by the authorities, Candomblé and its practitioners are increasingly viewed, at least by intellectuals and many enlightened Brazilians, as powerful symbols of the African cultural contribution to Brazilian society. In some instances, particularly for the large and prosperous terreiros in Salvador, Candomblé has emerged from its humble and oppressed origins to take its place as an acceptable spiritual alternative to Christianity. And part of this legitimacy appears to be derived from a declining emphasis on the practice of magic. As fear is gradually replaced by respectability, many practitioners no longer feel the need to conjure occult forces. Because the positive social role provided by the community terreiro is, in the eyes of many, compromised by continuing such activities, the practice of black magic appears to be on the decline.

Evil Eye

Among the myriad magically derived problems affecting Bahians, perhaps the most common among Candomblé believers and nonbelievers is mau-olhado, the 'evil eye.' A few special people, it is believed, are born with the innate ability to cast the evil eye, even if inadvertently. Mau-olhado originates as a form of exaggerated envy for the material possessions of others, such as animals, house plants, or pets. Small children are particularly susceptible. Often without realizing it, the perpetrator transfers negative fluids directly to the object of his or her desire, resulting in the injury, ill health, or even death of relatively defenseless beings, such as small birds and children. Every family seems to have experienced the effects of evil eye at one time or another. Ever vigilant against this dangerous force, Bahians are immediately suspicious of exaggerated compliments from friends and neighbors.

Olho grande, or big eye, represents a variety of evil eye, except that in this case the negative effects occur more in the area of business and finances. Failed business ventures, decreasing sales, and lack of professional promotion are all signals that the jealousy of a peer is blocking the path to advancement and success. Unlike mau-olhado, however, olho grande is considered to be intentional rather than accidental.

Both of these afflictions are more easily avoided than treated. The traditional means of fending off evil eye is to summon the occult powers of the plant kingdom to provide the necessary prophylaxis. The first line of defense involves the placement of specified ornamental plants in the entryways to private residences and businesses and at various points in the terreiro. The most common plants for this use include the woody herb vence tudo Africano (*Justicia gendarrussa*); the bowstring hemps espada-de-Ogun and espada-de-Oxóssi (*Sansevieria* cf. *aethiopica*); the woody aroid comigo-ninguém-pode (*Dieffenbachia maculata*); the shrubs abre-caminho (*Baccharis* sp.), pinhão roxo (*Jatropha gossypifolia*), and vence tudo (*Rolandra fruticosa*); and the fern samambaia (*Lygodium volubile*).

Although most of these species represent common pantropical cultivars, all are endowed with special significance within Candomblé. Each of these plants is said to "belong" to one or another of the gods of fire—deities whose nature is aggressive, bellicose, and masculine. It is not the power of the plants themselves but rather that of their owners that provides the necessary protection. The relevant gods include Ogun, with his power to clear paths; Oxóssi, the hunter; Omolu, the feared god of smallpox; and Caboclo, the indigenous god of the Brazilian forest. If it is to attack its intended victim successfully, evil eye must be able to navigate a gauntlet of spiritual protection.

Individuals can partially protect themselves against evil eye by carrying a sprig of arruda (*Ruta graveolens*) or laranja-da-terra (*Citrus aurantium*) somewhere on their bodies. Arruda in particular has a lengthy history of magical and medical use, extending well before the colonization of Brazil. It served as a panacea for all ailments during Greek and Roman periods,[54] and Roman ladies are reported to have hidden cuttings from this small cultivated shrub in their clothing to fend off evil eye.[55] Ferdinand Magellan carried arruda, probably for good luck, on his unlucky voyage of discovery.[56] In the 1830s, the French traveler Jean Baptiste Debret reported that African slaves sold arruda on the streets of Rio de Janeiro to buyers who hid small cuttings inside their turbans or behind their ears as protection from bad luck.[57] Arruda continues to serve precisely the same purpose, and the scene described by Debret has changed little in 160 years. Arruda is still available on the streets of Rio as well as in the herb markets of Salvador, and Baianas can still be seen with pieces of this magical plant tucked in the folds of their turbans or behind their ears.

Another line of personal protection against evil eye, as well as against other forms of bad luck, is provided by wearing or possessing various protective amulets. The horns of animals, strategically placed, have long represented lines of defense against unseen malevolent forces. For the European ancestors of Brazilians, horns symbolized "sexual energy, fecund impulse, and physical energy."[58] The use of horns to repel evil eye was common in Iberia at the turn of the century, as it has been among the African Yoruba in recent times.[59] The practice was also common in early nineteenth-century Brazil,[60] and it continues in Bahia today, where many Candomblé terreiros situate oxhorns in their gardens to repel evil eye.[61]

The most common Bahian amulet is the figa, represented by a small wood carving of a human fist with the thumb inserted between the index and middle fingers. Although some figas are crafted from bone, stone, or even plastic, the wood of guiné, arruda, native fig, and other spiritually powerful species is preferred.[62] Dating from at least as far back as Roman times, the use of the figa symbol against evil eye was common at the turn of the nineteenth century in Lisbon and Madeira,[63] and it is still displayed for this purpose in Portugal. Figa amulets in Brazil have been recorded since the early 1900s. Robert Walsh reported from Rio de Janeiro that illness in children that could not be explained through physical causes was "attributed to the effects of an evil eye," and that as a precaution, mothers "suspended over the head of the child to be protected, a little hand, with the thumb placed between the fingers, which they call a figa."[64] In late nineteenth-century Salvador, the figa was probably the most common form of amulet.[65] Today this tiny carving represents one of the most visible symbols of continued deference to the occult powers. Small figas are worn around the neck or as bracelets, and almost every Bahian household has one on display, even if only for decoration.

Another frequently used protective amulet is the **patuá**,[66] a small cloth pouch hung around the neck containing sacred objects, devotional messages, and plant parts. In the past these were fashioned from leather, but today they are usually made from cotton or synthetic cloth. **Patuás** have a considerable history of use among Europeans and African Muslims. Ancient Egyptians inscribed lengthy magical verses on their papyrus amulets well before the Christian era, and medieval Europeans carried various types of sacred objects with mystical messages hidden on their bodies for protection against magic.[67] In late nineteenth-century Bahia, Black Muslims—the descendants of Hausa slaves—carried protective talismans inscribed with Koranic messages to "close the body against all the evils."[68] The Hausa traders in West Africa were considered, at least until recently, "great salesmen" of these magical packets,[69] and such talismans are still commonly employed by Muslims throughout the world. Ever prepared to fortify his own arsenal of magical powers, the non-Muslim African readily incorporated these Islamic charms "to enrich and fortify his own magic."[70] Like most forms of protection against evil eye, the use of **patuás** is not restricted to followers of Candomblé; conversely, not all Candomblé followers subscribe to their use.

The foliar components of the **patuá** are fairly consistent. The ones I've seen prepared include a piece of rhizome from **dandá** (*Cyperus rotundus*) cut into the shape of a figa. This figure is then sandwiched between small leaves of arruda (*Ruta graveolens*) and guiné (*Petiveria alliacea*) and sewn into the tiny cloth bag. Christian prayers on small scraps of paper may also be included. West African **akokô** (*Newbouldia laevis*) also finds its way into **patuás**, as do pieces of garlic, clove, abre-caminho (*Baccharis* sp.), vence tudo (*Rolandra fruticosa*), and other herbs.[71]

In houses that experience chronic problems with evil eye or new homes whose owners seek to avoid these problems, a Candomblé healer may be called to do a limpeza, or cleaning. This process consists of, among other things, shaking specified leaves in the house and symbolically wiping away any negative fluids or envy that may have accumulated. The bundled leaves, which are always fresh, often include caiçara (*Borreria verticillata*), São Gonçalinho (*Casearia* sp.), coerana (*Cestrum laevigatum*), murici (*Byrsonima sericea*), and candeia branca (*Miconia hypoleuca*).

The treatment for those suffering the effects of evil eye, aside from the herbal baths described earlier, is Christian prayer. For Candomblé priests and priestesses, most of whom were baptized as Catholics, the recitation of Christian prayers does not seem to represent a spiritual conflict. Rather, it is simply a matter of administering the appropriate medicine for the specified affliction. In one such healing ceremony, the afflicted places cuttings from one, two, or three plants in a glass of water. These can be arruda (*Ruta graveolens*), vassourinha (*Scoparia dulcis*), salsa-da-praia (*Ipomoea pes-caprae*), pinhão roxo (*Jatropha gossypifolia*), fedegoso (*Senna occidentalis*), or alfazema (*Vitex* sp.). The person then places one hand over the heart, saying at the same time, "In the name of the father, son, and holy ghost." The participant then recites the following verse:

[Name of the participant],
God generated you,
God created you,
God frees you from the affliction that affects you.
Open life, open death,

There is nothing stopping you.
If it's because of your smile,
If it's because of the way you speak,
If it's because of the way you walk,
If it's because of your beauty,
If it's because of your ugliness,
If it's because of the way you study,
If it's because you work so well, . . .

Then the afflicted person continues to state all the possible sources of the evil eye.[72]

Aside from evil eye, a host of other complaints, most of magical origin, afflict the population as well. One of these is quebranto, which is described as a type of physical lassitude, a general pain in the body, and a lack of urge to do anything; it is one of the more common culture-specific illnesses. Manifesting flu-like symptoms without a viral source, quebranto is believed to be caused by the entrance into the body of negative fluids. Another common ailment is espinhela caida, described as a weakened condition of the arms and upper body, with pain typically in the thoracic area. The presence of the illness is diagnosed by measuring from the tip of the index finger to the elbow, and then comparing this length to the distance from the edge of one shoulder to the other. If the two measurements do not correspond closely, then the patient is believed to be suffering from espinhela caida. Vento caido is a common childhood illness. It is characterized by fever, diarrhea, and symptoms of dehydration, again without apparent organic cause. Diagnosis is made by passing a finger over the child's forehead and tasting it. If it tastes sour, or if the child's two feet are not the same size, then vento caido is indicated.

Because these health problems are not African in origin, their treatment is largely outside the arena of Candomblé spiritual medicine. The usual remedy involves spiritual purification by means of herbal baths, fumigations with incense, and Christian prayers. For example, cobreiro is a common affliction that lies outside the purview of Western medicine. Thought to be caused by the touch of a spider, toad, or snake, cobreiro manifests as an unexplainable outbreak of rashes and skin eruptions, something like water blisters. One of the treatments includes repeating the following prayer three times:

I came from Rome, from Romaria,
curing cobreiro, and cobraria,
with a green branch, and cold water.
We cut our head, we cut our tail,
in the name of God and of Maria.[73]

After saying the prayer, the patient dips three small stems of arruda in cold water and passes the moist leaves over the area affected by cobreiro.[74] Although the recitation of this and other healing prayers does not necessarily place this cure in the realm of magic, the inclusion of the ritual with arruda, a plant with no particular Christian significance but with a lengthy history in the realm of conjure and sorcery, does.[75]

While many of these magically derived ailments are as common today as in the past, other treatments appear to be dying out through lack of relevance. One such practice involves the use of mamona (*Ricinus communis*), the castor bean plant, to alleviate painful lactation. According to one elderly Candomblé pai-de-santo, in the past, small sections of the stem of mamona were cut and hung around the necks of women as amulets in order to stop lactation. This practice was apparently common during Brazil's colonial era, when large numbers of African and mulatto women were rented out as wet nurses to care for abandoned children in cities such as Salvador.[76] For those women who chose not to spend much of their adult lives breast-feeding hungry infants or who found sustained lactation to be painful, the mamona amulet was believed to provide a temporary respite. Aside from one description of mamona's past use, I saw no evidence of the plant's being used for this purpose.

The most complete erosion of magical practice involves the issue of fertility. In the literature on Yoruba as well as general African ethnomedicine, the subject of maximizing fertility in men and women assumes a prominent position. Children, for the Yoruba, are "the crown of life," and for a woman there is no greater dishonor or social calamity than to be pronounced barren.[77] Considered to be the work of witches or malevolent spirits, infertility is traditionally treated with the spiritual assistance of a **babalaô** (father of mysteries), a **babalorixá** (father of the **orixás**), or an herbalist. The functions of many of the Yoruba medicinal incantations recorded by Pierre Verger are self-explanatory: "Owner of Penis and Testicle," "Draw Semen," "Huge" (to get children), "It Cuts, It Cuts" (to make a man's sperm stay in the body of a woman), and others.[78] This preoccupation with fertility was, however, never elicited in my discussions with Candomblé priests. Other than a few plants thought to possess aphrodisiac powers (which of course are of marginal importance to the issue of fertility), no mention was ever made of plants or other means for increasing fertility. When I posed the question to Pai Ruy, he said that among most Afro-Brazilian women, many of whom are poor and without reliable husbands, the most significant issue was how to stop fertility, not how to enhance it. He could never recall having been approached by a client hoping to increase her fertility. A historical explanation for this lack of interest in procreation was offered by anthropologist Roger Bastide, who asked pointedly, "What was the good of asking the gods to make women fruitful when they could bear nothing but infant slaves?"[79]

Medicine for Wealth

The ritual use of plants to increase wealth or enhance business success is also common in Candomblé terreiros. Financial problems are a never-ending source of hardship for much of the Afro-Brazilian population, and not surprisingly, Candomblé priests have retained those rituals associated with acquiring and keeping money. One frequent method used is the banho de desenvolvimento 'development bath.' This ritual, as noted earlier, is similar to the purification baths, and like them it uses an odd number of sacred leaves in the recipe. The difference is that these leaf baths are specifically employed to improve the financial or commercial success of clients. People who are about to begin new businesses or are hoping to improve their current financial situation can seek to improve their chances by taking banhos de desenvolvimento as prescribed by a pai- or mãe-de-santo.

Financial status may be improved as well by employing the power of plants that chama dineiro 'call money' to them, such as vintém (*Drymaria cordata*), **akokô** (*Newbouldia laevis*), and folha-da-fortuna (*Kalanchoe pinnata*).[80] Folha-da-fortuna, the 'leaf of fortune,' has the remarkable ability to reproduce viviparously, sprouting roots and tiny buds from the serrations of the leaf margins—hence its English name, "everlife" or "neverdie."[81] This ability seemingly to produce something from nothing led to its magical association with attracting money in West Africa, as noted in the following Yoruba magical incantation directed at folha-da-fortuna:

> Abamoda [folha-da-fortuna], my aspiration will be accomplished
> Orisa Oke [**Orixá Okê**] accept the aspiration of the chameleon
> I aspire to money.[82]

The special qualities of this species are also attested to in the following oral text recorded in Bahia:

> It is said that in the beginning of the world, all the leaves of the forest were told to make the above **ebó** (he goat, cocks, **obí**, **orobo**, etc) in order that each one might live as comfortably as possible under the prevailing circumstances. But none of them took heed except Ologaman (leaf of fortune) who made up his mind to dispatch such an **ebó**. As a consequence,

he was endowed with all the magical powers of Osanyin and became a miraculous leaf among all others which even today sprouts so admirably that it is the most powerful leaf in the occult sciences.[83]

Having diffused from West Africa, the understanding of the powers of this leaf are retained as Candomblé collective knowledge. In Salvador, I have seen a leaf of folha-da-fortuna nailed to a Candomblé priest's door in the belief that this would attract money. I was told that if one plants the leaf in a pot over a single coin in the soil, its roots will eventually draw the financial energy of the coin and thereby attract money.

The power to influence people, either financially or otherwise, is attributed to the weedy sedge **dandá** (*Cyperus rotundus*). In Nigeria, in addition to a host of traditional medicinal uses, the aromatic tuber of **dandá** is chewed by people who seek to influence others by their words. Defendants in court cases will conceal pieces in their cheeks as charms to secure acquittal.[84] The magical use of **dandá** has survived intact among the Afro-Brazilian population in Bahia.[85] At the suggestion of a pai-de-santo, I tried chewing the root while giving a talk at a conference, with results that were distinctly unsuccessful.

Magical Powder

One of the magical practices for which Candomblé priests have been most renowned is the production and use of magical pó, or powder. At least until recently, a highly regarded pai- or mãe-de-santo was seen as one "who has all the leaves in his nail."[86] This appellation referred to the alleged practice of reducing powerful plants, either poisonous or magical, to a powder. Concealed in the hand or under a fingernail, the pó was transferred to a victim while shaking hands. Pai Vicente stated that this practice was common "in the old days," and that was why he chose not to shake hands with other priests. Pai Balbino reported that people from Itaparica Island were particularly suspect, and that he never ate food, drank water, or touched anyone when such people were visiting for fear of being poisoned. Every pai- or mãe-de-santo has a story about other unscrupulous Candomblé practitioners who used powders to kill or harm their enemies, although few were willing to admit that they themselves employed them. Not all magical powders are necessarily employed for nefarious ends, however, as Nina Rodrigues noted that magical powder was also used in amulets for protection.[87]

One of the best known magical powders is prepared from the seeds of pimenta-da-costa (*Aframomum melegueta*). These small, reddish seeds, which have been an item of trade between West Africa and Iberia since about the thirteenth century, have been imported from West Africa to Salvador at least since the mid-1800s.[88] Small plastic containers containing pimenta-da-costa can still be purchased in a few open markets. Frequently referred to as **atarê** among Candomblé priests, the seeds of this plant have retained their African magical uses in Brazil. Among West Africans and their diaspora, the species is employed to create domestic problems. The Yoruba soak the seed in special medicine and place it in a position to be stepped on by the intended victim, who will become diseased.[89] It is also placed in the home of a victim, again to be stepped on, in order to bring general disorder to the occupants.[90] This practice appears to have survived in Louisiana, among the descendants of Vodun practitioners, as well.[91] In Bahia, Manuel Querino noted in the 1930s that crabs prepared with this seed were used to create domestic discontent.[92] I was told by a pai-de-santo that simply placing the powder of pimenta-da-costa on the floor of the victim's home was sufficient to create havoc in his or her personal life.

There seems to be an endless list of recipes for magical powders employed to attract or dissuade someone's romantic attention. These are often prepared from the standard macabre fare of dried frogs and snakes, eggs, human body hair, fingernails, menstrual blood, and poisonous parts. A small packet of the powder is placed strategically in or near the victim's house, often near the doorway or under the bed.[93] In Ilhéus, a filha-de-santo described a case in which a husband was desperate to get his wife to leave him. He had tried everything, but she refused to leave. Finally, he consulted a pai-de-santo, who gave him the following formula: Collect seven small handfuls of sand from the grave of a recently buried man and put it in a sack. Then buy a package of pemba de Exu (a magical powder sold in religious shops). Collect some corredeira (*Borreria* sp. or *Irlbachia purpurascens*), and slowly grind all the ingredients together until they make a fine powder. Take the powder to a place frequented by Exu, such as a crossroads, and tell him that this powder belongs to the slave (individual Exu) of your deity. Then put the powder somewhere in the house of the victim. According to the filha-de-santo, the woman left within three days, never to return.

A very common type of magical affliction, which is not exactly either intentional or accidental, involves a process known as troca da cabeça 'exchanging heads.' This complicated and well-guarded ritual facilitates the transfer of some negative spirit that has been picked up by a client to an animate or inanimate object. It is not unusual, for example, for a person to be possessed by an unwanted spirit—perhaps a spirit of the dead, an **egun**—or to acquire the spiritual presence of an inappropriate **orixá**—perhaps picked up while passing an **ebó** on the street. In this type of affliction, which can only be positively identified through consultation with a Candomblé priest, the client needs to exorcise the spirit and transfer it to an alternative host. The usual medium is a sacrificed chicken. After the transfer is effected, the dead animal is placed at one of the haunts of Exu, usually a crossroads. However, as noted earlier, the negative energy in the decaying bird is highly vagile and is likely to leap into the body of any vulnerable passerby—a dog, a cat, or a human—initiating the need for another troca da cabeça. And so on.

The troca da cabeça, according to two pais-de-santo, can also serve a more sinister purpose. As the symbolic owners of their filhos or filhas, pais- and mães-de-santo have both the power and the right to exchange life forces with their supplicants. An aging or seriously ill priest can thus effect a troca da cabeça in order to trade his or her illness and limited life span for the health and longevity of a younger and stronger adherent. It is rumored, for example, that a famous mãe-de-santo in Salvador took the lives of seven of her filhas in this way, so that each died prematurely in order to provide another year of life to this elderly priestess. Seven deaths for seven years of extra life, or so the story goes.

Candomblé etiology charts a complex passage through the parallel worlds of the material (**aiê**) and the spiritual (**orun**). Because illness is seen as reflecting a dysfunctional relationship between the gods and their mortal followers, it follows that prevention and treatment is effected through direct intervention by the spirits or their proxies. However, aside from their presence during possession trance, when the **orixás** ride about the barracão on the backs of their supplicants, the gods are not present in any physical sense in order to implement their wondrous magic. Rather, they have endowed certain natural elements with sufficient **axé** to combat illness in all its forms—spiritual, magical, and organic. Among all the elements of creation, it is the sacred leaves that most directly manifest the healing power of the deities.

Ossâim

Ossâim, guardian of the sacred leaves and medicine, is the deity most intimately involved in health and healing. His domain is the forest and the field, wherever curative plants grow spontaneously. Often in the company of Oxóssi the hunter, with whom he is said to trade medicine for meat, Ossâim is the dedicated but reticent steward of the vegetal realm. Among the Yoruba and their New World diaspora, his image is one of absurd physical disability—one eye, one leg, one enormous ear, and a humorous high-pitched voice.[1] His symbol is a piece of iron with seven points, with the central point mounted by a

6.1   The seven-pointed iron symbol of Ossâim. (Photo: Robert Voeks)

magical bird (Fig. 6.1). The following legend, related by Pai Ruy, describes how Ossâim came to master the secrets of the healing forest:

> When Obatalá created Earth, the land lived under a blanket of clouds. And the plants were not green, but white. Then, the **ara aiê**, the created human beings, began to get sick. And Obatalá needed to acquire a medicine so that his creations would not get sicker. He left **aiê** and entered **orun** seeking help. And Ossâim was disposed to assist him. When Ossâim arrives in **aiê**, he looks up into the sky, and sees the sun completely obscured by clouds. And he said, "The first thing that is necessary is to blow away the clouds." So Obatalá instructed Iansã to blow away the clouds with her winds, and the sun began to shine on the world. It was in this way that the plants became green. Ossâim then went traveling through the world seeking a place to live in **aiê**. And the place that he liked the most was among the plants, because now the plants had become green. But no one else wanted to go live with him. The other **orixás** preferred their own territories: Iansã, the wind; Oxum, the sweet water; Yemanjá, the ocean; Xangô, the stone quarry. Ossâim preferred to stay concealed in the forest. Thus hidden among the vegetation, he created an intimacy with the green beings. And he learned the personality, the characteristics, the properties, and the magical power of each of the green beings. In this way, when the other created beings needed a curative element, it was only Ossâim that had this knowledge. Thus, when any type of illness affects an animal of creation, only Ossâim knows how to treat it.[2]

Ossâim's exclusive possession of the sacred leaves was not to persist. His medicinal knowledge, according to legend, was coveted by other deities who sought to share his secrets. The following oral text, well known in the terreiros of Bahia and also recorded in West Africa by Pierre Verger and in Cuba by Lydia Cabrera,[3] describes how the **orixás** came to possess individualized plant pharmacopoeias:

> There is a legend of rivalry between Ossâim, the **orixá** of medicine and leaves, and Iansã, the **orixá** of stars, winds, and storms. Everything began as a result of jealousy. Iansã went to visit Ossâim. Ossâim is very reserved, quiet, silent. Iansã wanted to know what he was doing. When Ossâim has the opportunity, he explains things. But Iansã is always rushed, she wants everything done immediately. She is always asking questions, and she needs to know everything that's going on. When Iansã arrived at the house of Ossâim, he was busy working with his leaves. It happens that there are certain types of work with leaves that you can't talk about, you

need to remain silent. Iansã started asking, "What are you doing? Why are you doing this? Why are you doing that?" And Ossâim remained silent. "Alright, if you don't want to tell me what you're doing, then I'll make you talk." That's when Iansã began to shake her skirt and make the wind blow. The house of Ossâim is full of leaves, with all of their healing properties, and when the wind began to blow, it carried the leaves in every direction. Ossâim began to shout "**Ewe O, Ewe O!**" [My Leaves, My Leaves!]. Ossâim then asked the help of the **orixás** to collect the leaves, and the **orixás** went about gathering them. And it happens that every leaf that an **orixá** collected, every species, he or she became the owner of that leaf.[4]

Scattered in all directions by the winds of Iansã, the sacred leaves drifted into the provinces of the other deities. Oxum collected leaves near her rivers; Yemanjá, by the sea. Oxalá gathered white leaves; Exu, those that burned and pierced the skin. While Ossâim retained the mysterious power of the vegetal kingdom—he alone comprehends the inherent meaning of each leaf—each deity nevertheless came to possess his or her personal healing flora.[5]

The resultant correspondence between gods and leaves represents a fundamental element of Candomblé ceremony and ritual. Each plant, at least in principle, belongs to a single **orixá**. For a devotee who belongs to some deity, healing may be mediated through recourse to the inherent **axé** of his or her guardian's leaves. An **abô** for one of Oxum's followers, for example, will usually include either three or seven of Oxum's species. A leaf-whipping intended to clean the negative fluids from a filha or filho of Ogun will include some of Ogun's leaves. On the other hand, if a client suffers from an ailment associated with another deity, such as Xangô's anxiety or Oxum's material obsession, then the priest will incorporate leaves from the appropriate **orixá**.

The annual terreiro festival devoted to a particular god makes liberal use of that deity's pharmacopoeia. Flowers and leaves dedicated to the **orixá** adorn the barracão. Others are sprinkled on the floor to neutralize negative fluids. Likewise, during the long months of initiation, novices slowly assimilate the foliar **axé** of their guardian deities. Each devotee passes the night sleeping in a bed of the leaves dedicated to his or her deity and takes a nightly **abô** consisting of sixteen or twenty-one of these leaves. His or her sacred necklace is ritually washed with sabão-da-costa, a black soap imported from West Africa, and a concoction of appropriate leaves. In the ceremony in which the **orixá** is firmly planted in the head of the initiate, his or her head is shaved and washed with sacred leaves and splashed with the blood of a sacrificial dove or chicken.

As earthly embodiments of the Yoruba pantheon, Candomblé plants exhibit one or more features that link them with their corresponding deities. Most of these features are clearly evident, but some are obscure or lacking entirely. For example, the archetypes of the deities are divided according to temperament: masculine **orixás** are hot-tempered and volatile, while feminine **orixás** are cool and balanced. This opposition of hot and cold finds ready association among the healing flora. Some leaves retain perceived heating properties; they are thin, hard, and, if taken internally, tend to produce sweat or increase blood pressure. Cool leaves are fleshy and moist and produce cooling medicinal influences; they reduce blood pressure, break a fever, or calm anxiety. Further possibilities for correspondence are provided by the symbols, preferences, and prohibitions (**euó**) of the **orixás**: their choices of color for clothing and sacred beads, their preferred foods, their icons, and their geographical locations.

The following is a summary of the principal characteristics employed to divide the Candomblé ethnoflora among the Yoruba deities. It should be noted, however, that not all plants used in Candomblé are associated with an **orixá**. Priests divulged the god-plant correspondences for only 105 of the 140 liturgical and medicinal species identified. Of the plants not possessed by a deity, the majority (roughly 71 percent) are employed primarily to treat organic health problems—headaches, toothache, obesity, and the like. This is consistent with the idea that the treatment of purely medical problems by Candomblé priests is a secondary occupation, one inherited as part of their role as community healers. Most of these species form part of the collective folk medicine of the region, which is known by many in the community, particularly older women, who have no direct connection with Candomblé. Representing a healing flora that retains little or no ritual significance within the terreiro, these medicinal plants are considered useful, but far from sacred.

Gods and Leaves

As the god of love and peace, Oxalá embodies the white dimension of nature. His color preference represents the major organizing force in his pharmacopoeia. The white infructescence of cultivated algodão (*Gossypium barbadense*) places this shrub within the domain of Oxalá, along with the aromatic white racemes of sabugeiro (*Sambucus australis*). The pantropical herb boa noite (*Catharanthus roseus* var. *albus*) has both white flowers and milky latex. With its showy white flowers, corneta (*Datura metel*) also clearly belongs to Oxalá (Fig. 6.2). The weeds candeia branca (*Miconia hypoleuca*), purga-do-campo (*Hybanthus calceolaria*), and cambara branca (*Lantana camara*) likewise display white flowers, while jambo branco (*Syzygium jambos*), a domesticate from Asia, produces pale-colored fruit.

6.2   The white corolla of <u>corneta</u> (*Datura metel*) brings this shrub within the domain of Oxalá. (Photo: Robert Voeks)

Unlike most of the masculine deities, whose temperaments are hot and war-like, Oxalá is most intimately associated with the female entities, spiritual forces that serve to soothe and cool. One of the healing roles of this deity and of his associated flora is to counteract illness associated with overheating, a condition that frequently troubles adherents and clients who are connected to the hot deities. Thick-leaved plants that exude liquid when crushed, such as folha-da-costa (*Kalanchoe integra*), are considered to have cooling properties and are thus usually associated with the cool-tempered **orixás** like Oxalá (Fig. 6.3). In addition to its use in cooling foliar baths, this plant is also em-ployed as a remedy for headache—perceived as a hot symptom—by placing the leaf as a poultice on the patient's forehead. Its coolness, along with the belief that Oxalá controls illness associated with the head, places this species firmly within his domain.[6] Another of his species, the medicinal grass capim santo (*Andropogon schoenanthus*), is prepared as an infusion to treat hyperten-sion, another illness associated with heatedness. Other cooling, thick-leaved species dedicated to this pacifist god include folha-do-ar (*Mikania glomerata*), alfavaquinha-de-cobra (*Peperomia pellucida*), and tapete-de-Oxalá (*Plectran-thus amboinicus*), the leaves of which are so densely pubescent as to appear white.

Oxum is the feminine **orixá** of running water. She is a voluptuous fertility figure who is anatomically associated with the female organs and the stomach. Vain and materialistic, Oxum adores gold, jewelry, and perfume. Reflecting her love of perfume, nearly all of her leaves and flowers are sweetly fragrant. These aromatic plants are added to baths for their soothing properties, underscoring Oxum's cooling influence. The mint family, noted for its essential oils, is rep-resented in her pharmacopoeia by alecrim (*Hyptis fruticosa*), poejo (*Mentha pulegium*), and patchulí (*Pogostemon* cf. *cablin*). Other aromatics associated with Oxum include sabugueiro (*Sambucus australis*), **macaçá** (*Brunfelsia uni-flora*), jasmin-do-brejo (*Hedychium coronarium*), and beti cheiroso (*Piper* sp.). Laranja-da-terra (*Citrus aurantium*), which has fragrant flowers and leaves, retains a cooling medicinal influence as a sedative when taken as an infusion. Water retention is believed to be a hot ailment; hence Oxum owns arrozinha (*Zornia* cf. *gemella*), a plant employed medicinally as a diuretic. Leopoldina (*Alpinia zerumbet*) is particularly well suited to Oxum. Its flowers are prepared into an infusion that is believed to have a tranquilizing effect, diminishing the heatedness associated with anxiety, whereas its scented leaves are frequent components of perfumed baths. The leaf extract of vassourinha santa (*Scoparia dulcis*) is employed to reduce fever, an obvious hot symptom—hence its pos-session by a cool deity.

6.3 The fleshy leaves of <u>folha-da-costa</u> (*Kalanchoe integra*) suggest association with one or more of the cool deities. (Photo: Robert Voeks)

Oxum's remaining flora reveals her obsession with wealth. Her love of gold is symbolized by the bright yellow flowers of arrozinha (*Zornia* cf. *gemella*), mal-me-quer (*Wedelia paludosa*), maravilha (*Caesalpinia pulcherrima*), cambara amarella (*Lantana camara*), and acocí (*Wulffia baceata*). Oxum's material interests also account for her association with folha-da-fortuna (*Kalanchoe pinnata*), a cool species. As noted earlier, the 'leaf of fortune' has the curious habit of sprouting roots and seedlings viviparously at its leaf margins; hence it is perceived as having the ability to create something from nothing, explaining its connection to a materialist goddess. Another of Oxum's leaves, vintém (*Drymaria cordata*), which carries the name of a twenty-réi coin of the colonial period, is employed for similar material ends.

Yemanjá is another fertility figure, but her aquatic home is the ocean. Her preferred geographical location is the shoreline. Warm, maternal, and stable, Yemanjá is the archetype mother image. The beads of her necklace are transparent or crystal blue, symbolic of her watery domain. She shares most of her leaves with the other cool **orixás**, and nearly all are aromatic. These include alecrim (*Hyptis fruticosa*), **macaçá** (*Brunfelsia uniflora*), patchulí (*Pogostemon* cf. *cablin*), manjericão (*Ocimum canum*), and **dandá** (*Cyperus rotundus*). The latter, an African sedge, often inhabits coastal wetlands, reflecting Yemanjá's physical domain. Marianinha (*Commelina diffusa*) has pale blue flowers, Yemanjá's color choice, and is employed to treat inflammation, a hot symptom.

Like Oxum, Yemanjá is connected with problems of the uterus and other female organs. This may explain the inclusion in her flora of transagem (*Plantago major*), a garden cultivar that is prepared as an anti-inflammatory tea for uterine problems. Yemanjá is a maternal figure, often referred to as "the milk **orixá**"; her portraits, which often adorn the walls of the barracão, show her with abundant breasts. This intimate connection with mother's milk may account for her association with mamona (*Ricinus communis*), which (as noted earlier) was used as an amulet in the past to stop painful lactation in wet nurses. The use of this weedy shrub to treat lactation problems is widespread in both the Old and the New World.[7] Derived from the verb mamar 'to suckle,' mamona in colloquial Portuguese refers to a female baby who nurses well, again suggesting this plant's connection with mother's milk and hence with Yemanjá.

The leaves of unha-da-vaca (*Bauhinia ovata*), also associated with Yemanjá, are prepared as an infusion to treat diabetes, a hot disease. The connection of this plant to a feminine deity may also stem from its rounded leaf form, a common characteristic of the plants of female deities. Roundness also characterizes the emblems of the cool female deities, such as the **abebé**, the rounded fan of Yemanjá and Oxum.[8] This shape stands in sharp contrast to the more phallic icons associated with the masculine gods—usually lances and knives—and the shapes of their associated flora.[9]

Nanã is the aged female goddess of rain, swamp, and soil. She is referred to as the grandmother of the **orixás**, and in some legends is said to be the wife of Oxalá. Like the other cool deities, she is associated with regenerative properties. Her preferred colors are lavender, or blue, and white. Nanã's leaves are mostly aromatic, including neve cheiroso (*Hyptis suaveolens*), hortelã (*Mentha* sp.), alecrim (*Hyptis fruticosa*), beti cheiroso (*Piper* sp.), patchulí (*Pogostemon* cf. *cablin*), and **macaçá** (*Brunfelsia uniflora*). Her other two plants, bom dia (*Catharanthus roseus*) and salsa-da-praia (*Ipomoea pes-caprae*), both display large lavender-colored corollas, representing her color preference, and round leaves, characteristic of the feminine flora.

Iansã is the female deity of wind, storms, and stars. Unlike the cool female deities, Iansã can be either hot or cool, bellicose or compassionate, depending on her mood. Her fiery disposition is aptly personified by her preference for red. The leaves of Iansã, characteristic of her violent mood swings, vacillate between the extremes of hot and cool. Several are sweetly aromatic, such as **macaçá** (*Brunfelsia uniflora*), beti cheiroso (*Piper* sp.), and patchulí (*Pogostemon* cf. *cablin*), which she shares with the water **orixás**—Yemanjá and Oxum. The majority of her leaves, however, symbolize her warlike qualities. Many have an acrid or foul smell (common among the masculine ethnoflora) as well as long, tapering apices, representing her lance. These species include aroeira (*Schinus terebinthifolius*), which has bright red, acrid-smelling berries; fedegoso (*Senna occidentalis*), which has strong-smelling leaves shaped like daggers; and mastruz (*Chenopodium ambrosioides*), which also has pointed, rank-smelling leaves. Folha-do-fogo-de-Iansã (*Tibouchina* cf. *lhotzkyana*), literally 'Iansã's fire leaf,' has acuminate leaves and is covered by a thick layer of reddish pubescence, representing her color choice. Iansã's nature is best elicited by guiné (*Petiveria alliacea*). Aside from having acrid-smelling leaves, this herb is used medicinally as a tranquilizer and somniferant—hence its cooling dimension. If ingested for prolonged periods, however, the root extract of guiné is reported to produce anxiety, hallucinations, and even death.[10] Thus, like its female guardian, guiné swings unpredictably between the extremes of hot and cold.

Omolu is the dreaded god of smallpox, pestilence, and all dermal ailments. His image is ancient, bent, and arthritic, with skin so horribly scarred by smallpox that he conceals his appearance in a rough suit of palm straw. His colors are generally black and white. Omolu's leaves, such as balainho-do-velho (*Centratherum punctatum* ssp. *punctatum*), candeia branca (*Miconia hypoleuca*), canela-do-velho (*Miconia* sp.), and **capeba** (*Pothomorphe umbellata*), have rough and punctate surfaces, suggesting his own pockmarked skin. One of Omolu's plants is known as sete chagas (*Philodendron* sp.), or 'seven sores,' although the connection of this taxon with skin disease is unclear. Quitoco (*Pluchea suaveolens*) represents a medicinal treatment for rheumatism, one of Omolu's noted afflictions, and has acrid-smelling leaves, a signal that the species belongs to a masculine god.

Popcorn is one of Omolu's principal offerings and healing bath ingredients. With its contorted shape, popcorn symbolizes the skin eruptions associated with smallpox. Its explosive kernels may also be seen as reflecting Omolu's volatile temper. Avoiding the proper name of this plant for fear of invoking Omolu's wrath, devotees refer to popcorn as flor 'flower' within the confines of the terreiro. Mamona (*Ricinus communis*) is another of his plants. The spiny red fruits of this species suggest Omolu's skin condition, as well as, perhaps, his piqued anger.[11] The explosive nature of mamona's fruit, which can send its seeds flying several meters, reflects this god's violent temperament. Pinhão roxo (*Jatropha gossypifolia*), a species with a history of magical application in Brazil,[12] has reddish-tinged leaves and petioles, again reflecting Omolu's temperament. The large palmate leaves of **embaúba** (*Cecropia pachystachya*), a common second-growth treelet, are often referred to as the 'hands of Omolu.' The leaves are used as trays to serve the foods that are sacred to this ominous god.

Xangô is the volatile god of thunder, lightning, and fire. He is geographically associated with lofty locations, and his colors are red and white. Xangô's furious temper is reflected by the bright reddish-purple floral display of some of his species, such as **akokô** (*Newbouldia laevis*), bico-de-papagaio (*Centropogon cornutus*), and cordão-de-São Francisco (*Leonotis nepetifolia*). Folha-do-fogo (*Clidemia hirta*), or the 'leaf of fire,' is covered with reddish pubescence.

Xangô's flora is further distinguished by its abundance of trees and treelets. Sixty-four percent of his flora is arborescent, compared to less than 21 percent of the combined Candomblé pharmacopoeia. His tree flora includes bico-de-papagaio (*Centropogon cornutus*), São Gonçalinho (*Casearia* sp.), murici (*Byrsonima sericea*), **embaúba** (*Cecropia pachystachya*), betis branco (*Piper aduncum*), **akokô** (*Newbouldia laevis*), and **orobô** (*Garcinia kola*). Xangô's link to arborescent as opposed to understory vegetation may stem from his association with high places, the source areas for thunder and lightning. It may also follow, as one informant suggested, from the fact that trees are frequently struck by lightning, the source of energy for Xangô, and thus his **axé** is transferred from the skies via arboreal conductors to the sacred foliage inhabiting the ground.

The masculine deities Oxóssi and Ogun are brothers, according to legend.

Oxóssi, who holds sway over the hunt and the forest, shoulders an iron bow and arrow. His colors are green and red. Ogun is the god of iron and war. Forever hammering out his iron implements at the forge, Ogun is by nature very hot. He is the consummate warrior figure, fending off evil, opening up passages, and winning battles. His colors are green or blue.

The leaves of these brother deities, many of which they share, are characterized by long blades and pointed apices, representing the spears and arrows of these two warrior gods. These species are exemplified by **peregun** (*Dracaena fragrans*) (Fig. 6.4) and the two bowstring hemps, espada-de-Oxóssi and espada-de-Ogun (*Sansevieria* cf. *aethiopica*). The vernacular names of other leaves associated with Ogun and Oxóssi evoke these gods' aggressive archetypes and their ability to solve the problems of their followers. These species include abre-caminho 'opens the way' (*Baccharis* sp.), vence tudo 'conquers everything' (*Rolandra fruticosa*), comigo-ninguém-pode 'no one overpowers me' (*Dieffenbachia maculata*), tira teima 'takes away stubbornness' (*Zanthoxylum* sp.), and vence demanda 'achieves objectives' (*Vernonia* cf. *cotoneaster*). Ogun's association with **dandá** (*Cyperus rotundus*) reflects the perceived magical attributes of this plant, as both West Africans and Afro-Brazilians chew the rhizomes of **dandá** in order to influence the opinion of others.[13]

Exu is the deity of passageways and crossroads. Capricious and at times malicious, Exu serves as messenger to the **orixás**, the conveyor of **axé** from mortals to gods. Although he is a notorious troublemaker and considerable effort is expended to placate him, Exu is also the god of potentiality, the catalyst that make things happen. Properly propitiated, he clears obstructions to human wants and desires. Ignored, Exu brings calamity with a vengeance. Symbolic of his temperament, Exu's colors are red and black.

The leaves of Exu are as threatening as his personality. Many impart a burning sensation when touched, and most are employed for malevolent purpose— to dissolve intimate relationships, to bring bad luck, and to create general chaos. Covered with spines and prickly pubescence, several are painful to the touch, including urtiga (*Dalechampia ilheotica*), cansanção (*Cnidoscolus urens*), folha-do-fogo (*Clidemia hirta*), the fronds of **dendê** (*Elaeis guineensis*), and the stems of malissa (*Mimosa pudica*). The razor-sharp leaf margins of *tiririca* (*Scleria* sp.), another of Exu's species, cut the skin of those who brush against it. The prickly diaspores of *tiririca*, along with those of carrapicho (*Bidens pilosa*), cling to the legs of passersby, by this means finding transport to trails and roads, the preferred haunts of Exu.

Nearly all of Exu's leaves enter into black magic formulas. The red seeds of **atarê** or pimenta-da-costa (*Aframomum melegueta*), as noted earlier, are ground into powder and scattered in the homes of victims in order to create

6.4 A <u>filho-de-santo</u> collecting leaves of **peregun** (*Dracaena fragrans*) in the garden of Axé Opó Afonjá. Its lance-shaped leaves indicate ownership by a warlike **orixá**. (Photo: Janira Voeks)

disorder, a practice still carried out in Nigeria. Likewise, the nearly black flowers of corredeira (*Irlbachia purpurascens* and *Borreria* sp.), symbolizing Exu's dark side, are ground into a powder, combined with grave dirt, and slipped into the home of an unsuspecting victim.

From the foregoing examples, it appears that the Candomblé system of plant classification is based on morphological and, to a lesser extent, medicinal properties that are perceived to be associated with the individual personalities of the Yoruba pantheon. The gods and their personal pharmacopoeias are roughly divided between those perceived to be hot and those perceived to be cool, and between masculine and feminine. Hot **orixás** exhibit fiery personalities—aggressive, warlike, and volatile—and their respective floras personify these behavioral attributes. Leaves and stems are spiny or prickly. Flowers and fruits are red or black, reflecting their hot temperaments. Leaves exhibit linear blades, acuminate tips, foul or acrid aroma, and/or rugose surfaces. The feminine deities, on the other hand, represent cooling and calming influences. They are maternal, sensual, fecund, and materialistic. Their floras are characterized by sweetly aromatic leaves and flowers with white, gold, blue, or lavender corollas. Leaves tend to be rounded and fleshy and to produce abundant sap. Several species enter into medicinal prescriptions to cool down illness associated with the hot deities.

Candomblé plant classification bears little or no resemblance to its Western scientific counterpart. Floral structure is seldom considered, and phylogenetic hierarchy plays no role whatsoever in classification.[14] Salience is wholly defined by those features—tactile, olfactory, visual, geographical, or medicinal—that suggest association with the archetypes of one or another deity. Closely related taxa, such as manjericão (*Ocimum canum*) and **quiôiô** (*O. gratissimum*), pertain to different **orixás**, as do varieties of the same species, such as bom dia (*Catharanthus roseus*) and boa noite (*C. roseus* var. *albus*).

Considerable differences of opinion exist about which species are associated with which deities. Part of this diversity stems from the fact that I chose to work with terreiros from several different traditions. Informants included priests and priestesses from Jeje, Ketu, Ijexá, and Angola. While this method afforded a broad view of the healing methods and the use of plants within Candomblé, it nevertheless led to the inclusion of terreiros with little common ancestry. Not only were there many differences between these different 'nations' in the plants used, but in some cases the deities themselves varied. Oxumarê, a Dahomean deity represented by a serpent, occurs in some but not all terreiros. The Yoruba deity Odudua appears occasionally, but is poorly developed in most terreiros. The Caboclo spirit, which is native to Brazil rather than West Africa, is frequently accepted into the smaller, more proletarian terreiros, but is generally banned from larger Candomblé houses. Katende is an Angolan spirit that is infrequently encountered. Thus, at least some part of the variability in plant-deity connections stems from the fact that terreiros of different traditions do not retain exactly the same pantheons.

It is also true that a surprisingly large percentage of species are shared by two or more deities, a situation that seems inconsistent with Ossâim's legend. The explanations I was offered by pais- or mães-de-santo, however, were not very compelling. One pai-de-santo noted that closely connected deities, such as husbands and wives, or brothers, tended to share their floras. A mãe-de-santo suggested that floras were shared by **orixás** pertaining to the same realm of nature—gods of fire, for example, or goddesses of water. Others just shrugged their shoulders. The answer, I suspect, is found in the nature of myths that are maintained as oral tradition. They are subject to inconsistencies, and they change through time. Whatever is learned by the novice during the years of initiation is considered sacred knowledge, regardless of whether it conflicts with other beliefs. Inconsistencies exist only in the minds of nonbelievers.

Candomblé terreiros are fiercely independent, and competition rather than cooperation characterizes their relationship. As terreiros live and die by the number of followers they manage to attract, there is nothing to be gained by sharing secrets of any sort with competing pais- and mães-de-santo. There is thus limited exchange of knowledge between terreiros and, as a result, nothing approaching a Candomblé collective medicinal knowledge. Bahia's first pais- and mães-de-santo, exposed to a diverse and largely unknown flora, determined independently which species belonged to which deities, based on the legend of Ossâim's leaves as well as their own perceptions of the essence of each plant. Some of these god-plant correspondences may have arrived with early Yoruba priests and priestesses, particularly in the case of taxa that were common to West Africa and Brazil, although this is difficult to prove. Whatever the source, these decisions were passed on to devotees, who founded their own temples and continued to assimilate additional taxa. This independent origin is clearly evidenced by the Candomblé liturgical floras, which, although organized by means of the same conceptual framework, nevertheless exhibit limited floristic overlap from one adherent to another and from one terreiro to another.[15]

Hot and Cold Medicine

The opposition between hot and cold personified by the archetypes of the Yoruba pantheon represents one of the organizing principles in the Candomblé medicinal plant classification system. As the gods gravitate toward one perceived temperature state or the other, so also do their associated illnesses and healing plants. Hot deities are prone to hot illness, whether physical or psychological, and their medicinal treatments are often drawn from the pharmacopoeias of the cool goddesses. The leaves of hot gods are, at least in principle, employed to heat the cool deities.

From the perspective of a cohesive ethnomedical system, however, the hot-and-cold scheme suffers from noticeable irregularities. First, the characteristics of several Candomblé plants fail to conform to the behavioral attributes of their associated gods. Assa peixe branco (*Pluchea sagittalis*), for example, is one of Ogun's leaves. However, this plant produces a white floral display, suggestive of Oxalá's color preference, and is employed medicinally as a febrifuge, a treatment for a hot symptom that should place this taxon within the purview of a water deity. Likewise, whereas sabugueiro (*Sambucus australis*) is shared by Oxalá and Oxum, both cool-tempered deities, the medicinal use of this plant to treat skin problems suggests an association with Omolu, a hot god. These apparent inconsistencies, at least in some cases, reflect the range of properties that characterize individual taxa. For example, one informant connects the aromatic sedge **dandá** (*Cyperus rotundus*) with Yemanjá, suggesting the physical domain of this deity. Two other informants place **dandá** with Ogun, a god known for his ability to clear obstructions blocking his supplicants. This latter correspondence reflects the perceived magical properties of this species. Other apparent inconsistencies in god-plant associations, however, are not so readily explained.

The classification and treatment of hot versus cold illness exhibits further problems. Although a host of hot medical problems are associated with masculine gods, and cooling prescriptions are associated with cool deities, the reverse situation is relatively rare. That is, few of the leaves used to treat cool illness are connected to the hot deities. This is not for lack of cool medical problems, which include colds, flu, hypotension, and hypoglycemia, nor for lack of plant prescriptions to treat these ailments. Healers discussed the use of mamão (*Carica papaya*), capim estrella (*Rhynchospora nervosa*), malva branca (*Sida cordifolia*), and other plants to treat a cold, a cool illness, although none of these species corresponds to a masculine deity. They are simply medicinal plants with no perceived spiritual significance. Avocado (*Persea americana*) is likewise not associated with a deity, although the leaves of this New World cultigen are prepared as a diuretic, perceived as a heating property. For reasons that are unclear, the hot plant–cool illness concept is poorly developed within Candomblé.

The hot-cold scheme is not unique to Brazilian Candomblé. This ancient concept is at the heart of early European and Asian health and healing theories, and it is a dominant organizing principle in many Latin American and African American folk medical systems as well.[16] Although the presence of a hot-and-cold etiology among Hispanic Americans can be attributed to diffusion from Old World sources, the existence of this concept among Mesoamerica's pre-Hispanic civilizations—the Mayas, Aztecs, and Zapotecs—as well as among isolated indigenous South American societies argues for the independent evolution of the hot-cold paradigm in the New World.[17]

The origin of the hot-cold dichotomy within Candomblé ethnomedicine is problematic. Although hot and cool temperature states are among the features used to categorize the dispositions of the Yoruba deities both in Africa and in Brazil,[18] evidence is lacking that Candomblé's hot-and-cold etiology traces its roots to Africa. This binary system does not appear among the sacred oral texts of the Yoruba **babalaô**.[19] Nor do the incantations recited by the **babalaô** to invoke the vital energy of the medicinal leaves allude to any hot or cold properties.[20] Yoruba herbalists, a separate class of healers who tend to organic rather than spiritual and magical illness, prescribe medicines that are bitter, sweet, sour, or peppery. But like their **babalaô** counterparts, herbalists do not classify either illness or medicine along hot or cold lines.[21]

There is no evidence one way or the other regarding the possible contribution of Amerindian health and healing concepts to Candomblé's hot-versus-cold opposition. Motivated by practical concerns—particularly the virgin soil epidemics that decimated the indigenous population—sixteenth-century Bahian planters and Jesuit missionaries went to considerable efforts to document the local Tupinambá plant pharmacopoeia.[22] Other contemporary observers described how the indigenous shamans directed the women to sing and dance in a circle, after which they fell into trance and were "able to foretell future things," ceremonies that are highly reminiscent of those currently carried out in Candomblé.[23] Focused only on what was considered useful or exotic, these early reports, not surprisingly, failed to explore the more theoretical dimensions of indigenous etiology and healing.

Among Brazilians of European descent, however, the concept of environmental control of illness, and particularly the deleterious effects of heat and cold, has a long pedigree. In the early 1600s, Dutch physician Guilherme Piso counseled recent arrivals to Brazil against the overuse of hot and cold baths.[24] And throughout Brazil's colonial period, excessive heat was blamed for a multitude of venereal and childhood disorders.[25] Today a seemingly endless array of illness episodes, including some that are life-threatening, are attributed to the environmental effects of imbalanced temperature states. Activities such as drinking cold water on a hot day, taking a cool shower after a hot meal, or sitting in a recently vacated warm chair are all perceived as unnecessary health risks.[26]

Centuries of culture contact and miscegenation in the Northeast of Brazil have blurred the racial and cultural distinctions that once separated Europeans from Africans. In the area of religion and magic, Africans borrowed liberally from their oppressors, particularly when the beliefs were found complementary to their own. Incorporating alien materials and beliefs represented a survival mechanism—Catholicism was Brazil's only sanctioned religion—as well as actual change in the convictions of adherents. This flexibility is characterized by the syncretism of African **orixás** and Catholic saints, a process that was well advanced in Bahia by the late 1800s.[27] Such a fusion of spiritual images and meanings was facilitated by the nearly parallel roles played by the African pantheon and Catholic hagiology in the attainment of practical goals, such as warding off disease, increasing fertility, and maintaining good health.[28] The malleability of African healing systems—the ability to change and adapt as social, economic, and biological conditions necessitate—is further underscored by the wholesale adoption of European and Amerindian medicinal and magical species by Afro-Brazilian healers.

This process of redefinition and assimilation may well have extended into the conceptual dimensions of ethnomedicine. Two components of the hot-and-cold system—the division of the Yoruba deities into hot and cold categories and the correspondence of deities with liturgical and medicinal species—arrived with African priests and priestesses during and after the slave trade. Adherents who strayed from the archetypal equilibrium imposed by their guardian deities became overheated or overcooled and, in so doing, opened the door to spiritual retribution. The simple elegance of this opposition was, in a sense, preadapted to the addition of (and modification by) complementary concepts. One such concept is the belief that physical and emotional distress was at least partly mediated through relations with the spirit world, to which both belief systems already subscribed. Another logical extension was the hybridization of hot and cold deities, an African concept, with the folk belief that illness is often the outcome of hot and cold imbalance, concepts that are in all likelihood of Portuguese origin.

7 THE CANDOMBLÉ FLORA

Salvador, the Black Rome of Brazil, teems with houses of Candomblé worship. A few of these are well known and well funded, such as Gantois, Engenho Velho, and Bate-Folhas, which have pedigrees reaching into the previous century. But far more ubiquitous are the innumerable small candomblés—"proletarian candomblés," as Roger Bastide called them[1]—which summon forth the **orixás** and heal the ailing in nearly every neighborhood. Although there are no census figures available, the Federação Baiano dos Cultos Afro-Brasileiros estimates that over two thousand Bahian terreiros are registered with their group, and many of them are in Salvador (Fig. 7.1).

With so many rituals involving plants taking place, a tremendous demand exists for medicinal and liturgical species. In smaller cities with sizable Candomblé communities—such as Cachoeira, Ilhéus, and Itabuna—adequate gardens, open space, and forest habitat still exist to supply the foliar components necessary to most ceremonies.[2] But in Salvador, the situation is different. With a population approaching two million, the city's few remaining forests and open spaces are decreasingly able to furnish the herbs needed by sacred and secular healers. Even the most precarious sites for construction, such as steep escarpments and ridge crests, where secondary forests previously met the needs of herbalists, are now chock-full of the hovels of recent migrants. The wealthy traditional houses of worship, which still retain their own gardens or at least have adequate resources to fund journeys to distant collection sites, feel

7.1 The Pelourinho section of Salvador. Today a popular tourist destination, the Pelourinho was originally where African slaves were whipped and beaten in public. (Photo: Barbara Weightman)

the pinch of plant scarcity less acutely than do the more modest terreiros. For the myriad proletarian terreiros, economic necessity requires that they resort to local casas de folhas 'houses of leaves' for their medicinal and sacred floral needs.

Houses of Leaves

Leaf houses are located in all of the major feiras, or open markets. Smaller feiras move to a different location in the city each day of the week, whereas others, such as the expansive Feira da São Joaquim and the Feira da Sete Portas, represent permanent fixtures in the Salvadoran cityscape. A small herb stand in Sete Portas run by Sr. Djalma Santana has been operating for sixteen years. His as well as four other herb stands at Sete Portas cater to all the plant needs of their clients, both sacred and medicinal. As of 1989, Djalma's young son Robson had been apprenticing for six months. Even more leaf houses operate at São Joaquim (Fig. 7.2). Some, such as that run by Dona Isabella, focus more on the medicinal plants employed in traditional herbal teas. One stand displays a placard announcing that the owner serves "All the Nations," meaning all the Candomblé traditions (Ketu, Caboclo, etc.). The well-known shop of Sr. Edson Souza—who is known as "Caboclo"—deals exclusively with the plants and other material needs of Candomblé. Caboclo has been in his location for about thirty years, and is assisted by his daughter and others. He usually has about thirty or forty liturgical species on display. Because the **axé** of the plant is found in the sap—the symbolic blood—of the leaves, only fresh and green plants are sold. Along with the leaves, Caboclo also keeps a supply of the animals used in sacrifice, especially white doves, chickens, Guinea fowl, and sometimes male goats. He also stocks many of the other items used in Candomblé, such as **obí** and other seeds, iron emblems dedicated to the deities, snail shells, and the beads used by initiates (Fig. 7.3). As the best known of the Candomblé leaf brokers in the city, Caboclo has been featured in newspaper and television reports.

The operators of Salvador's leaf houses seldom have the time or inclination to collect their own plants. Although most began their careers as modest purveyors of self-collected medicinal plants, today they purchase their stock of leaves, flowers, roots, bark, and seeds from herb collectors. Their sources range

7.2 Collection of liturgical plants, dried and fresh, for sale in a Salvador leaf stand. (Photo: Robert Voeks)

7.3 Candomblé gourds, seeds, and shells for sale at the Mercado Modelo in Salvador. (Photo: Robert Voeks)

from the <u>mato</u>, or secondary forest and other disturbed areas surrounding Salvador, to medicinal gardens. Medicinal gardens include neighborhood <u>quintais</u>, or backyard gardens, as well as moderate-sized commercial enterprises. Dona Antônia, an aged black woman living in a tiny adobe house near my home in Ilhéus, cultivated dozens of medicinal plants in her <u>quintal</u>. Cuttings were made available to anyone in the neighborhood who needed them, including my family, who made frequent use of her healing herb teas. If she didn't possess the necessary plant, she always knew of a neighbor who did. One commercial garden, located on the outskirts of Ilhéus, contains all of the common plants used in traditional medicine as well as liturgical species used in religious ceremonies. These species are cultivated on simple raised hills, usually as a polyculture, without the aid of pesticides or herbicides. The owners had learned these methods from reading magazines on organic gardening techniques. They ran their own small herb stand in the local market and sold plants to individuals as well. The husband-and-wife team were both devout members of the Assembly of God Church, a Christian group that is known in the region for its rigid intolerance of African-derived religions. They justified the cultivation of magical plants by noting that it was part of their

Christian duty to bring happiness to others, regardless of their religious affiliation.

Collectors arrive at the <u>feiras</u> early each morning with whatever plants they have been able to find and sell them to leaf houses that are in need of particular species. Because fresh leaves are the most significant plant parts used in healing and ritual ceremonies, there is a constant need to replenish the deteriorating stock. In the tropical sun, leaves last no more than a few days on the trays that line the fronts of the leaf houses. It is not uncommon, however, for the collectors' efforts to go unrewarded.

I spent a few days in the field with Tonia, a woman in her late thirties who collects plants for the leaf houses. She lived in a tiny two-room shack in the suburbs of Salvador, where she was raising her eight children alone. Good-natured in spite of her situation, Tonia supplemented her income as a <u>jogo-de-bicho</u> ticket seller[3] by collecting plants for the leaf houses. She had never been involved in Candomblé, which she deprecated as just another means of fleecing the poor of their money, but rather had just picked up her knowledge of plants bit by bit. On a good day, she would probably net four to five dollars.

The houses of leaves serve commercial as well as social roles. For the priests and priestesses of Candomblé, they supply plants and animals that are increasingly difficult to locate. Particularly preceding a <u>terreiro</u> celebration, there are endless lists of materials that need to be acquired immediately. I once drove Maria das Loudres to the Feira de São Joaquim before her <u>festa do escravo</u>. We returned with some candles and flowers, a few plants that she had been unable to locate near her <u>terreiro</u>, a trunk full of sacrificial chickens, and a live goat that she had purchased from Caboclo.

Clients purchase one or more packets of fresh leaves for their medicinal teas or healing baths. Often the leaf prescription is scribbled on a slip of paper, the product of a consultation with a Candomblé priest. It is just as common, however, for the customer to seek the advice of the leaf-house owner for his or her medical or magical dilemma. Such exchanges elicit not only the depth of knowledge of the herb trader, but also the means by which ethnomedical beliefs are reinforced in the Afro-Brazilian community. These encounters can develop into lively debates, with the customer relating his or her successes and failures with certain plant medicines, and the herb salesperson countering with his or her own experiences.

The mutually beneficial relationship between leaf houses and Candomblé <u>terreiros</u> is characterized nevertheless by an undercurrent of condescension and mistrust. Priests and priestesses are adamant in proclaiming the superiority of their liturgical plant knowledge. Plant retailers, they argue, have not passed through initiation, do not know proper collection techniques, and are not able to recite the incantations necessary to elicit the **axé** of the leaves. They are, in short, wholly ignorant of the fundamentals.

Leaf-house operators view the situation differently. Having spent much of their adult lives collecting and selling medicinals, they affirm their roles as community herbalists and ritual plant specialists. During a single day, they may well work with dozens of different species, attending to the disparate plant needs of clients from all the different Candomblé nations and from the secular public as well. Particularly in Salvador, where priests are drawn from a population with little or no experience with the floristic landscape, the notion that Candomblé practitioners retain a superior level of plant knowledge is difficult for the herb traders to accept. This rivalry serves to underscore the point that competition rather than cooperation characterizes those who would claim the social roles of herbalists and magicians.

Besides locally gathered herbs, there remains a minor market in liturgical products imported from Yorubaland. The Mercado Modelo in Salvador has traditionally maintained a few stalls catering to the needs of Candomblé adherents. Until a few years ago, Salvadoran merchants traveled to West Africa to purchase marketable ceremonial items. Today, the trip has become too expensive, and merchants now depend on Nigerian embassy staff and other visitors from West Africa to supply their needs. Among the materials still being imported is palha-da-costa, the fiber of an African raffia palm that filhas of Omolu wear when in trance to cover his horribly disfigured body. They also trade in sabão-da-costa, a type of dark-colored African soap made with ashes, which is used by Candomblé priests to ritually purify the beads of novices. Limo-da-costa, a type of vegetable fat sacred to Oxalá, can often be found in the market, as can pano-da-costa, the brightly colored cloth sarong worn by filhas-de-santo during terreiro ceremonies.

Several species of plants have been imported since colonial times to meet the liturgical and magical needs of Africans. The seeds of **obí** (*Cola acuminata*), **orobô** (*Garcinia kola*), and **atarê** (*Aframomum melegueta*) were being imported into Salvador in the nineteenth century[4] and later in this century, when Donald Pierson carried out his research.[5] All these seeds are still available in the refurbished Mercado Modelo. Although **obí** has been successfully planted so that there is now a domestic source of the seed, many priests still hold that African **obí** retains more **axé** than the local product. **Orobô** and **atarê** failed to bear fruit in the New World, and so imports continue to be the only source.[6]

Finally, an increasing number of shops also stock packaged powders, herbal

7.4   Commercial plant preparations for sale in a Candomblé leaf house. (Photo: Robert Voeks)

preparations, and even aerosol sprays dedicated to the **orixás** (Fig. 7.4). Simply push a button, and the foliar power of the African deities is immediately brought to bear. These "over-the-counter" concoctions, viewed with horror by most Candomblé priests, nevertheless serve a function. The client avoids the time and cost of a consultation with a <u>pai-</u> or <u>mãe-de-santo</u>, which can be considerable. He or she also avoids the difficulty of locating rare liturgical leaves, some of which need to be sought out in distant forests.[7]

The Humanized Flora

Candomblé priests discussed with me the medicinal or magical properties of roughly 200 species. Of these, I collected or otherwise identified 140 taxa. Perusal of the species list (Appendix 1) reveals that the Candomblé pharmacopoeia is floristically rich. The 140 taxa are distributed among 117 genera in 54 families. Ninety-six of the genera, or nearly 70 percent, are represented by a single species. Only three of the genera, *Vernonia*, *Ocimum*, and *Sida*, include three or more species. By any index of measurement and at any level of taxonomy, this is a diverse assemblage of plants.

Although it is tempting to interpret this taxonomic diversity in terms of the region's general species richness, such an assumption would miss the mark entirely. Neither the habitats occupied by this healing flora nor the life histories of the species support this view. This flora is *in* the most floristically diverse forest to date identified, but not *of* it. The Candomblé flora is, in every sense, the product of human modification of the landscape.

At least 60 of the taxa, or about 43 percent, are cultivated or otherwise encouraged to grow. Many of these, such as **urucum** (*Bixa orellana*), jaca-de-pobre (*Annona muricata*), papaya (*Carica papaya*), and sabugueiro (*Sambucus australis*), are domesticated species that depend entirely on humans for their existence. Others exist naturally outside of cultivation, usually in disturbed habitats, such as mamoeira (*Ricinus communis*), transagem (*Plantago major*), corneta (*Datura metel*), and aroeira (*Schinus terebinthifolius*); in addition, these are often purposely planted in backyard gardens as ornamentals or for medicinal use. Still others occur spontaneously in gardens as weeds, but are spared because of their perceived value; these include bom dia (*Catharanthus roseus*), fedegoso (*Senna occidentalis*), and quebra-pedra (*Phyllanthus amarus*). The sacred arboreal dwelling of Iroko (*Ficus* sp.) is never purposely planted, according to Yoruba custom, but is always spared if it begins to grow spontaneously.

A second obvious feature of this flora is the dominant presence of species that are not native to Brazil. Of the 122 taxa for which origins are known or strongly suspected, 25 percent are of Old World origin. A few of these, including **obí** (*Cola acuminata*) and **akokô** (*Newbouldia laevis*), were purposely introduced from Africa and naturalized for use in Candomblé worship. Others, such as **orobô** (*Garcinia kola*) and **atarê** (*Aframomum melegueta*), never bore fruit in Brazil and so continue to be imported from Nigeria. Still others were brought for commercial purposes by the Portuguese colonists and were incorporated by Afro-Brazilian healers, such as the African oil palm (*Elaeis guineensis*), known by the Yoruba term **dendê** among Afro-Brazilians, and jambo branco (*Syzygium jambos*), a fruit tree introduced from Asia. The Portuguese also introduced a host of Old World ornamentals and potherbs that ultimately found their way into the Candomblé pharmacopoeia, such as leopoldina (*Alpinia zerumbet*) and vence tudo Africano (*Justicia gendarrussa*). Finally, early European settlers took a keen interest in bringing a portion of their own healing flora to Brazil, and several of these plants were ultimately adopted by the Afro-Brazilian community, including erva doce (*Pimpinella anisum*), losna (*Artemisia* cf. *absinthium*), and several taxa in the mint family, such as manjericão (*Ocimum canum*), **quiôiô** (*Ocimum gratissimum*), and poejo (*Mentha pulegium*).

The most compelling evidence for the human etiology of this flora comes from a look at the habitats and life histories of its members. The dominant class is the herbs, with 55 percent of the species, followed by shrubs with 15 percent. Few, if any, of these taxa are located in old-growth forest. Rather, most are characterized by weedy life histories—being small in size, reproducing rapidly, and being poor competitors—and are plants that owe their abundance and diversity to removal of the native forest rather than to its inherent species richness. These plants occur most often in secondary forests, in cattle pastures, on plantations, along roadsides, and in kitchen gardens. Many are recognizable as noxious weeds of pantropical proportions, such as quitoco (*Pluchea suaveolens*), malissa (*Mimosa pudica*), and guiné (*Petiveria alliacea*).

The Atlantic coastal rainforests are dominated, floristically and physiognomically, by trees and treelets. Arborescence does not, however, characterize the Candomblé pharmacopoeia, in which trees and treelets make up less than 14 percent and 11 percent, respectively, of the taxa. Many of these species (41%) are exotic rather than native, and several of the native trees are domesticated or are otherwise managed. Less than 10 percent of the Candomblé flora was collected in old-growth rainforest, and several of these, including pau pombo (*Tapirira guianensis*), aroeira (*Schinus terebinthifolius*), and canela-de-velho (*Miconia* sp.), are much more abundant in secondary forests. The primary forests of the region, dominated by native trees, treelets, lianas, and epiphytes, clearly hold little to draw the attention of local herbalists foraging for medicinals. Thus, rather than a natural outgrowth of the region's protean tropical biodiversity, the Candomblé plant pharmacopoeia is highly representative of the changes this region has witnessed during the last five centuries: it is cultivated, it is exotic, and it is opportunistic.

There is a tendency among Brazilians to denigrate the value of Afro-Brazilian medicinal knowledge. This negative view, as noted earlier, stems from the long-standing association of Afro-Brazilian healers with the occult sciences, and especially with the perceived use of exotic materials and deadly poisons in magical ceremonies.[8] Over the centuries, while observers marveled at the wealth of medicinal knowledge retained by the indigenous population, most denied entirely the legitimacy of African ethnomedicine. In his review of the history of Brazilian medicine, Lycurgo Santos Filho surmised that because Africans were unable to introduce their native pharmacopoeia, "African medicine was quite inferior to indigenous medicine."[9] Narciso Cunha, while lauding the diversity of medicinals found in Salvador's herb stands in the 1940s, only remarked in passing that there were also "inevitably those charms and drugs used in the cults of African origin."[10] Gilberto Freyre offered perhaps the kindest view of Afro-Brazilian medicine, noting that it was in no way inferior to that doled out by colonial physicians, who were known to include excrement, urine, hair, toads, and other noxious ingredients in their prescriptions.[11]

This view also follows from the knowledge that Africans are not native to Brazil and are, in effect, strangers to the forest. The fact that most of the pharmacopoeia is derived from species found in disturbed and cultivated areas, rather than species from primary forests, tends to reinforce this belief. Weeds, potherbs, garden cultigens, and secondary forest taxa carry little of the pharmacological mystique associated with the mysterious jungle, where, according to many, the cures for what ails society wait to be discovered.

Jungle Medicine

The view that primary tropical forests harbor potentially valuable drug plants follows in part from their legendary species richness and in part from their apparently high incidence of pharmacologically active compounds.[12] As an evolutionary response to elevated and protracted levels of herbivory by insects and other tropical forest creatures, plant species have developed complex chemical-based defense systems to avoid being eaten.[13] These secondary metabolites, such as alkaloids and simple phenols, have been shown to appear with greater frequency in tropical as opposed to temperate forest plants, leading to the designation of tropical forests as potential "pharmaceutical factories."[14] Given the successful development of powerful and economically valuable drugs from various tropical plants, there is considerable interest in tapping indigenous knowledge of the jungle pharmacopoeia.[15]

This race to reveal the pharmacological secrets of the primary rainforest in no way negates the bioactive nature or the value, to folk healers, of the lowly weeds, cultivated plants, and disturbance species. There is, in fact, little evidence to suggest that the primary forest represents an inherently more important source of folk medicinals than disturbed habitats. For although tropical forests are geographically richer in pharmacologically active compounds than their temperate zone counterparts, it appears that the smaller, faster-growing taxa most often employ metabolically inexpensive chemical lines of defense, such as alkaloids and phenols, whereas climax forest trees have more often opted for expensive structural defense systems, such as cellulose and lignin.[16] Secondary-forest species, weeds, and perhaps even garden cultivars may represent a more likely source of bioactive compounds, and hence of potentially useful drug plants, than primary forest taxa. It is worth noting that even the celebrated Madagascar periwinkle (*Catharanthus roseus*)—known as <u>bom dia</u> and <u>boa noite</u> in Bahia—from which a cure for childhood leukemia and Hodgkin's disease was developed, is nothing more than a noxious weed of pantropical distribution.[17] Familiar, accessible, and pharmacologically rich, disturbance vegetation may well constitute the most sensible habitat for Candomblé and other healers to forage in for medicinals.[18]

The spiritual ancestors of the priests and priestesses of Candomblé, African shamans and herbalists who arrived during the slave trade, were obviously unable to introduce their Old World medicinal packages directly. Rather, as they gradually came to occupy the vacated positions of medical and spiritual healers, Afro-Brazilian <u>curandeiros</u> crafted a novel New World pharmacopoeia. Folk taxonomic names were taken from the Portuguese, such as <u>transagem</u> (*Plantago major*), <u>losna</u> (*Artemisia* cf. *absinthium*), and <u>melão-de-São Caetano</u> (*Momordica charantia*); from the West Africans, such as **akokô** (*Newbouldia laevis*), **ewe susu** (*Bidens pilosa*), and **dendê** (*Elaeis guineensis*); and, to a lesser extent, from the Tupi, such as ***embaúba*** (*Cecropia pachystachya*), ***janaúba*** (*Himatanthus phagedaenicus*), and **urucum** (*Bixa orellana*). Thus, all three races contributed to the evolving medicinal lexicon. Some knowledge of indigenous medicinals was undoubtedly assimilated during the early years of contact between African and indigenous plantation laborers. Jesuit missionaries absorbed some elements of the native pharmacopoeia, and this information, in time, was passed on to become part of the general collective medicinal knowledge. Early Portuguese colonists imported the more common elements of their native *materia medica* to the kitchen gardens of colonial Bahia, and many of these European medicinals were ultimately incorporated into the Afro-Brazilian pharmacopoeia.

African slaves and freedmen, however limited by their socioeconomic position, contributed to the development of the regional healing flora as well. Constrained by limited mobility, they must have experimented with and incorporated the ordinary plants immediately at hand—that is, disturbance species and domesticated cultivars. In addition, African weeds such as **dandá** (*Cyperus rotundus*) that arrived during the course of the slave trade were recognized and adopted and became known in Bahia by their Yoruba as opposed to Portuguese or Tupi vernacular names. Finally, the relative floristic similarity between West Africa and eastern Brazil allowed incoming Africans the opportunity to substitute taxonomically similar Brazilian taxa for well-known African medicinals that failed to reach the New World. For example, with its characteristic rounded and cleft leaves, *Bauhinia ovata*, a member of a pantropical genus, was early recognized and adopted by Afro-Brazilian shamans.

7.5   Pata-de-vaca (*Bauhinia ovata*), also known as **abafé**, growing along a roadside near Ilhéus. (Photo: Robert Voeks)

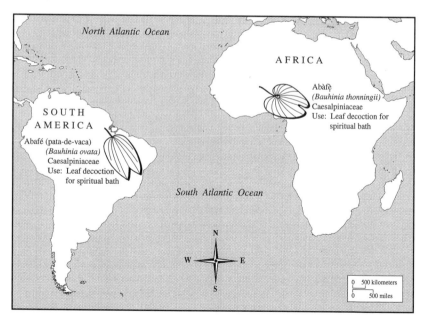

7.6   Similar leaf structure of West Africa's **abàfè** (*Bauhinia thonningii*) allowed for its substitution by a Brazilian congeneric, **abafé** (*Bauhinia ovata*).

To this day, this species is known among some Bahian healers by its Yoruba name, **abafé**, and continues to be employed for similar medicinal ends in West Africa and eastern Brazil (Figs 7.5 and 7.6). The eventual outcome, both in Brazil and in other points in the African American landscape, was a floristically rich New World healing flora that served the needs of the sick and ailing, but that drew little from the decreasingly common primary rainforests.

8 AFRICAN RELIGION IN THE AMERICAS

The existence in Brazil of the Candomblé religion—a set of beliefs and practices that are, at their foundation, of West African origin—requires explanation. On the one hand, the problem falls squarely into the arena of migration and diffusion studies: the movements of people and their culture over space; adjustment to new physical, social, and economic conditions; retention or abandonment of native ideas, materials, and technologies; and absorption or rejection of innovation.[1] Candomblé is thus, in many respects, a case of simple cultural diffusion. At the same time, two features distinguish this as well as other elements of the New World African diaspora. First, the actors were unwilling participants in the migration, and second, cultural retention occurred both in spite of and partly as a result of the gauntlet of barriers to diffusion that were erected by European society. In the face of seemingly insurmountable obstacles placed in their paths, including forced removal from their homeland and forfeiture of their material culture, the horrors of the transatlantic crossing and plantation slavery, and the imposition of an alien society and religion, how and why did Africans retain so much of their traditional culture? The answers, it seems, do not fall into a single category, but rather draw from each of the factors—economic, social, political, and environmental—that made the African diaspora unique among the world's great migrations of people and ideas.

African Migration

The migratory features of the slave trade most clearly delimited the diffusion of African religious and medical systems to one or another point on the Atlantic coast of the Americas. Where the volume and duration of the slave trade were heavy and protracted, African-based ethnomedicine not only survived, but in some cases came to predominate. This was clearly the case in Brazil, which absorbed over four million African immigrants, or about 40 percent of the total slave population to arrive in the New World, over the course of the four centuries of slave trafficking. The old Spanish Main received roughly five million Africans, and the existence of such orthodox expressions of African belief systems as Santeria in Cuba and Vodun in Haiti, both major destinations for slaves, underscores the evident importance of numbers. North America, on the other hand, having received scarcely 500,000 Africans during the entire slave trade—roughly 5 percent of those reaching the New World—witnessed limited survival of African-based religious and ethnomedical systems.[2] These figures, combined with the fact that throughout most of its colonial period Brazil was dominated numerically by Africans,[3] give a rough idea of why African cultural traditions have persevered there. For example, the population of Salvador in 1807 was recorded as 28 percent white, 20 percent mulatto, and 52 percent black.[4] By 1824, after many Portuguese had fled Brazil following independence, whites constituted less than a quarter of Bahia's total population.[5] At least in purely racial terms, Bahia was settled by Africans.

The ethnicity of the incoming African immigrants and particularly the timing of the slave imports were critical to the eventual hegemony of Yoruba over other African beliefs and practices that arrived in Bahia. Although there was considerable diversity of source regions during the course of the slave trade,[6] the preferences of the planters, merchants, and miners, as well as the changing economic and political environment in Africa, resulted in regional pulses of slave imports. Pierre Verger divides slave arrivals to the Captaincy of Bahia into several cycles (Fig. 8.1).[7] The Guine Cycle, covering the period from the dawn of slaving activities until the end of the sixteenth century, witnessed mostly arrivals from the Guine coast. This early trickle of bondsmen, amounting probably to no more than seven thousand individuals, left little imprint on the evolving cultural landscape. The Angola and Congo Cycle, which tapped mainly into Bantu populations south of the equator, subsumed most of the seventeenth century. The large number of Bantu imports during this period, as well as their reported attitude of assimilation rather than resistance, translated into considerable contributions to the language, religion, and culture of

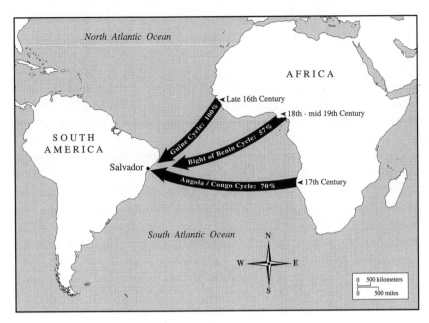

8.1 Principal source regions for African slaves arriving in Bahia. Verger's (1987) last two phases are consolidated into a single Bight of Benin cycle. Percentages are of all slaves taken to Brazil during each cycle.

the region.[8] The Mina Coast Cycle, lasting to the latter quarter of the eighteenth century, developed as a result of the demand in old Dahomey for Bahian tobacco. Bypassing the usual triangular trading pattern, Bahia exchanged its coarse-grade tobacco directly for Mina slaves. Relations were so good that in 1795 and 1805 Dahomey posted an ambassador in Salvador.[9]

The last cycle, which persisted until the arrival of the final slave ship in 1851, focused on the Bight of Benin. By agreement with Britain, which was exerting increasing pressure to end the slave trade, the Portuguese crown agreed to confine its slaving acquisition after 1815 to ports south of the equator, and by 1830 to halt slave imports altogether. While Rio de Janeiro, in accordance with the agreement, limited most of its imports to West Central and East Africa during this period,[10] Bahian imports increasingly came from north of the equator, particularly from the feuding West African kingdoms of the Yoruba and the Dahomeans. Bahia in this period was in the midst of a resurgence in its sugar economy after many decades of decline. The need for chattel workers for plantation and mill skyrocketed just as the region's principal source areas were on the verge of closure.[11] Thus, rather than gradually winding down their slave imports during the waning years of slavery, planters and other slave-owners rushed to purchase as many Bight of Benin captives as possible before the final deadline. This regional preference persisted after 1830, as clandestine slave ships began dumping their ill-treated "pieces" at deserted stretches of beach away from the watchful eyes of the authorities. During the final four decades of slave trafficking to Bahia—including twenty years of illegal imports—an estimated 242,800 West Africans arrived in Bahia, or just over 6,070 per year.[12]

The numerical dominance during the eclipse of the Bahian slave trade of the Yoruba and Dahomeans, groups which through centuries of contact in Africa had come to share many of the gods and beliefs that would ultimately take root in the New World, was a major factor that led to the ascendancy of their cosmology over the beliefs of others that had preceded them. Other African religious survivals, such as Vodun in Haiti and Santeria in Cuba, were each also derived from the ethnic group that dominated the last wave of immigrants.[13] Regions where no particular group predominated, such as Venezuela, preserved aspects of African religious expression, but to a much lesser extent.[14] In Bahia, the cultural traits and traditions of the millions of Africans who lived and died before the last cycle of slave importation would remain, becoming absorbed and redefined by Candomblé and by greater Brazilian society, but the foundation of African religion in Bahia was to be shaped by the Yoruba.

Slave Life

The conditions of existence imposed by slavery also helped determine the continued demand for large numbers of African laborers, as well as the degree to which their cultural attributes eventually persisted in Brazil. Austrian traveler Johann Rugendas gave Brazilian slave-owners generally high marks, noting that their slaves "are infinitely better treated" than those in the English colonies.[15] Anglican chaplain Robert Walsh observed that, at least in terms of access to hospital facilities, there was no separation of patients according to race or social standing.[16] The benign paternalism that, according to early scholars, tended to characterize Brazilian slavery was the fruit of long association between the Muslim Moors and the Spanish and Portuguese prior to the fifteenth-century Iberian Reconquest. Centuries of cultural exchange and miscegenation with people of color, it was believed, had left Iberians incapable of the level of brutality meted out by the English slavocracy. The Portuguese who colonized Brazil, according to historian Gilberto Freyre, constituted "a people existing indeterminately between Europe and Africa, and belonging uncompromisingly to neither one."[17] In any case, even if human compassion and dignity were not overriding concerns for the average slave master, plantation slavery was surely subject to the laws of benefits and costs. Fair and decent treatment of chattel slaves could be justified by simple economics. Or could it?

The conditions of slave life clearly varied from region to region, from plantation to plantation, and from urban to rural settings. Not all slaves were treated poorly, and not all owners were tyrants.[18] Many estate slaves were allowed to cultivate their own plots of land and even sell any surplus in markets.[19] As a rule, they were allowed one free day to work their garden plots, just as had been the practice in Africa.[20] Petty private enterprise made it possible for many slaves to buy their own manumission, a strategy supported by many masters. By providing decent working conditions and a chance for freedom, the plantation owner could count on many years of diligent work and obedience and, eventually, the return of his original investment when the slave's strength was waning.[21]

Slave conditions appear to have been better on sugar estates operated by the Christian orders. In his analysis of the Santana sugar plantation near Ilhéus, which was owned by Jesuits, historian Stuart Schwartz suggests that reasonably stable family units were the rule among chattel laborers. In 1731, the majority of slave households included a man, a woman, and one or more children. In 1752, following two decades of a pro-family policy, roughly 80 percent of Santana slaves lived in family units. Although the underlying objective of these Jesuit policies may have been to counter the perceived "moral failings and sexual laxity of the slaves,"[22] the results, at least for some African slaves, were conditions that may have been marginally tolerable.

Taken as a whole, however, slave conditions in colonial Brazil appear to have been as brutal as anywhere in the New World. According to Nuno Marques Pereira, an early eighteenth-century traveler to Brazil, rural slaves were required to work not only during the day, "but also at night, ragged, naked, and without sustenance."[23] Beasts of burden, according to one observer, were treated better than African slaves were in Brazil.[24] Slaves were branded, whipped, chained, raped, dismembered, and, as an example to coworkers, occasionally tossed kicking and screaming into the sugar furnaces.[25] Noses and ears were routinely chopped off. At least one African was punished by being hung by his testicles until he died.[26] By any index of inhumanity, the inventory of instruments of torture was chilling.[27] Body mutilation, scars, and physical deformities resulting from beatings and overwork were widespread. Life expectancy for Brazilian-born slaves was a mere twenty-three years,[28] and self-destruction was a tragically common means of escape.[29]

Merciless working conditions, in concert with other features of Brazilian slavery, had serious implications for slave demographic patterns. Planter preference for young male laborers left the black population with a heavily male-dominated sex ratio. Plantation sex ratios in Bahia approached two to three males for every female.[30] Marriages were generally not encouraged, and infant and child mortality among the black population bordered on astronomical.[31] The results were predictable. The slave population, rather than growing gradually through natural increase, declined by 1.5 to 3.0 percent per year. Population losses were balanced by further imports. This demographic attrition ironically made perfect economic sense for the estate owner. Throughout much of the slave trade African slaves were a bargain, and the owner doubled his initial investment if the slave survived a brief five years of captivity.[32] It appears that slave-owners, rather than protecting their work force and encouraging its multiplication, viewed the importation of "fresh hands" as economically preferable to the cost of maintaining healthy chattel.

Disease took its toll as well. The debilitating effects of overwork and chronic malnutrition militated against whatever natural resistance to pathogens Africans might have retained.[33] Smallpox epidemics raced through the population every ten to twenty years until the early 1800s, when outbreaks were finally controlled by vaccination programs.[34] Measles, tuberculosis, bronchitis, and dysentery were common as well. Although frequently misdiagnosed, beriberi was apparently rampant in the slave community.[35] High mortality among the slave population in nineteenth-century Rio de Janeiro was attributed to the effects of tuberculosis, dysentery, and smallpox, all compounded by the effects of malnutrition.[36] African-borne diseases, such as elephantiasis and Guinea worm, arrived on the slave ships and continued to plague the black community in the New World.[37] Syphilis was also common among the slave population, a circumstance Gilberto Freyre attributes in part to the belief among whites in the Northeast of Brazil that sexual intercourse with an African virgin girl was the best purge for this chronic disease.[38] The verdict on the conditions of Brazilian slavery, with notable exceptions, is unequivocal. For most African slave laborers, life was brutal and brief, a sustained state of misery in a New World purgatory.

As a direct consequence of poor working conditions, disease, and suicide, the average slave survived a brief seven years in captivity, and his or her life expectancy was a mere twenty-three years.[39] The combined effects of high mortality and of fertility rates below replacement level generated an incessant demand for fresh captives during the four centuries of slavery. In Rio de Janeiro, for example, even after three centuries of sustained slave traffic, over 73 percent of its 1832 slave population was born in Africa as opposed to Brazil.[40] According to João José Reis, the "typical slave in Bahia in the nineteenth century was then male, young . . . and African born."[41] As a result, the captive labor force was, throughout much of the slave trade, numerically dominated by people whose worldview was shaped by their African heritage.[42] The insidious byproduct of this circumstance, at least from the point of view of the ruling class, was that each shipload of fresh slaves reintroduced African cultural practices and beliefs just as they were in the process of eroding and, just as important, gave renewed status to the value of African culture among the population. This cultural rescue effect meant that traditional religious values were continuously being reinforced among the African slave and free population in Bahia.

African Connections

Among the Yoruba and their descendants in Brazil, the rejuvenation of African cultural beliefs was a function, however, of much more than negative population growth rates. It was also a result of the conscious effort of Africans to keep in close contact with their homeland, to cultivate and disseminate the beliefs and practices of their forebears in Brazil, and to remain true to a worldview that set them apart from the rest of Brazilian society. Although the cumulative effect of this process came to represent a direct challenge to Portuguese ideology, constituting a conspiracy of resistance on the part of an oppressed race, it is important to remember that the actors were individuals with their own motivations and agendas. Some must have earnestly felt the evangelistic calling to expand the worship of the **orixás**. Others strove for the power and prestige associated with religious leadership. Others, perhaps, simply wanted to make a profit.

The cultural connection between West Africa and Bahia in the decades following the end of slavery was probably more direct than that of any of the other peoples of the African diaspora. As Melville and Francis Herskovitz observed a half century ago, for Afro-Bahians "Africa is no vague mythical land. . . . It is a living reality, whence many of the objects they use in their rituals are imported, where people they know have visited and . . . where their fathers or grandfathers came from."[43] Some of the slaves emancipated when slavery was finally abolished in 1888, as well as some of the African slaves who had managed to purchase their freedom or had otherwise been emancipated in the decades before, returned to their homes in Africa. Exactly when this repatriation process began and how many chose to return is uncertain. But by the early 1850s, applications by ex-slaves for passports began to appear, along with classified announcements in the local newspapers of their imminent departure for "the coast of Africa." For example, in an 1858 copy of the *Diário da Bahia*, an ad announced that "The liberated African Benedicto, of the Nagô [Yoruba] nation, returning to the coast of Africa, is declared to be allowed to leave."[44]

For many of these repatriates, bitter memories of a lifetime of forced servitude must have been partially erased by putting Brazil and all that it meant permanently behind them. For others, however, who left friends, family, and commercial opportunities behind—not to mention a familiarity of place that must have long before supplanted the memory of Africa—Brazil was not so easily abandoned. A number of repatriated Africans, upon returning to Africa, recognized the business potential of transatlantic trade in goods appreciated by those who remained in Brazil. For example, José Francisco dos Santos returned to Wydah, Dahomey, and established an import-export business that operated from the 1840s to the 1870s. His 112 surviving letters show that he shipped over six hundred slaves before 1851, mostly to Salvador, while in the subsequent period he focused on **obí**, pano-da-costa, and other items in demand among the black population in Bahia. He also kept up with the lives of his old friends and business associates and frequently handled remittances of money and other valuables being sent by friends in one direction or the other.[45] In another case, a black women born in Cachoeira, Bahia, named Isadora Maria Hamus, moved to Lagos, spent eight years learning Yoruba and English, and returned to Bahia to become a leader of a house of Candomblé. In intellectual circles, perhaps the best known repatriate was Sr. Martiniano do Bonfin. His father had been illegally brought to Bahia from Nigeria as a slave in 1842, but was freed by Governor's decree in the early 1850s and later purchased his wife's freedom. In 1875, he journeyed to Lagos with young Martiniano, in order that the boy receive a proper education and learn the religion of his ancestors. Eleven years later, fluent in Yoruba and English, Sr. Martiniano returned to Salvador. He went on to become a respected consultant on matters of African ritual for the most powerful houses of Candomblé.[46] And finally, as noted earlier, several of the most important houses of Candomblé were founded by African repatriates who eventually returned to Bahia.[47]

Such individual initiative was necessary for the perpetuation of African cultural beliefs and, by extension, for the formation of houses of worship. Disseminated in an environment that was, throughout much of its history, numerically dominated by Africans and their descendants, these kernels of cultural continuity were likely to sprout and take root, provided that there were cracks in the matrix of social control instituted by the authorities. Such openings of opportunity, narrow and inadvertent as they were, were provided by the nature of the Brazilian slavocracy and the strategies it employed to maintain power.

Black Brotherhoods

The spark of potentiality provided by individual initiative was able to catch fire in Brazil in part because of some of the nuances of the evolving Brazilian economy, society, and religion. One of these was the colonial government's policy of encouraging the formation of Catholic brotherhoods that were segregated according to ethnic affiliation. Dating from the thirteenth century in Portugal, these fraternal organizations were intended to uphold proper Christian virtues, to provide for the welfare of members and their dependents, and to promote charitable activities. For Africans in Brazil, both slave and free, the brotherhoods served as the only officially sanctioned means through which they could reestablish a measure of the corporate identity lost from the old continent and rigorously prohibited in the new. Although membership in some brotherhoods was open to all, others enforced an exclusive policy of ethnic standards—admitting, for example, only Jeje from Dahomey, or Ketu from Yorubaland. Each brotherhood retained its own ruling body, provided for the Christian education of its members, honored its patron saints, and generally served as a symbol of the successful integration of African pagans into European society.

While on the one hand upholding proper white Christian values, the brotherhoods on the other hand constituted one of the few legal means by which African language, customs, and ideas could be perpetuated. Here were islands of African space, congenial environments where people of similar language and worldview could support each other and be supported. Here was a parallel social structure wherein the bonds of oppression were temporarily loosened, an African meritocracy where hard work and perseverance might be rewarded with an elected high station. Here were the personal contacts between ethnic compatriots that fostered the perpetuation of African religious beliefs. The fact that these organizations were dedicated to Christian beliefs probably represented only the minutest of contradictions for its membership, who then, as now, viewed each belief system as an adjunct or even a logical extension of the other.[48]

The white authorities' lack of control of the black population, particularly in urban areas, has been cited as a factor that further facilitated the preservation of African culture and language. This was particularly the case regarding dancing and singing in native African languages. A certain level of tolerance was advocated by ecclesiastics and government officials on the grounds that a contented laborer was likely to be more productive and less prone to attempt escape. Others argued that African dances stirred the libidos of the slaves and thus encouraged reproduction.[49] How such opinions were weighed by plantation owners must have varied greatly. However, in cities like Rio de Janeiro and Salvador, slaves and freedmen were commonly seen dancing the **batuque** and the **lundú** in the early hours of the morning, to the annoyance of some but apparently not all of the white population. There were occasionally arrests in Salvador, as a municipal code ostensibly prohibited such public demonstrations, but in most of these cases the perpetrators appear to have been drunk and disorderly.[50] Johann Rugendas describes seeing the dances of the Africans, including the **lundú**, which "the Portuguese also dance."[51] The general indifference on the part of the authorities was reflected in angry letters from Bahian merchants to the Prince Regent. One correspondence suggested that "Perhaps we should ask them on our knees not to dance the **batuque** and not to convert this country into a new Mina Coast, as they have been doing up to this time."[52] From the point of view of the government, however, allowing Africans to associate openly with their ethnic kindred, whether by singing and dancing or in the more structured environment of the brotherhood, was part of a long-standing policy of divide-and-rule, a strategy to avoid conspiracies against the ruling order by encouraging historical sentiments of antagonism between the different African "nations."[53]

The Church

Lax enforcement of colonial and, later, imperial policy found its religious parallel in the area of ecclesiastical education. Comments by most contemporary observers were in agreement that Africans seldom received more than the barest rudiments of religious training, a circumstance that seems irreconcilable with the principle that Brazil was colonized in order to bring the one true god to the heathens. Slaves were baptized either before being loaded in Africa or shortly after arrival in Brazil, and for many this gesture represented the beginning and end of their Christian education.[54] For the planter, pastoral attention to the laborers translated into diminished productivity, and whether slaves were permitted to observe the Sabbath and other religious holidays depended on the disposition of the master.[55] Catholic missionaries, who waged a fierce battle for the souls of the indigenous population, seldom directed their efforts at the Africans. As major slave-holders themselves, the Jesuits, Franciscans, and

Benedictines served more as pastoral apologists, counseling the oppressed blacks to seek their salvation in the hereafter. It fell on the chaplain, the master, and his overseers to impart a few simple prayers and the commandments to their slaves. Without a forceful program of indoctrination, it is less than surprising that so many Africans clung tenaciously to the religious beliefs of their homeland.

Not only the generally low intensity of Christian evangelism but also the particular brand of Catholicism that arrived in Brazil weighed heavily in the capacity of Africans to appear to acquiesce to the religion of the whites while continuing to practice the religion of their ancestors. Removed from the rigid and ascetic Catholicism of Rome, Iberia had preserved a medieval Catholicism of the Counter-Reformation, a folk religion grounded in a hagiology of hands-on, miracle-working saints. Through prayers and votive offerings, white colonists called upon patron saints like St. George, St. Emiliano, and St. Sebastian—often pictured as military men "on horseback and sword in hand"—to open paths and conquer their enemies, or they besought the Virgin Mary, often depicted wearing a thin, provocative gown, to bring health and good looks to newborns.[56] Direct appeals to the saints for help in solving health problems found pastoral support in the words of Pope Innocent III, who stated that "many times bodily illness is due to spiritual indisposition, and applying a remedy to the ailment of the soul, our Lord sends health to the body."[57]

It was this cult of the saints, the adoration of a pantheon of spiritual entities that solved earthly problems, that Africans came to know as Catholicism. This obvious correspondence between the archetypes of saints and **orixás** was early perceived and capitalized on by the African population, who by the late nineteenth century were actively engaged in the process of associating their own deities with those of the Catholic hagiology. St. Barbara, the patron saint of storms and lightning, became one with Xangô, the Yoruba god of thunder. Oxalá, the most highly regarded of the Yoruba deities, became linked with Jesus Christ.[58] Which saint came to be associated with each **orixá** varied considerably from terreiro to terreiro, from nation to nation, and from period to period as well.[59] It was, as Nina Rodrigues could readily perceive in the late nineteenth century, "precisely this fact that gives the illusion of the Catholic conversion of the Negroes."[60] The long-term result, regardless of which spiritual correspondences came to predominate, was to give blacks the license to worship their own gods.

The polytheistic nature of Brazil's Catholicism was complemented by a series of other structural similarities to the religion of the Yoruba. Whereas the simple rituals of North America's Protestant churches, dominated by Methodist and Calvinist ideals, stood in sharp contrast with the complex structure of African religious practice, "the pomp and display of the Catholic liturgy gave the Africans a basis for identification and correspondence."[61] Elaborate rituals and offerings, belief in magic and divination, ancestor worship, votive offerings and sacrifices, and the adjuration of gods to deal with real-world problems—all fundamental to African religious structure—found their ready parallels within Catholicism. Even the sign of the cross, the most pervasive and seemingly exclusive emblem of the Christian faith, was already a traditional sacred symbol to slaves who hailed from Dahomey.[62] In addition, unlike its Protestant counterparts, the Catholic Church maintained an implicit policy of tolerance toward pagan rituals and deities. Converting the heathens to the one true religion was best effected, not by destroying their icons and suppressing their ceremonies, but rather by the gradual substitution of Catholic symbols and rituals.[63] In this way, Africans could continue to carry out pagan rites, now disguised as Catholic liturgy, and to honor their own gods, now absorbed by the names of Catholic saints. In Protestant North America, where the clergy rigorously attacked African "heathenism,"[64] the religion of the slaves was for the most part extinguished.[65] In Catholic Brazil, the similarities between the religious practice of the whites and those of the black population, combined with a general policy of tolerance and gradual religious assimilation, allowed Africans to build a facade of Catholicism while at the same time maintaining the fundamentals of their belief system.

Resistance

The nuances of the slave trade, the conditions of life on plantations and in the cities, and the peculiarities of the evolving Brazilian social structure facilitated the continuation as well as the mutation of African cultural beliefs and practices. But while these features created windows of opportunity for African cultural retention, it was the aggressive actions of individuals from a marginalized social stratum, struggling to improve their lot in life or even to recreate the society from which they had been uprooted, that formed the basis of African cultural preservation. The avenues of resistance ranged from purely symbolic to physical attacks on the prevailing social structure: work slowdowns on the plantations, suicides, armed insurrections, and the formation of **quilombos**, or communities of escaped slaves.[66] Viewed in an ideological framework, such actions represented highly rational responses on the part of individuals and groups to unacceptable living and working conditions. The persistent attempts to reassemble African religious systems in Brazil were motivated in part by similar material desires, but they also drew much of their inspiration from the specific inability of the Catholic faith to address the primary concerns of its people. Because these religious assaults challenged Catholicism—the spiritual cornerstone of Catholic civilization, underpinning the economic and social interests of the dominant class—these fronts of resistance were particularly insidious and revolutionary. Structural similarities and levels of syncretism notwithstanding, the Yoruba spiritual worldview was diametrically opposed to its Catholic counterpart in ways that must have attracted both slave and free blacks during the course of Brazilian history, and that today draw adherents from all social and racial backgrounds.

At center stage of the challenge was the contrast in the roles that each religion offered to Brazilians—between a European folk religion that justified the earthly status quo through eventual salvation, that put off the promise of progress until the next life, and that sought solace through a distant and unknowable god, and an African religion that empowered its members, that sought to level the social and economic playing field through direct action during this life, and that allowed its members to dance with the deities. Solutions to the problems of everyday life—health, love, jealousy, and finances—were the issues most relevant to the African population, and these were precisely what was offered by Candomblé.

Magical medicine constituted perhaps the most potent weapon of the Africans, first as executed by isolated priests and magicians, and later as a collective effort within houses of Candomblé worship. In the otherwise one-sided context of the master-slave relationship, the ability to tap into the occult forces came to represent one of the few powers that Africans held over their owners—as well as over their fellow bondsmen. Early Portuguese settlers came from a world in which the practices of magic and witchcraft were viewed as routine, day-to-day activities, and it was only later that such practices became associated with the work of Satan. But while the Inquisition drove these practices underground in the Old World, belief in the power of magical medicine found fertile soil on the isolated frontiers of a new continent,[67] a landscape where uncertainty and lack of control underscored the lives of Africans and, to a lesser extent, of the Portuguese population. African priests, who had long been considered masters of these unseen forces, moved to fill this social niche vacated by the demise of the indigenous *pajés*. It may be, as reported elsewhere, that initial perceptions of the magical power of Africans actually expanded over time, feeding on the fears and superstitious nature of both races. Such an expansion may have also been fostered among the black population in response to the complete power exercised by the white population, a power that in the minds of many could only be explained by the magical power of the Europeans.[68] On the one hand, African priests drove fear into both the white and the black population; on the other hand, both races firmly believed that certain Africans retained these powers, and at one time or another both races found cause to seek out their services. This situation has changed little over the years, as many Bahians, both black and white, refer to Candomblé priests with a mixture of fear and contempt, and yet are known on occasion to seek their counsel.

Beginning with the formation of the first Candomblé terreiros in the early nineteenth century, the knowledge of magical medicine retained by individual Africans became collective knowledge, kept alive and passed on from generation to generation—however modified—by the hierarchy of the terreiro. A few traditional terreiros have zealously preserved what they perceive to be the purely African elements of these ethnomedical systems, whereas the multitude of smaller, proletarian terreiros, which at least by force of numbers constitute the true Brazilian Candomblé, have acted as clearinghouses for African as well as various fringe medical and magical beliefs. Adherents as well as secular clients now seek out a host of ethnomedical services, searching for the cause, the diagnosis, and the prescription for problems ranging from spiritual and magical to purely organic. There are few illnesses or immediate social problems for which one or another Candomblé priest cannot offer an explanation and a remedy. And there are few, if any, healing rituals that do not depend on the use of the liturgical and medicinal flora. "Without the leaves," as one priest noted, "there is no Candomblé." Thus, social and economic factors notwithstanding, the physical environment into which Africans were transported was a pivotal factor in their ability to recreate their belief system.

Gods in the Forest

The religion that the Yoruba brought to Brazil was fundamentally animistic. Unlike universal religions of conversion and salvation, such as Christianity and Islam—which embrace proselytization, spiritual hegemony, and geographical expansion as central tenets of their earthly mission—the Yoruba belief system was firmly attached to place. It was associated with a specific, nation-sized area, and it was tightly integrated with the functioning of local governing bodies. Most importantly, the Yoruba religion was spiritually committed to the features of its immediate physical surroundings. Its gods were nature gods, personifications of physical elements: wind, thunder, water, trees, and soil. Reverence and meaning were attached to sacred spaces: towns, hills, forests, and rivers.

Unlike the religions that developed in Africa's nearby savannas and deserts—wide-open landscapes where worship was directed toward the celestial vastness of the heavens, toward the sun, the moon, and the stars—the religion of the Yoruba was a closed forest religion, drawing its inspiration, as Una McClean describes, from "a myopic, green landscape where close-up detail predominates."[69] Firmly rooted in place, the religion of the Yoruba, like other ethnic belief systems, represented an unlikely candidate for wide-scale diffusion.[70]

These barriers to diffusion were partially cleared by the nature of the Yoruba slave migration and by the characteristics of its destination. As unwilling participants in an insidious European enterprise, Africans were forced to travel by long-distance saltation rather than incremental expansion. Disengaged from one tropical forested region and deposited in another, Africans bypassed many arid physical habitats that would have proved less inviting to their pantheon. Coastal Bahia, although distant from the known world of the Yoruba, presented an array of physical features complementary to the ones to which they had previously attached cosmological significance. Oxum found a home in the region's deep perennial streams. Frequent thunderstorms suggested the presence of Xangô, and the accompanying rain, winds, and lightning indicated the presence of his mythological wife, the unpredictable Iansã. Oxóssi and Ossâim, the hunter and the herbalist, found refuge in Bahia's broadleaf evergreen rainforests. Devastating smallpox epidemics, as bad as those that had swept across native Africa, testified to the New World existence of Omolu. At least for the Yoruba pantheon, Bahia's tropical forest landscape presented nearly all the physical ingredients necessary for animistic correspondence and substitution.[71]

The New Land

Biogeography represented a more formidable obstacle to successful diffusion. Because the religion of the Yoruba is centered around a practical, this-worldly motif, bringing fertility, happiness, and good health to its followers, arriving African priests faced the material challenge of how to perpetuate a plant-based healing system in an alien floristic landscape. Over two thousand miles of ocean and 100 million years of evolution separated healers from their healing flora. African captives were obviously in no position to convey their ethnoflora during the Middle Passage, and as slave laborers and later as poor freedmen, Afro-Brazilians were severely constrained in their ability to import liturgical plants from their homeland. Although the successful introductions **obí** (*Cola acuminata*) and **akokô** (*Newbouldia laevis*) are ritually significant, these trees constituted a tiny fraction of the necessary plant arsenal. While their Portuguese masters went about transplanting their temperate agrosystems to tropical Brazil, however impractical the task and maladapted the species, African priests must have recognized early that the ability to practice magic and medicine in the Americas depended upon their capacity to adopt the flora immediately at hand. This ethnobotanical puzzle, as has been suggested in previous chapters, was solved by various means.

At the rank of plant family and genus, Africa and South America exhibit a reasonable degree of propinquity. This taxonomic similarity was the product of the Cretaceous separation of the West Gondwana plate into Africa and South America, vicariant continental rafts that dragged kindred floras in opposing directions. In subsequent millennia, pulses of climatic change and plant evolution dissolved much of the original floristic similarity. Native species that had once inhabited both banks of the incipient Atlantic, probably without exception navigated unique evolutionary paths. As a result, arriving priests and priestesses may well have been disappointed, at least at the species level, by the vicariant pre-Columbian flora they encountered.

At the level of plant genus, however—the rank that is most salient in terms of human cognition[72]—and certainly at the plant family level, eastern Brazil and western Africa would not have seemed so very different. Some of the most ubiquitous families in the Atlantic forests of Brazil are common components of West Africa's flora, for example, Myrtaceae, Sapotaceae, Euphorbiaceae, Lauraceae, Melastomataceae, and Moraceae, to mention only a few. The list of genera common to both floristic provinces is even more impressive, providing a wealth of possible candidates for substitution. These included *Aristolochia*, *Bauhinia*, *Casearia*, *Ficus*, *Mimosa*, *Piper*, *Sida*, *Vernonia*, and *Vitex*, all of which enter into the **odu** of Yoruba **babalaô** and all of which, in time, were incorporated into the Candomblé spiritual flora.[73] For example, the West African **abafé**, *Bauhinia thonningii*, was replaced by the morphologically similar *Bauhinia ovata* of Brazil. The African **aloma**, *Vernonia senegalensis* and *V. amygdalina*, became Candomblé's **alumã**, *Vernonia condensata* and *V. schoenanthus*.[74] Because the Yoruba system of liturgical plant taxonomy is based mainly on sensory attributes—visual, tactile, and olfactory—the presence of slightly variant flower or fruiting structures on newly encountered Brazilian species probably would not have severely impeded their acceptance into the neo-African ethnoflora.

The vegetative similarity between the two distant continents transcended this floristic affinity. Both exhibit coastlines that are, or at least were, mantled by moist tropical forests, habitats that provided similar structural elements for the ethnofloral replacement process: tall broadleaf evergreen trees, great spreading buttresses, and branches festooned with lianas, stranglers, and epiphytes. The diffusion of the Yoruba god Iroko to the New World represents perhaps the best example of this substitution process.

Sacred Trees

The peoples of West Africa hold many tree species to be sacred. In the distant past, defacing one of these "tree gods" constituted a capital offense.[75] West Africa's most sacred tree, perhaps, is the silk cottonwood *(Ceiba pentandra)*,[76] a species fortuitously native to West Africa, the Caribbean, northern South America, and perhaps Southeast Asia.[77] Recognized and immediately re-adopted by arriving Africans, the silk cottonwood became the dwelling place of African spirits in Venezuela, of the god Loco in Haiti, and of duppy spirits in Jamaica.[78] For these constituents of the African diaspora, the task of transferring their principal tree deity was solved by the vagaries of long-distance seed dispersal or plate tectonics long before they themselves arrived. For the Yoruba, however, the process required more creativity.

One of the most sacred trees of the Yoruba is the **iroko** *(Chlorophora excelsa)*, dwelling-place of the god Iroko. Among African Yoruba, Iroko is a male deity associated with peace, whose primary role is to settle disagreements between human beings.[79] Temples were once built wherever the **iroko** tree was seen to germinate spontaneously, and it was thought that the tree would not survive if purposely planted.[80] Like many of the other **orixás**, in Brazil Iroko assumed a somewhat different archetype. He became the god of time and eternity.[81] According to Ruy Póvoas, Iroko and his adepts are difficult to work with, generally out of equilibrium, and thoroughly disconnected from the daily regimen of existence. You will "wait the lifetime of a vulture to get a reply from Iroko." Like the other deities, he retains his own preferences and prohibitions and has his dedicated days. The principal difference is that this god resides in a tree—a tree species that occurs only in West Africa, and that at least in the past was believed to be recalcitrant to intentional transplant.

The response of believers was to adopt a completely different species, a tree that lacked any transatlantic connection but exhibited certain structural and taxonomic similarities with the original African **iroko**. The species chosen was the Brazilian native gameleira branca *(Ficus* sp.), a species that apparently held no particular spiritual import for the native Tupinambá (Fig. 8.2).[82] Both the African and the adopted Brazilian **iroko** are in the mulberry family (Moraceae), and both bleed abundant white latex when cut.[83] Like its West African counterpart, the Brazilian **iroko** is a formidable tree, broad and commanding, surrounded by abundant niches in its buttresses for the placement of votive offerings.[84] For many traditional as well as proletarian terreiros, a towering

8.2   The sacred **iroko** (also known as **loco** among Jeje [Vodun] adherents), dwelling-place of the Yoruba god Iroko. The African species (*Chlorophora excelsa*) was replaced in Bahia by gameleira branca (*Ficus* sp.). (Photo: Robert Voeks)

iroko near the <u>barracão</u> represents a necessary landmark in their sacred African space.

However compelling as a framework for ethnobotanical diffusion, this substitution process in fact contributed only a relatively small number of plants. The opportunities for floristic and physiognomic substitution were considerable, but the process was infrequently carried out. This is particularly the case with regard to Bahia's old-growth rainforests, which are notable for their absence from the Candomblé healing flora. Indeed, of the few primary-forest taxa that were adopted into Candomblé, most are equally or more abundant in heavily disturbed sites. Native trees constitute a small minority of perceived useful Candomblé plants, and epiphytes are completely absent. Structural attributes of the coastal rainforest vegetation, however similar to the vegetation in West Africa, do not appear to have played a dominant role in the diffusion of an alien ethnomedical package.

In principle, floristic similarity at the species level could have been augmented by waif dispersal after Africa and South America separated. As richly illustrated by the flora of the Hawaiian Islands, plants have the capacity to disperse away from their immediate surroundings, sometimes by prodigious leaps. The two most likely candidates for long-distance dispersal are the bottle gourd (*Lagenaria siceraria*) and the beach morning-glory (*Ipomoea pes-caprae*), species with specialized flotation devices that in all likelihood facilitated their transatlantic colonization. The bottle gourd, of such great symbolic value to the Yoruba as a perfect representation of the parallel worlds of the material and the spiritual, may well have suggested the presence of the **orixás** in the New World. But aside from these limited exceptions, the vast majority of the pre-Columbian flora would have presented a medicinal mystery for newly arrived Africans. It was, rather, the arrival of Europeans and their wholesale transformation of the New World bioscape that allowed the diffusion of African ethnobotany.

Plants and People

By the time Yoruba priests were arriving in large numbers, in the latter eighteenth and early nineteenth centuries, and particularly during the period when the first houses of Candomblé worship were being established, the Bahian flora had already been irreparably damaged—or, depending on your philosophical bent, significantly enhanced—by human intervention. Responsive to successive boom-and-bust economic cycles of extraction and plantation, the primary forests had been cut, burned, and transformed for generations by waves of settlers. The old-growth forest frontier was already well away from the coast.

And the human floristic landscape, comprising the habitats with which people were most intimately familiar—the plantations, the pastures, the roadsides, and the kitchen gardens—was brimming with species that were familiar to Africans. At the species level, nineteenth-century Bahia was not so strange at all.

The full significance of the effect of human actions is revealed by reviewing the Candomblé species list (Appendix 1). Nearly half of the species employed in Candomblé ritual and ceremony inhabit both sides of the Atlantic, a biogeographical homogenization that was the result of human rather than natural processes. When species in the same genera are included in this calculation, nearly 60 percent of the Candomblé ethnoflora is also employed by present-day Yoruba healers in Africa.[85] Several of these are Old World taxa that arrived in Bahia and were being employed medicinally by the mid-1500s.[86] Most, or perhaps all, of the other species that would later find their way into the Candomblé ethnoflora were present by the early 1800s.[87] Their modes of transport varied. Many were purposely transplanted in Brazil—not by Africans, but by their European captors. Fruit- and oil-producing species, like **dendê** (*Elaeis guineensis*), jambo branco (*Syzygium jambos*), mango (*Mangifera indica*), and mamona (*Ricinus communis*), were introduced for commercial purposes and to enhance the number of useful species in the region. By the late 1500s, Friar Vicente do Salvador boasted that Brazil was blessed with more food plants than any other tropical country because it received "the crop plants of all the others."[88] Garden herbs, imported for culinary and probably also medicinal and magical purposes, included poejo (*Mentha pulegium*), manjericão (*Ocimum canum*), arruda (*Ruta graveolens*), and perhaps transagem (*Plantago major*). Other garden cultivars, such as **peregun** (*Dracaena fragrans*), leopoldina (*Alpinia zerumbet*), and espada-de-Oxóssi (*Sansevieria* cf. *aethiopica*), must have been brought for their ornamental qualities. A host of other Old World plants arrived with the Portuguese as stowaways, opportunistic Old World weeds that colonized the increasingly disturbed Brazilian landscape with a vengeance. These included **dandá** (*Cyperus rotundus*), jasmin-do-brejo (*Hedychium coronarium*), and others, all of which found their way into the Candomblé pharmacopoeia. By whatever means and for whatever motivation it reached the Americas, much of what African Americans would eventually adopt as their own ethnoflora owes its presence to the unintentional actions of the ruling class.

However significant these Old World imports, the majority of Candomblé species are in fact of New World origin. Some had been transported to Africa earlier, during the course of European colonization, either as weeds or cultigens, and were there incorporated into Yoruba healing. When Africans arrived in Brazil, they discovered many of these familiar healing plants, of New World origin, but long important elements in Yoruba healing recipes. New World maize, for example, which arrived in West Africa early, was assimilated into Yoruba **babalaô** recipes for good luck, wealth, and healthy births.[89] Other cultigens included cotton (*Gossypium barbadense*) and tobacco (*Nicotiana tabacum*) as well as a long list of weeds, such as malissa (*Mimosa pudica*), guiné (*Petiveria alliacea*), and alfavaquinha-de-cobra (*Peperomia pellucida*).

The opportunities for ethnobotanical diffusion resulting from these processes of floristic homogenization are exemplified by the composition of the house **abô**. Fundamental to initiation among the Yoruba and their Brazilian diaspora, the house **abô** would not seem to have been open to wholesale floristic reformulation. Examination of the **abô** of three terreiros suggests that continuity, by whatever means, was largely the rule (Appendix 2). Among those taxa for which origins can be determined, over half occur in West Africa and also in eastern Brazil. Some, such as **akokô** (*Newbouldia laevis*), the espadas (*Sansevieria* cf. *aethiopica*), **macaçá** (*Ocimum canum*), and leopoldina (*Alpinia zerumbet*), were purposely introduced for various ends. Others, such as cordão-de-São Francisco (*Leonotis nepetifolia*) and **dandá** (*Cyperus rotundus*), were Old World taxa that arrived as weeds. Still others were New World weeds that had long ago attained amphitropical distributions, including pinhão roxo (*Jatropha gossypifolia*) and fedegoso (*Senna occidentalis*).[90] Among the remaining **abô** species not found both in Africa and in the Americas, most are at least represented by pantropical genera. Whether by biogeographical or by cognitive processes, ethnobotanical continuity was maintained.[91]

Because many of the species used in Candomblé continue to be endemic to the Americas, it appears that African healers were capable of assimilating entirely new species from their immediate surroundings. This ethnobotanical flexibility was provided, at least in part, by the Yoruba system of medicinal plant organization. In West Africa, liturgical and medicinal species correspond with one or another of the ancient deities, a relationship mythically underpinned by the legend of Ossâim's leaves. The nature of these god-plant associations, which are encoded in the medicinal recipes and incantations of the **odu**, are maintained as oral text and recited during divination by **babalaô** priests, the most respected class of Yoruba healers. Although the specialized role of the **babalaô** failed to survive in Brazil, the conceptual framework provided by their system of association did. Whether any of the original Yoruba god-plant correspondences survived in Brazil is not clear. What was most important, however, was that pais- and mães-de-santo were able to justify conceptually the incorporation of hitherto unknown New World plants into their pharmacopoeias. The newly assigned god-plant associations were based upon a broad suite of characteristics corresponding to the personalities, physical appearances, and preferences of each of the African **orixás**.

Candomblé in Brazil

The existence in a neo-European landscape of Candomblé, a religion reconstituted and perpetuated by African slaves and their descendants, is clearly not a puzzle at all. Indeed, given the interplay of so many supportive processes—social, economic, political, and geographical—it would be a mystery if it had failed to take root and prosper. Although encompassed by a Portuguese social structure, Bahia was and continues to be dominated numerically by people of African descent. Wave upon wave of forced immigrants arrived at the Bay of All Saints, introducing and reintroducing the traditions and language of their homeland. These last human pulses, driven by the ethnic preferences of planters and urban elites, were dominated by Yoruba and Dahomey people, African cultures with cosmologies and traditions that rivaled those of their European captors in complexity and resilience. The incessant infusion of African ways was fostered, ironically, by the horrific conditions and consequently the abbreviated life spans of Brazilian slaves, as well as by the voluntary movements of black freedmen back and forth across the Atlantic. Diffusion was facilitated further by the structural similarity of Brazilian Catholicism, a folk religion that emphasized saint worship and extravagant ceremony, to the religion of the **orixás**. The similarity of Bahia and West Africa's floristic landscapes, supplemented exponentially by the transatlantic exchange of cultigens, weeds, and sacred species, allowed for the continuation of African healing practices as well as the assimilation of those of European origin. This biological correspondence encouraged the diffusion of African ethnobotanical practices to Brazil, accompanied by the corresponding Yoruba system of beliefs.

However effective at laying the foundation for cultural diffusion, these features and processes could not have functioned without the perseverance of individual Afro-Brazilian leaders. Candomblé terreiros did not establish themselves. They were the products of individual initiative, mostly by unknown priests and priestesses who refused to buckle under the pressure of European spiritual hegemony. While most of the seeds of their resistance withered and died, a few survived and ultimately multiplied, providing sacred space within which the oral wisdom of the African gods could be cultivated, hybridized, and disseminated to future generations.

APPENDICES

1 CANDOMBLÉ SPECIES LIST

Vernacular names are listed in order of most common usage: Portuguese terms are <u>underlined</u>, African names are in **bold**, Tupi names are ***italicized and boldfaced***, and common English names are listed in brackets.

Associated deities: number in parentheses indicates number of informants (if more than one) identifying god-plant relationship.

Life form is what I observed when the plant was collected.

Voucher numbers: as stored at the herbarium, Centro de Pesquisas do Cacau, Itabuna, Bahia, Brazil (NC = Not Collected).

Family name	Scientific name	Vernacular name(s)	Magical/ spiritual use
Acanthaceae	*Justicia gendarrussa Burm* f.	<u>vence tudo Africano</u>	living plant as ornament for protection against <u>olho grande</u>
Agavaceae	*Dracaena fragrans* (L.) Ker-Gawl	**peregun**; <u>nativo</u>	decoration; <u>sacudimento</u> in house; presence in house keeps away bad spirits; flowers in **abô**; <u>camarinha</u>; <u>banho de descarga</u>
	Sansevieria cf. *aethiopica* Thunb.	<u>espada-de-Ogun</u>; **ida orixá** [bowstring hemp]	**abô**; decoration; to guard house against evil eye
	Sansevieria cf. *aethiopica* Thunb.	<u>espada-de-Oxóssi</u> [bowstring hemp]	**abô**; decoration; to guard house against evil eye
Anacardiaceae	*Mangifera indica* L.	<u>manga</u> [mango]	

Organic medical use and preparation	Associated deities	Origin (ecological status): life form	Voucher no.
	Caboclo	Old World (cosmopolitan ornamental): shrub	173, 225, 241
	Ogun (4), Oxóssi, Ossâim	Old World (cosmopolitan ornamental): woody herb	172, 301
	Ogun (4)	Old World (cosmopolitan ornamental): herb	NC
	Oxóssi (4)	Old World (cosmopolitan ornamental): herb	NC
	Ogun	Asia (cosmopolitan food plant): tree	NC

Family name	Scientific name	Vernacular name(s)	Magical/ spiritual use
	Schinus terebinthifolius Raddi	aroeira; **ajobiewe; perôko**	**abô**; banho de descarga sacudimento in house; camarinha; magic; scattered on floor of barracão
	Tapirira guianensis Aubl.	pau pombo	**abô**; sacudimento in house; leaves scattered on floor of barracão
Annonaceae	*Annona muricata* L.	jaca-de-pobre; **apa oka** [graviola]	
Apiaceae	*Pimpinella anisum* L.	erva doce [anise]	
Apocynaceae	*Catharanthus roseus* (L.) G. Don	bom dia [Madagascar periwinkle]	
	Catharanthus roseus var. *albus* Sweet	boa noite [Madagascar periwinkle]	
	Himatanthus phagedaenicus (Mart.) Woodson	**janaúba**	
Araceae	*Dieffenbachia maculata* (Lodd.) G. Don	comigo-ninguém-pode [dumb cane]	living plant is displayed against evil eye
	Philodendron sp.	sete chagas	
Arecaceae	*Elaeis guineensis* Jacq.	**dendê; mariuô** [African oil palm]	spines used for Exu work; leaves burned to take away bad spirits; fruit oil in offerings; young leaves (**mariuô**) hung at entrances to barracão
Aristolochiaceae	*Aristolochia trilobata* L.	jarrinha; **joco mojé**	
Asteraceae	*Achyrocline satureoides* (Lam.) DC.	marcela	
	Ambrosia artemisiifolia L.	artemesia [artemisia]	**abô**; banho de descarga; banho de desenvolvimento

Organic medical use and preparation	Associated deities	Origin (ecological status): life form	Voucher no.
women's problems; leaf baths for hemorrhages and external injuries	Ogun, Iansã (2)	New World (cosmopolitan weed): treelet	191, 220
	Oxalá (2)	New World: tree	354, 389
leaf tea for treatment of diabetes		New World (cosmopolitan food plant): treelet	291
raw leaves to be chewed or leaf tea for gas; leaf tea for anxiety		Mediterranean (cosmopolitan potherb): herb	197
	Nanã	New World (cosmopolitan weed and ornamental): woody herb	398
	Oxalá	New World (cosmopolitan weed and ornamental): woody herb	399
latex is rolled into pills and ingested for general illness		New World: shrub	299
	Ogun	New World (cosmopolitan ornamental): woody herb	222
bath for losing weight	Omolu	New World: climber	260
	Exu, all the **orixás**	West Africa (cosmopolitan plantation crop): palm	NC
flower tea taken for rheumatism and hernias		New World (ornamental): climber	216
whole-plant tea for liver and stomach ailments		New World: herb	285
leaf tea for stomach and liver problems, and as a diuretic		New World (weedy): herb	194

Family name	Scientific name	Vernacular name(s)	Magical/ spiritual use
	Artemisia cf. *absinthium* L.	losna [wormwood]	
	Baccharis sp.	abre-caminho	**abô**; decoration against evil eye; sacudimento in house
	Bidens pilosa L.	carrapicho; picão; **ewe susu**	
	Blanchetia heterotricha DC.	selva-de-Ogun	
	Conocliniopsis prasiifolium (DC.) K. & R.	cama-de-coelho	**abô**
	Mikania glomerata Spreng.	folha-do-ar	**abô**
	Pluchea sagittalis (Lam.) Cabrera	assa peixe branco	leaves scattered on floor of barracão
	Pluchea suaveolens (Vell.) O. Ktz.	quitoco	**abô**; banho de descarga
	Rolandra fruticosa (L.) Kuntze	vence tudo	**abô**; potherb guards house against evil eye; banho de descarga
	Vernonia condensata Baker	**alumã; ewe auro**	**abô**
	Vernonia cf. *cotoneaster* Less.	vence-demanda	banho de descarga
	Vernonia schoenanthus L.	**alumã; ewe auro**	**abô**
	Wedelia paludosa DC.	mal-me-quer; **bai joco**	
	Wulffia baceata (L. f.) Kuntze	acocí	**abô**

Organic medical use and preparation	Associated deities	Origin (ecological status): life form	Voucher no.
leaf tea or bath for women during menopause and for fever relief; leaf extract taken internally as vermifuge		Old World (cosmopolitan ornamental): woody herb	196
	Ogun (3), Oxóssi	New World: shrub	151
leaf tea for kidney problems, fever, and as a diuretic	Exu (2)	New World (cosmopolitan weed): herb	204, 259
	Ogun (2)	New World: herb	154
		New World: herb	277
leaves and stem in foot bath for pain	Oxalá	New World: climber	334
leaf tea for kidneys and gas, to reduce fever	Ogun	New World: herb	286
tea or bath for relief of stomach ache, rheumatism, or women's problems	Omolu, Ossâim	Unknown: herb	213, 236
	Ogun (3), Oxóssi	New World: herb	263
leaf tea for stomach and liver complaints and dyspepsia	Ogun, Omolu	New World: treelet	177, 243
	Ogun	New World: herb	249
leaf tea for stomach and liver complaints and dyspepsia	Ogun, Omolu	Unknown: treelet	190
whole-plant tea with salt for oral inflammation; leaf kneaded in alcohol and rubbed on rheumatic area; leaf juice rubbed directly on cut to form scar tissue; leaf extract with honey and egg yolk taken for tuberculosis	Omolu, Oxum (2)	New World: herb	383
	Oxum	New World: shrub	265

Family name	Scientific name	Vernacular name(s)	Magical/ spiritual use
Bignoniaceae	*Newbouldia laevis* Seem.	**akokô**	**abô**; leaf attracts money; in amulets for luck
Bixaceae	*Bixa orellana* L.	***urucum***	
Boraginaceae	*Cordia* sp.	baba-de-boi	
Burseraceae	*Protium warmingianum* March.	amescla	**abô**; incense
Caesalpiniaceae	*Bauhinia ovata* Vog.	unha-da-vaca; pata-de-vaca; **abafé**	**abô**; banho de descarga
	Bauhinia cf. *smilacina* Steud.	escada-de-macaco	
	Caesalpinia pulcherrima (L.) Sw.	maravilha; barba-de-barata	
	Senna occidentalis (L.) Link	fedegoso [wild senna]	**abô**; incense; praying against evil eye
Campanulaceae	*Centropogon cornutus* (L.) Druce	bico-de-papagaio; crista-de-peru; **ewe akuko**	initiation
Caprifoliaceae	*Sambucus australis* Cham. & Schlecht.	sabugueiro	**abô**
Caricaceae	*Carica papaya* L.	mamão [papaya]	
Caryophyllaceae	*Drymaria cordata* Willd. ex. Roem. & Schult.	vintém	leaf rubbed on head of birds before sacrifice; leaf attached to front door to attract money
Chenopodiaceae	*Chenopodium ambrosioides* L.	mastruz [wormseed]	

Organic medical use and preparation	Associated deities	Origin (ecological status): life form	Voucher no.
	Xangô	Africa (intentionally introduced to Bahia): tree	319
seed extract mixed with oil rubbed on skin for protection against sunburn		Tropical America (cosmopolitan crop and ornamental): shrub	282
	Oxalá	New World: tree	352
leaf tea for espinhela caida		New World: tree	328
leaf tea for diabetes and women's problems	Ogun, Yemanjá, Exu	New World: treelet	245, 373
stem in warm bath for relief of rheumatism; garrafada is taken internally for general weakness, or as an aphrodisiac		New World: liana	330
	Oxum	New World (cosmopolitan cultivar): herb or shrub	309
bath to reduce fever	Iansã	New World (cosmopolitan weed): herb	184
leaf juice mixed in milk taken internally for stomach ulcer	Xangô (2)	New World: tree	158, 297
leaf tea or bath to relieve skin problems; leaf extract taken internally to relieve gas; tea to treat flu symptoms	Oxalá, Oxum	New World: shrub	254
syrup made from male flowers for chest cold; leaf tea from mature leaves taken internally for relief of rheumatism		Central America (cosmopolitan food plant): treelet	240
	Xangô, Oxum	Unknown (pantropical weed): herb	160
leaf tea and juice for women's problems, bruises, internal pain; whole plant juice with milk, honey, egg yolk, and powdered cinnamon for bronchitis, inflammation	Xangô, Iansã	New World (cosmopolitan weed): herb	238, 244

Family name	Scientific name	Vernacular name(s)	Magical/ spiritual use
Clusiaceae	*Garcinia kola* Heckel	**orobô** [bitter kola]	bori
Commelinaceae	*Commelina diffusa* Burm. f.	marianinha; **opodô odô**	
Convolvulaceae	*Ipomoea pes-caprae* (L.) Sweet	salsa-da-praia; **aboro aibá** [beach morning-glory]	**abô**; praying against evil eye along with arruda and vassourinha
Crassulaceae	*Kalanchoe integra* (Medic.) O. Kuntze	folha-da-costa; **ewe dudu**	**abô**
	Kalanchoe pinnata (Lam.) Pers.	folha-da-fortuna; milagre-de-São Joaquim; saião; **oju orô**	magical powder; leaf on forehead for headaches; leaf hung on wall to attract money; planted in pot with a coin to attract money
Cucurbitaceae	*Lagenaria siceraria* (Mol.) Standl.	cabaça [bottle gourd]	musical instrument; symbolism; magical container of Ossâim
	Momordica charantia L.	melão-de-São Caetano; **ejinrin**	
Cyperaceae	*Cyperus rotundus* L.	**dandá**; **dandá**-da-costa [nutgrass]	magical powder; chewed for influence; put in amulets; **abô**
	Scleria sp.	*tiririca; tiririca*-de-Exu; **labe labe**	magic powder made from roots to stop actions of bad neighbors
	Rhynchospora nervosa (Vahl) Boeck.	capim estrella	**abô**
Euphorbiaceae	*Aleurites moluccana* (L.) Willd.	nogueira	
	Centratherum punctatum Cass. ssp. *punctatum*	balainho-do-velho	**abô**
	Cnidoscolus urens (L.) Arthur	cansanção; **jojofá**	banho de descarga; magic; work with Exu; sacudimento of initiates

Organic medical use and preparation	Associated deities	Origin (ecological status): life form	Voucher no.
	Xangô, all the **orixás**	Africa (introduced to Bahia, seeds imported from Africa) : treelet	300
leaf tea or bath to relieve inflammation	Yemanjá	New World (cosmopolitan weed): herb	385
leaf bath for relief of rheumatism	Nanã	Unknown (cosmopolitan beach colonizer): creeping herb	384
leaf syrup for cough; leaf poultice on forehead for headache	Oxalá, Yemanjá (3), all **orixás**	New World (cosmopolitan cultivar and weed): herb	169, 224
leaf syrup for relief of flu symptoms	Oxum, all **orixás**	Old World (cosmopolitan ornamental and weed): herb	175
		Old World (pre-Columbian pantropical cultivar): climber	NC
leaf bath or hot leaves applied to body for general aches, injuries, or rheumatism		Old World (cosmopolitan cultivar and weed): climbing herb	183
root tea (including other uncollected plants) for cerebral hemorrhage	Oxalá, Ogun (2), Yemanjá	Old World (cosmopolitan wetland weed): herb	392
	Exu (2)	Unknown (weedy in Old and New Worlds): herb	320
whole plant in syrup for relief of whooping cough		Unknown: herb	234
leaf tea taken internally or oil pressed from seeds rubbed on skin for relief from rheumatism		Southeast Asia (cultivated): tree	315
	Omolu	New World: herb	250
	Exu (5)	New World: herb	170, 180

Family name	Scientific name	Vernacular name(s)	Magical/ spiritual use
	Dalechampia ilheotica Wawra.	urtiga; **esimsim**	magic; work with Exu
	Jatropha curcas L.	pinhão branco	**abô**
	Jatropha gossypifolia L.	pinhão roxo	decoration to remove evil eye, with prayer against evil eye, ar-de-morte
	Pera cf. *glabrata* (Schott.) Baill.	açoita cavalo	initiation; magic
	Phyllanthus amarus Schum. & Thonn.	quebra-pedra	
	Ricinus communis L.	mamoeira; **ewe lara** [castor bean]	banho de descarga; stem piece used to be hung around the necks of wet nurses to stop painful lactation
Fabaceae	*Erythrina poeppigiana* (Walp.) O. F. Cook.	**mulungú**	floor of seita
	Machaerium angustifolium Vog.	sete capote	work with Exu; magic
	Machaerium salzmannii Benth. sp. aff.	arco-de-barris	
	Zornia cf. *gemella* (Willd.) Vog. vel aff.	arrozinha	
Flacourtiaceae	*Casearia* sp.	São Gonçalinho	**abô**; sacudimento in house against evil eye; scatter leaves on floor of barracão
Gentianaceae	*Coutoubea spicata* Aubl.	papai nicolau	camarinha
	Irlbachia purpurascens (Aubl.) Mass	corredeira	black magic
Lamiaceae	*Hyptis fruticosa* Salzm. ex. Benth.	alecrim	incense

Organic medical use and preparation	Associated deities	Origin (ecological status): life form	Voucher no.
leaf tea for kidneys and rheumatism	Exu (4)	New World: climber	281
		New World: treelet	218
	Omolu	New World (cosmopolitan ornamental and weed): shrub	226
	Exu	New World: treelet	257
whole plant tea for kidney ailments		New World (cosmopolitan weed): tiny herb	186
oil from seed as purgative	Yemanjá, Omolu (Abaluaiê)	Old World (cosmopolitan weed and crop plant): shrub	NC
leaf tea for sore throat, tooth ache, somniferant, relaxant	Omolu, Exu	New World (cultivated as shade tree): tree	310
	Exu	New World: tree	271
leaf tea or bath for relief of rheumatism; leaf bath to soak sore feet		New World: scandent vine	353
whole-plant tea as diuretic	Oxum	New World (cosmopolitan weed): herb	256
	Oxóssi, Xangô, Iroko	Unknown: treelet	306
whole-plant tea for stomach problems	Oxalá	New World: herb	253
	Exu (3)	New World: herb	264
leaf tea for rheumatism and ovarian and uterine problems; leaf syrup for flu; leaf bath for general weakness	Oxalá, Oxum, Nanã, Yemanjá	New World: herb	255

Family name	Scientific name	Vernacular name(s)	Magical/ spiritual use
	Hyptis suaveolens (L.) Poit.	neve cheiroso	
	Leonotis nepetifolia (L.) Ait. f.	cordão-de-São Francisco	**abô**
	Mentha sp.	hortelã grosso	banho de descarga
	Mentha pulegium L.	poejo	**abô**, scatter leaves on floor of barracão
	Ocimum campechianum Mill.	alfavaca-de-galinha	
	Ocimum canum Sims	manjericão; catinga-de-criola	leaves scattered on floor of barracão; **abô**; banho de desenvolvimento
	Ocimum gratissimum L.	**quiôiô**; alfavaca-cravo	**abô**; plant placed under bed to take away bad spirits
	Ocimum selloi Benth.	elixer paragorico	
	Plectranthus amboinicus Lour.	tapete-de-Oxalá	**abô**
	Pogostemon cf. *cablin* Benth.	patchulí [patchouli]	root made into perfume
Lauraceae	*Persea americana* C.F. Gaertn.	abacate [avocado]	
Lythraceae	*Cuphea racemosa* (L. f.) Spreng.	barba-de-São Pedro	
Malpighiaceae	*Byrsonima sericea* DC.	muricí	**abô**; sacudimento in house; leaves scattered on floor of barracão
Malvaceae	*Gossypium barbadense* L.	algodão; **ewe oxu** [cotton]	

Organic medical use and preparation	Associated deities	Origin (ecological status): life form	Voucher no.
	Nanã	New World: herb	164
leaf decoction as vaginal douche to stop hemorrhaging	Ogun, Xangô	Old World (cosmopolitan weed): herb	229
leaf syrup taken for cold symptoms	Nanã	Unknown: herb	205
whole-plant tea for stomach problems and flu	Oxum (2), Yemanjá	Old World (cosmopolitan cultivar): herb	233, 318
whole plant in boiling water, vapor breathed in to relieve congestion		New World: herb	198
postpartum leaf bath	Oxóssi, Yemanjá (3)	Old World (cosmopolitan potherb): woody herb	211
whole-plant tea or bath for relief of flu, women's problems, measles, or chicken pox	Xangô (2)	Old World (cosmopolitan cultivar and weed): shrub	219, 230, 247, 313
leaf tea for relief of stomach problems		New World: herb	199, 242
leaf tea for stomach and liver complaints, poor digestion	Oxalá (3)	Old World (cosmopolitan cultivar): herb	152, 304
	Oxum (2), Oxumarê, Nanã, Yemanjá, Iansã	Old World (pantropical cultivar): herb	206
leaf tea as diuretic to treat urinary retention and general swelling		Central America (cosmopolitan food plant): tree	NC
	Iansã	New World: woody herb	280
	Ogun, Oxóssi, Xangô	New World: tree	294, 349
leaf extract or tea taken internally for inflammations and stomach problems	Oxalá (2)	New World (cosmopolitan cultivar): shrub	NC

Family name	Scientific name	Vernacular name(s)	Magical/ spiritual use
	Sida carpinifolia L. f.	vassourinha-de-relógio; **missi missi**	**abô**
	Sida cordifolia L.	malva branca	
	Sida glomerata Cav.	vassourinha-de-relógio; **missi missi**	**abô**
	Sida linifolia Cav.	lingua-de-teiú	
Melastomataceae	*Clidemia hirta* (L.) D. Don.	folha-do-fogo; **ewe ainã**	magic
	Miconia hypoleuca (Benth.) Triana	candeia branca	sacudimento in house
	Miconia sp.	canela-de-velho	**abô**; leaves scattered on floor of *barracão*
	Tibouchina cf. *lhotzkyana* (Presl.) Cogn.	folha-do-fogo-de-Iansã	magic
Mimosaceae	*Mimosa polydactyla* HBK	malissa	magic
	Mimosa pudica L.	malissa [sensitive plant]	magic
Moraceae	*Cecropia pachystachya* Trécul	***embaúba*; abaô**	
	Ficus sp.	**iroko; loco;** gameleira branca	center of ceremonies, sacred tree
Myrtaceae	*Eugenia uniflora* L.	pitanga	scatter leaves on floor of barracão
	Syzygium jambos (L.) Alston	jambo branco [jambo]	
Passifloraceae	*Passiflora alata* Dryand.	***maracujá*** [passion fruit]	leaf in **abô**; banho de descarga

Organic medical use and preparation	Associated deities	Origin (ecological status): life form	Voucher no.
leaf tea for sore throat and flu		New World: herb	223
leaf tea for relief of toothache		unknown (cosmopolitan weed): herb	248
leaf tea for sore throat and flu		New World: herb	251
	Oxóssi	unknown (cosmopolitan weed): herb	258
	Xangô, Exu (2)	New World: herb	159, 363
	Oxalá, Omolu	New World: tree	356
leaf tea for stomach and intestinal ailments	Omolu (3)	New World: shrub or treelet	178, 276
	Iansã (2)	New World: shrub	279
		New World: herb	214
whole-plant decoction is gargled for sore throat and oral inflammation	Exu	New World (pantropical weed): herb	268
leaf bath for general health; leaf decoction for relief of urinary problems	Omolu, Xangô	New World: treelet	355
	Iroko (6)	New World: tree	NC
leaf bath for low blood pressure; leaf tea for flu and general weakness	Katende	Brazil (cosmopolitan cultivar): treelet	189
bark boiled into syrup for cough relief	Oxalá	Southeast Asia (cosmopolitan fruit tree): tree	394
leaf extract to relieve gas and for asthma relief; fruit extract for relief of constipation	Oxumarê	Brazil (cosmopolitan fruit plant): climber	NC

Family name	Scientific name	Vernacular name(s)	Magical/ spiritual use
Phytolaccaceae	*Petiveria alliacea* L.	guiné; *pipi;* ojusaju	**abô**; banho de descarga; used in amulets
Piperaceae	*Peperomia pellucida* HBK	alfavaquinha-de-cobra; **oriri; irirí**	**abô**; use to attract money
	Piper aduncum L.	betis branco	banho de desenvolvimento
	Piper sp.	beti cheiroso	**abô**
	Pothomorphe umbellata (L.) Miq.	*capeba;* agogo iya	banho de descarga
Plantaginaceae	*Plantago major* L.	transagem [English plantain]	**abô**
Plumbaginaceae	*Plumbago* sp.	loquinho	work with Exu; magic
Poaceae	*Andropogon schoenanthus* L.	capim santo	
	Cymbopogon giganteus Chiov.	capim aruana	incense
	Cymbopogon cf. *martinii* (Robx.) W. Watson	capim caboclo	incense (burned with abre-caminho)
	Digitaria insularis L. Mez. ex. Ekman	capim açú	
	Lasiacis ligulata Hitchc. & Chase	taquara	
	Zea mays var. *rugosa* Bonaf.	pipoca [popcorn]	**abô**; offerings
Rubiaceae	*Borreria verticillata* (L.) G. Mey.	caiçara	sacudimento in house
	Borreria sp. (also see *Irlbachia*)	corredeira	black magic

Organic medical use and preparation	Associated deities	Origin (ecological status): life form	Voucher no.
bath for flu, general weakness; brewed with strong coffee and taken internally as an arborfactant; hot leaf massage for rheumatism relief	Ogun, Iansã (2)	New World (cosmopolitan cultivar and weed): herb	171, 295
whole plant in tea for heart palpitations, high blood pressure, and prostate swelling	Oxum, Oxalá	New World (cosmopolitan weed): herb	176
	Xangô	New World: treelet	210, 376
	Oxum, Oxumarê, Nanã, Iansã	unknown: shrub	283
leaf tea for liver ailments; warm leaves applied externally above liver for pain	Omolu (Abaluaiê)	New World: herb	231
leaf tea for stomach problems, sore throat, and women's problems	Yemanjá	Old World (cosmopolitan weed, occasionally cultivated): herb	208
	Iroko, Exu (2)	unknown: herb	165
leaf tea for stomach complaints, flu, and respiratory problems	Oxalá	Old World (cosmopolitan potherb): herb	187
	Caboclo	Old World (cultivated potherb): herb	289
		New World (cultivated potherb): herb	252
lower internodes brewed into tea as aphrodisiac		New World (weed): herb	387
	Oxóssi	New World: herb	314
	Omolu (4)	New World (cosmopolitan crop plant): herb	NC
	Ogun (2), Oxóssi	unknown (cosmopolitan weed): herb	275, 296
	Exu (3)	unknown: herb	269

Family name	Scientific name	Vernacular name(s)	Magical/ spiritual use
Rutaceae	*Citrus aurantium* L.	laranja-da-terra [bitter orange]	**abô**; carried on body as protection from evil eye
	Murraya paniculata (L.) Jack	murta-da-praia	
	Ruta graveolens L.	arruda [rue]	**abô**; carry sprig against evil eye
	Zanthoxylum sp.	tira teima	**abô**
Schizaeaceae	*Lygodium volubile* Sw.	samambaia; **ewe amin**	decoration against evil eye; banho de descarga
Scrophulariaceae	*Scoparia dulcis* L.	vassourinha santa, vassourinha, v.-da-Nossa Senhora	used in praying against evil eye; banho de descarga
Solanaceae	*Brunfelsia uniflora* (Pohl) D. Don.	**macaçá**	**abô**
	Cestrum laevigatum Schlecht.	coerana; **ikeregbe**	sacudimento in house
	Datura metel L.	corneta	
	Nicotiana tabacum L.	fumo [tobacco]	offering to Ossâim in forest for collecting leaves (rolled black tobacco preferred); fresh leaf in banho de descarga
	Solanum americanum Mill.	maria preta; erva Santa Maria	

Organic medical use and preparation	Associated deities	Origin (ecological status): life form	Voucher no.
leaf tea taken as a sedative	Oxum (2)	Southeast Asia (cosmopolitan fruit tree): treelet	NC
	Nanã	Southeast Asia: shrub or tree	217
leaf soaked in sterilized water as eye wash for inflammation; combined with losna, hortelã, poejo, and other (uncollected) herbs for postpartum discomfort, uterine pain; combined with erva cidreira as an abortive; used with prayer to cure cobreiro; combined with *Lippia alba* as an abortive; placed in amulets	Oxóssi, all **orixás**	Mediterranean (cosmopolitan medicinal): woody herb or shrub	201, 202
	Ogun, Oxóssi, Omolu	unknown: shrub	155, 273, 303
leaf bath to relieve rheumatism	Oxóssi, Caboclo	New World: herb	262
leaf extract ingested for fever relief, skin ailments	Oxum	New World (cosmopolitan weed): herb	207, 391
root decoction for relief of menstrual pain	Oxum (3), Oxumarê, Nanã (2), Yemanjá (4), Iansã	New World: herb	203, 317
		New World: shrub	188, 246
rolled, dried leaves smoked for asthma relief	Oxalá (2)	Old World (cosmopolitan cultivar and weed): herb or shrub	227
	Ossâim (2)	New World (cosmopolitan crop): herb	NC
leaf tea for cough; leaf extract or bath for bruises; leaf extract mixed with sulfur powder applied to areas with eczema outbreaks	Iansã	New World: herb	185, 215, 400

Family name	Scientific name	Vernacular name(s)	Magical/ spiritual use
	Solanum sp.	**jurubeba; agog ogum**	
Sterculiaceae	*Cola acuminata* (Beauv.) Schott & Endl.	**obí**; noz-de-cola [kola nut]	**bori**, divination
Verbenaceae	*Aegiphila sellowiana* Cham.	fidalgo	
	Lantana camara L.	cambara branca; cambara	
	Lantana camara L.	cambara amarella	
	Lippia alba (Mill.) N. E. Brown	erva cidreira; melissa	
	Stachytarpheta cayennensis (Rich.) Vahl	gervão	
	Vitex sp.	pau d'arco	
	Vitex sp.	alfazema	**abô**; incense; praying against evil eye
Violaceae	*Hybanthus calceolaria* (L.) Schulze-Menz	purga-do-campo	
Zingiberaceae	*Aframomum melegueta* K. Schum.	pimenta-da-costa; **atarê** [malaguetta pepper]	black and white magic; seeds scattered in home of enemy to bring disorder
	Alpinia zerumbet (Pers.) B. L. Burtt & R. M. Sm.	leopoldina	**abô**; banho de descarga; banho de desenvolvimento
	Hedychium coronarium J. König	jasmin-do-brejo	

Organic medical use and preparation	Associated deities	Origin (ecological status): life form	Voucher no.
fruit eaten for relief of liver and stomach problems, as well as general weakness; leaf tea as cough suppressant		unknown: herb	235
	Ifá, all the **orixás**	Africa (introduced to Bahia, seeds imported from Africa): tree	307
leaf in warm bath for relief of rheumatism		New World: shrub	290
syrup from flowers to relieve chest colds	Oxalá	New World (cosmopolitan weed): shrub	312; 396
	Oxum	New World (cosmopolitan weed): shrub	386
leaf tea as relaxant; combined with arruda as abortive		scandent shrub	182, 228
leaf tea as treatment for women's problems		New World (weed): herb	316
prolonged use of leaf tea as cancer treatment		unknown: treelet	292
leaf tea as diuretic and for stomach and liver problems; leaf macerated in alcohol with camphor and menthol, rubbed on rheumatic area	Oxum	unknown: shrub	232
roots made into tea for acid stomach and ulcers	Oxalá	herb	390
	Exu (3)	Africa (cultivated spice, seeds imported from Nigeria are sold in Bahia): shrub	NC
tea for shortness of breath, nervousness	Oxalá, Oxum, Odudua	Old World (cosmopolitan ornamental): herb or shrub	192
	Oxum	Old World (cosmopolitan wetland introduction): herb	305

2 HOUSE ABÔ FOR THREE CANDOMBLÉ TERREIROS

(1)	(2)	(3)
Brunfelsia uniflora	Alpinia zerumbet	Alpinia zerumbet
Byrsonima sericea	Brunfelsia uniflora	Cestrum laevigatum
Casearia sp.	Byrsonima sericea	Piper aduncum
Cyperus rotundus	Cymbopogon giganteus	Protium warmingianum
Kalanchoe integra	Jatropha gossypifolia	Sansevieria aethiopica
Leonotis nepetifolia	Leonotis nepetifolia	Schinus terebinthifolius
Newbouldia laevis	Mikania glomerata	
Ocimum canum	Protium warmingianum	
Rolandra fruticosa	Rhynchospora nervosa	
Sansevieria aethiopica	Rolandra fruticosa	
Schinus terebinthifolius	Sansevieria aethiopica	
Vernonia cf. cotoneaster	Schinus terebinthifolius	
Vitex sp.	Senna occidentalis	
Wulffia baceata	Vernonia schoenanthus	
	(or V. condensata)	

NOTES

1 Introduction

1 Beckwith 1969, pp. 88–103; Brown and Bick 1987; Cabrera 1971; Curtis 1980; Davis 1988; Hurston 1931; Mathews 1987; Pierre 1977; Pollak-Eltz 1972; Sandoval 1979; Scott 1978; Voeks 1993.
2 Maclean 1971, pp. 26–28.
3 For Islamic influence in fourteenth-century West Africa, see Ibn Batúta 1984 [1829], pp. 317–339. An overview of pre-fifteenth-century religious diffusion is found in Bentley 1993. See also Hallgren 1988 and Dantas 1982 on plurality and orthodoxy in Yoruba and Yoruba-derived religions.
4 Brown and Bick 1987; Creel 1988, pp. 43–44; Santos 1986, pp. 26–32; Leacock and Leacock 1975, pp. 48–49; Sandoval 1979, p. 138.
5 African American healing systems are seldom given much credibility and are usually discussed in a derisive tone. See, for example, Laguerre 1987, pp. 9–13, and Santos Filho 1947, p. 37.

2 The Bahian Landscape

1 Fine-tuning of these dates is critical to understanding the biogeographical relations of the two continents, as this period was precisely when angiosperms were beginning their explosive divergence. See Pitman et al. 1993, pp. 15–34; Szatmari et al. 1987.
2 Angiosperms grew from a tiny fraction of the Aptian flora to upward of 80 percent of the flora by the Albian period, a few million years later. See Crane 1987, pp. 107–144; also Raven and Axelrod 1974, pp. 539–673. For an alternative view of the origin of angiosperms, see Smith 1973, pp. 49–61. For the view that angiosperm evolution occurred after plate breakup, see Thorne 1973, pp. 27–47.
3 Early palm biogeography is outlined in Moore 1973, pp. 63–88. For origin of the Annonaceae family, known principally for the pawpaw (*Asimina triloba*), see Schatz and Thomas 1993, pp. 86–103.
4 Briggs 1983, pp. 85–100.
5 The pineapple, or Bromeliaceae family, with roughly 1500 species, is largely epiphytic and is endemic to the New World. A single species, *Pitcairnia feliciana*, occurs in West Africa. Only one species of cactus, *Rhipsalis baccifera*, is native to Africa, although it is a widespread epiphyte in the New World as well. See Thorne 1973, pp. 27–47.
6 Richards 1973, pp. 21–26.

7 Livingstone 1993, pp. 455–472.
8 Haffer 1969. A good description of the refugial theory is found in Haffer 1982, pp. 6–24.
9 For a largely supportive review of the Pleistocene refugial theory, see Prance (ed.) 1982. Evidence against the theory is presented in Colinvaux 1993, pp. 473–499; Leyden 1985; and Nelson et al. 1990.
10 Good 1974.
11 Thorne 1973, pp. 27–47.
12 Berlin 1992, pp. 52–101.
13 Gentry 1993, pp. 500–547.
14 The penultimate penetration of the sea into the land, dated at 123,000 Y.B.P., deposited a ridge of coral and other marine material 3.0 to 6.0 meters above current mean sea level. See Bernat et al. 1983; Bittencourt, Martin, and Boas, 1979, pp. 232–253.
15 Braun and Ramalho 1980; King 1956.
16 Matsumoto 1983; Vilas Boas et al. 1979, pp. 254–263.
17 These Holocene-dated terraces occur at 2.5 and 4.7 m, respectively, above current mean sea level. Vilas Boas et al. 1979.
18 Voeks 1987, pp. 163–166.
19 Kousky 1980; Ratisbona 1976, pp. 219–293.
20 Milde 1983; Santos 1962; Silva 1984.
21 Kousky 1979; Parameter 1976.
22 Voeks 1987, pp. 14–17.
23 Mori 1989, pp. 427–454; Myers 1988. A distribution map of the region's remaining forest patches is found in Beazley 1990, pp. 130–135.
24 Cunha 1975 [1944], p. 30. Further details on local floristic patterns can be found in Rizzini 1963; Veloso 1946; Vinha, Ramos, and Hori 1976, pp. 11–212; Voeks 1990.
25 Mori, Lisboa, and Kallunki 1982; Mori et al. 1983.
26 This figure for tree species richness is not completely comparable to other richness studies as it included individuals in smaller size classes. Thomas and Carvalho 1993; Mori et al. 1983. For comparison with other tropical forest plots, see Gentry 1988.
27 Peixoto and Gentry 1990.
28 Mittermeier 1986, pp. 298–315; Mori, Boom, and Prance 1981.
29 Brown 1982, pp. 255–308; Jackson 1978; Kubitzki 1977, pp. 231–236; Mori and Prance 1981; Prance 1987, pp. 46–65; Soderstrom and Calderón 1974.
30 Martin et al. 1980.
31 Cardim 1939 [1584], p. 172; Hemming 1978, pp. 77–86.
32 One of the initial descriptions of Brazil can be found in Braga 1968. For determination of several of Caminha's botanical observations, see Andrade-Lima 1984.
33 Hemming 1978, p. 181; Paraíso 1982.
34 Staden 1928, p. 137, 168.
35 Alcorn 1981; Denevan 1992; Gomez-Pompa, Flores, and Sosa 1987; Posey 1984; Unruh 1990.
36 Eder 1970; Johannessen 1966; Sauer 1963.
37 Hartley 1976.
38 Anderson 1983; Brinkmann and Vieira 1971; Voeks and da Vinha 1988.
39 Tomlinson 1979.
40 The "houses of the hill" of the Amazonian Desana are avoided at all times; see Reichel-Dolmatoff 1971, pp. 81–83. For ancient sacred forests, see Hughes 1984, pp. 331–343.

41 The West African **iroko** is *Chlorophora excelsa* (Moraceae); see Parrinder 1961, p. 11. The Jamaican ceiba is *Ceiba pentandra* (Bombacaceae); see Beckwith 1969, p. 89.

42 Dean 1995, p. 46.

43 Marchant 1942.

44 Leite 1938, vol. 1, pp. 17–19 . A review of the writings of Brazil's first Jesuit missionaries can be found in Forsyth 1983.

45 Vasconcellos 1865 [1663], vol. 2.

46 Schwartz 1992, pp. 84–93.

47 Manioc (*Manihot esculenta*) is a tuberous cultivar in the spurge family (Euphorbiaceae). It represented the staple food for natives throughout the New World tropics, and it was readily adopted by the incoming Portuguese and Africans. Its reported cultivation on infertile, spodosolic soils is consistent with the observation that decreasing soil fertility is associated with increasing tuber biomass in this species. See Conceição 1979. For reference to sandy soils and manioc cultivation in Bahia, see Antonil 1976 [1711], p. 101.

48 Schwartz 1992, p. 89.

49 Leão 1982; Oliveira 1985.

50 Atougia 1925 [1751], pp. 185–186; Lapa 1968, p. 92; Masefield 1906, p. 388.

51 Judge José Augusto Beirbosa Coelho to Senator Conselheiro João Lustosa[?] da Cunha Paranagua, 13 Oct. 1881. Colonial Section, Agriculture-Piassava, Public Archive of Bahia, Salvador.

52 Voeks 1988.

53 Curtin 1984, pp. 136–148.

54 Nóbrega 1886, p. 63.

55 Léry 1625, p. 1333.

56 Cardim 1939 [1584], p. 91.

57 Nóbrega 1886, p. 69.

58 Vicente do Salvador 1931 [1627?].

59 Sousa 1971, pp. 169–172.

60 Cardim 1939 [1584], pp. 93–94.

61 Soares 1966 [1594?], vol. 1, p. 17.

62 Knivet 1625 [1591], pp. 1312, 1319.

63 Anchieta 1933, pp. 125–128.

64 Piso 1948 [1648], p. 133.

65 Almeida 1975.

66 Orta 1913 [1563], p. 121.

67 An apothecary's list from sixteenth-century Guatemala indicates that the cost of imported plant medicinals was excessive. See Simpson 1937.

68 Knivet 1625 [1591], p. 1319.

69 DeBry 1625, p. 957.

70 Knivet 1625 [1591], p. 1310.

71 Bosman 1705, pp. 455, 459, 460, 462.

72 Johnson 1973; Sauer 1988, pp. 24–25; Sousa 1971, p. 187.

73 Nóbrega 1886, p. 81. Also see Sousa 1971, p. 206.

74 Bosman 1705, p. 462.

75 Sousa 1971, p. 206; Targioni-Tozzetti 1855, pp. 133–181.

76 Correa 1926.

77 Zohary 1982, p. 90.

78 Ferreyra 1735, p. 294.

79 Debret 1978 [1834–1839], vol. 3, p. 184.

80 Cabrera 1971, p. 539. Cabrera lists rue by its synonym, *Ruta chalepensis*.

81 Grimé 1979, p. 20.

82 Curtin (ed.) 1968, p. 266; Ferreyra 1735, p. 534.

83 Bancroft 1769, p. 53.

84 Morton 1981.

85 Although unnatural concentrations of alien plants and animals may occur along religious migration routes, the advertent transplantation of exotics for religious motives is rare. See, for example, Sopher 1967, pp. 32–33. A species that may owe its Mediterranean distribution to the Jewish Diaspora is discussed by Isaac 1959.

86 For early importation of medicinals from Africa and the Far East, see, for example, Constable 1994, pp. 151–155; also Stannard 1972.

87 Niane 1984, pp. 615–634.

88 Curtin 1984, pp. 53–56; Lovejoy 1980.

89 Bosman 1705, p. 462.

90 Curtin 1984, pp. 251–252.

91 Welwitsch 1965 [1862], p. 320.

92 Verger 1952. Other examples of commerce in kola by Afro-Brazilians can be found in Turner 1942.

93 Bondar 1937.

94 Barros 1983, pp. 48–49; Cabrera 1971, p. 405; Pierson 1967 [1942], p. 239; Abbiw 1990, pp. 72–73; Gill and Akinwumi 1986; Morton 1981, p. 550.

95 Letter dated 15 June 1555, *Cartas Avulsos* 1887, p. 141.

96 Antonil 1976 [1711], p. 101.

97 An excellent summary of weeds in the New World can be found in Crosby 1993, pp. 145–170.

98 Parsons 1970, p. 153.

99 Filgueiras 1990; Parsons 1972; Walsh 1831, vol. 1, p. 264.

100 Sofowora 1982, p. 9; Zohary 1982, p. 193.

101 Descourtilz 1827.

102 Martius 1843, p. 20.

103 Sauer 1988, p. 52. In his review of North American weeds, Baker suggests that the escape of introduced medicinals has been of minor floristic significance. See Baker 1986, pp. 44–57.

104 Ayensu 1978, pp. 136–139; Harris 1965; Oakes and Morris 1958.

105 Pierre Verger, personal communication, 1991. Also see Barros 1983, p. 133.

106 Holm et al. 1977, pp. 385–393.

107 Sauer 1988, p. 148.

108 Sagar and Harris 1964.

109 Stannard 1972, p. 466.

110 Sousa 1971, pp. 169–172.

111 Although plantain is normally a spontaneous weed, I have encountered it among Santeria adherents in Miami and Candomblé followers in Bahia only as a garden cultivar, never spontaneous.

112 Holm et al. 1977, pp. 8–24.

113 I saw one of my neighbors in Ilhéus wearing a folha-da-costa compress to treat headache. Among the locations where this plant is similarly employed are Middle America (Bougerol

1983; Morton 1981, pp. 258–259) and Ghana (Abbiw 1990, p. 160). I also saw <u>folha-da-costa</u> used as a headache compress among the Dusun in northwest Borneo in Dec. 1994. See also Brunei Darussalam, Department of Agriculture 1992, p. 31.

114 Verger 1976–1977.

115 Sauer 1988, pp. 18–21.

116 Vicente do Salvador 1931 [1627?], p. 35. See also Cardim 1939 [1584], p. 64, and Piso 1948 [1648], p. 114.

117 Cardim 1939 [1584], p. 64. He lists the Tupi name **tetigcucú**, but says it is the same as the "<u>machoação das Antilhas</u>," the beach morning-glory.

118 Pierre Verger, personal communication, 1991, reports that among the African Yoruba its name is **gboro ayaba**, and that it is associated with the **orixás** Oro, Logunedé, and Oxum. Also see Barros 1983, p. 132.

119 Richardson 1972.

120 Whitaker 1971, pp. 320–327.

121 Harris 1965.

122 Bondar 1949.

123 Morton 1981, p. xiv.

124 Abbiw 1990; Ayensu 1978, p. 61–63.

125 Burkill 1985, p. 260; Parrinder 1961, p.61.

126 Pierre Verger, personal communication, 1990.

3   Indians and Africans

1 Letter dated 10 Aug. 1549, Nóbrega 1886, p. 63.

2 Hemming 1978, p. 19.

3 Boxer 1962, pp. 10–11; Menezes 1957, pp. 13–16.

4 Vicente do Salvador 1931 [1627?], p. 36.

5 Rodrigues 1934, p. 95.

6 Dean 1995, pp. 28–35.

7 For recent review of disease in colonial Spanish America, see Lovell 1992.

8 Letter dated 10 Aug. 1549, Nóbrega 1886, p. 67.

9 Vasconcellos 1865 [1663], vol. 2, p. 65.

10 Schwartz 1985, p. 53.

11 Hemming 1978, p. 107.

12 Leite 1938, vol. 2, p. 574.

13 The vaccination program introduced in the early 1800s finally brought smallpox under control in Brazil. See Walsh 1831, p. 223. For an interesting environmental interpretation of Brazilian smallpox outbreaks, see Alden and Miller 1988, pp. 35–109.

14 Hemming 1978, p. 145.

15 Dean 1995.

16 Freyre 1986 [1948], pp. 383–385.

17 Santos Filho 1947, p. 145.

18 Hemming 1978, p. 468.

19 Rodrigues 1934, p. 116.

20 Leite 1938, vol. 2, pp. 570–583; Santos Filho 1947, pp. 23–32.

21 Monardes 1580 [1574], pp. 1–2.

22 Orta 1913 [1563], p. 105.

23 Sousa 1971, p. 23.

24 Vicente do Salvador 1931 [1627?], p. 62. Also see Rodrigues 1934, p. 117.

25 Leite 1938, vol. 2, pp. 21–22.

26 For a similar perception among the Spanish clergy in western Amazonia, see Taussig 1987, pp. 142–143.

27 Letter dated 10 Aug. 1549, Nóbrega 1886, p. 67.

28 Hemming 1978, pp. 112–113; Leite 1938, vol. 2, pp. 21–22; letter dated 5 July 1559, Nóbrega 1886, pp. 134–145.

29 Léry 1625, p. 1346.

30 Léry 1625, p. 1336.

31 Hemming 1978, pp. 55–60; Leite 1938, vol. 2, pp. 14–19.

32 Thevet, cited in Purchas 1625, p. 916. The authenticity of André Thevet's observations are questioned in Forsyth 1983, pp. 147–178.

33 Letter probably written in 1549, Nóbrega 1886, p. 71.

34 Staden 1928, p. 150.

35 Léry 1625, pp. 1337–1338.

36 Knivet 1625 [1591], pp. 915–916.

37 Léry 1625, p. 1338.

38 Sousa 1971, p. 206.

39 Knivet 1625 [1591], p. 1311.

40 Letter dated 6 Jan. 1550, Nóbrega 1886, p. 81.

41 Sousa 1971, p. 206.

42 Monardes 1580 [1574], p. 40.

43 Blowing tobacco smoke on the afflicted is still central to Amerindian healing ceremonies. In some cases, emergent African American religious groups in the Americas assimilated this tradition from indigenous groups, such as the Brazilian Umbanda, whereas among other African-derived religious groups, the tradition had clearly made the journey to Africa and back. See Bastide 1978, p. 173; Pollak-Eltz 1972, p. 104.

44 Letter probably written in 1549, Nóbrega 1886, p. 71.

45 Staden 1928, p. 149.

46 The Batuque Afro-Brazilian religion in Belém retains many traditional Amerindian healing methods, including blowing smoke on the patient, shaking a rattle gourd, and brushing the patient with macaw feathers. Leacock and Leacock 1975, pp. 250–283.

47 See for example Ferreyra 1735; Martius 1843; Sousa 1971, pp. 204–216.

48 Cunha 1941, p. 19. For changes in secondary compounds in relation to environmental factors, see review in Trease and Evans 1983, pp. 83–93.

49 Cardim 1939 [1584], p. 65, reported that "*Igpecacóaya*" was used as an antihemorrhage preparation. See Farnsworth and Soejarto 1992, pp. 25–51. For some current folk uses of these species in Brazil, see Cravo 1984.

50 Cardim 1939 [1584], pp. 54–65; Menezes 1957, p. 52; Piso 1948 [1648], pp. 81, 120; Vicente do Salvador 1931 [1627?], pp. 35–36.

51 The low level of bacterial infection and concomitantly small pharmacopoeia among the isolated Waorani of eastern Ecuador is discussed in Davis and Yost 1983. For the general lack of infectious disease among isolated indigenous societies, see Black 1975.

52 Leite 1938, vol. 2, p. 571.

53 Menezes 1957, pp. 28–30, 44.

54 Leite 1938, vol. 2, pp. 21–22.

55 Letter from Padre Anchieta, dated 1554, cited in Forsyth 1983, p. 155.

56 Letter to Padre Mestre Simão dated 1552, Nóbrega 1886.

57 Pierson 1967 [1942], p. 29; Schwartz 1978, pp. 72–78.

58 Thornton 1992, pp. 136–137.

59 Schwartz 1985, pp. 66 and 70.

60 Thornton 1992, p. 135.

61 Watson 1974. For the origins of many of these cultigens, see also Butzer 1988, pp. 91–109.

62 Childs and Killick 1993; Thornton 1992, pp. 45–52.

63 Akinjogbin 1967, pp. 13–14; Smith 1988, pp. 87–90.

64 Boxer (1962, p. 4) notes that these perceptions were not "unanimous" among slave-owners.

65 Antonil 1976 [1711], p. 89.

66 Ferreyra 1735, p. 55.

67 Cuban slave-owners refused to employ physicians and barbers for their slaves, allowing the African folk healers to continue their practice. See Danielson 1979, pp. 35–36. For description of North American slave healers, see Mathews 1987.

68 Debret 1978 [1834–1839], vol. 3, pp. 184, 360.

69 Karasch 1987, p. 264.

70 Walsh 1831, pp. 229–230.

71 Verger notes that the nineteenth-century Yoruba wars produced many captive priests and religious leaders who were ultimately sold into slavery. See Verger 1987, pp. 10–11. Menezes 1957, p. 91, mentions that curers arrived on the slave ships, but offers no examples. Dahomean priests are said to have been among the slaves brought to Haiti, and one of the leaders of the 1791 revolution, Toussaint-L'Ouverture, is reported to have been trained in herbal skills by his father, a petty African chieftain. See James 1963, pp. 21–22; Métraux 1959, p. 30; and Pierre 1977.

72 DeBry 1625, p. 960.

73 Bosman 1705, pp. 383–384, 427.

74 Buckley 1985; Durodola 1986; Maclean 1971.

75 Santos Filho 1947, p. 37.

76 Curtin (ed.) 1968, p. 260.

77 A few such discoveries were registered in North America, where, for example, a slave named Cesar was given his freedom and an annual stipend by the South Carolina legislature in the 1750s for discovering a remedy for rattlesnake bite. Likewise, a Virginia slave was freed and given an annual stipend for discovering a cure for venereal disease. See Laguerre 1987, pp. 27–30.

78 Pierre Verger, personal communication, 1990.

79 According to Spanish chargé d'affaires Mariano Alvarez, Vodun survived in Haiti because the flora had become so similar to that "which in Africa they employ in their incantations." Cited in St. John 1889, p. 234.

80 Cunha 1941, p. 22. See also Laguerre 1987, pp. 87–88.

81 Tyler 1958, vol. 1, pp. 110–116.

82 Bougerol 1983, pp. 73–85.

83 James 1963, pp. 86–87.

84 Creel 1988, pp. 148–165.

85 Jackson 1976, pp. 259–272.
86 Stedman 1963 [1796], p. 212.
87 Pollak-Eltz 1972, pp. 97–98.
88 Métraux 1959, p. 15.
89 Abreu 1922; Mendonça 1925.
90 Governor of Pernambuco report, cited in Ribeiro 1958.
91 Reis 1988a, p. 73.
92 Lapa 1978, p. 137.
93 Antonil 1976 [1711], p. 91.
94 Walsh 1831, p. 226.
95 Rugendas 1941, p. 200.
96 Bastide 1978, pp. 132–133.
97 Freyre 1986 [1948], pp. 334–337.
98 Debret 1978 [1834–1839], vol. 3, p. 184; Karasch 1987, pp. 262–263; Walsh 1831, p. 230.
99 Ben-Yehuda 1989, pp. 229–260.
100 Inquisition courts were held in Brazil, although they were apparently more interested in discovering Jews and punishing sexual offenders than in dealing with folk beliefs in magic. See Abreu 1922, p. 20.
101 Williams 1979, pp. 7–8.
102 Bastide 1971, pp. 131, 160; Freyre 1986 [1948], pp. 331–333.
103 Lewis 1986, pp. 66–69.
104 Bastide 1971, pp. 160–161.
105 Reis (1987, pp. 110–117) makes the important point that although the uprising was carried out by Muslims rather than by followers of the **orixás**, many of the conspirators were in fact Yoruba who had converted to Islam, either before or after arriving in Brazil.

4   *Religion of the Orixás*

1 Carneiro 1967 [1948], pp. 63–65; Verger 1981, pp. 28–29.
2 Reis 1988a.
3 Viana Filho 1946; Ramos 1980 [1939], pp. 11–12; Pierson 1967 [1942], pp. 31–37; Verger 1987, p. 9.
4 Bastide 1971, pp. 106–107.
5 For lexical continuity and change in houses of Candomblé, see Megenney 1991; Póvoas 1989.
6 Carneiro lists seventeen types of Candomblé extant in Bahia in the 1930s. Carneiro 1967 [1948], p. 59; see also Cacciatore 1977, pp. 80–81. On Candomblé de Caboclo, see Wafer 1991 and Omari 1984.
7 The Yoruba cosmology forms the framework of other neo-African religions in Brazil. See, for example, Bastide 1978; Brown and Bick 1987.
8 Parrinder 1961, pp. 13–25; Verger 1966.
9 According to Ruy Póvoas, the high figures found in Yoruba oral texts of **odu** should not be taken literally; rather, they simply suggest large numbers, like saying "I have a thousand and one things to do." Bascom 1980, p. 33.
10 An authoritative description of the Candomblé pantheon is provided by Verger 1981. See also Cacciatore 1977; Magalhães 1973.
11 Smith 1988, p. 30.
12 Thompson 1983, pp. 84–85.
13 Smith 1988, pp. 109–124.

14 Brown 1989, pp. 65–89; Simpson 1980, pp. 29, 65–66.

15 Simpson 1980, pp. 73–79.

16 Lépine 1981, pp. 11–31.

17 In West Africa, Iansã is known as Oyá.

18 Métraux 1959, p. 100; Sandoval 1979; Simpson 1978, p. 75.

19 Thornton 1988, p. 267.

20 Bastide 1978, pp. 261–262; Camara 1988.

21 Freyre 1986, p. 254. Also see Kieckhefer 1989, pp. 69–75.

22 René Ribeiro notes that Pope Gregory I had long ago advised that the idols of heathens should not be destroyed, but rather that Catholic idols should be substituted; that animal sacrifices should not be eliminated, but that they should be redirected toward commemorating the Catholic holy days. The Pope viewed these as more effective methods to bring pagans slowly into the fold. See Ribeiro 1958. Kieckhefer 1989, p. 45, gives an interesting example of how a magical phrase using a medieval German deity was replaced over time by the name of Christ.

23 Bastide 1971, pp. 156–159.

24 Many of the saints assumed military personas among Catholics in Portugal and later in Brazil. This curious set of associations is traced to the unholy alliance of church, state, and military that occurred during the protracted struggle to eject the Muslim Moors. See Freyre 1986 [1948], pp. 228–229.

25 The considerable variation among terreiros in correspondences between saints and **orixás** also resulted from the fact that each **orixá** is known to have various forms, or "qualities." Oxum has sixteen, Exu has twenty-one, and Xangô has twelve. Each quality, although a manifestation of the same entity, has a different age and appearance and even different likes and dislikes. Thus, where a terreiro gives more emphasis to a particular quality of an **orixá**, a different Catholic saint will seem to fit the characteristics of the African deity.

26 Many Candomblé temples—even those that consider themselves to be orthodox—require that potential members be baptized as Catholics before going through any level of initiation.

27 See Santos 1986, pp. 72–75.

28 See Bastide 1978, p. 196; Carneiro 1967 [1948], pp. 128–129.

29 Póvoas 1989, pp. 29–30.

30 Full initiation traditionally requires seven years, although many proletarian candomblés have of necessity adopted an abbreviated schedule.

31 In much of the literature, Candomblé and other New World belief systems are referred to as "cults" rather than religions. I avoid the term "cult" in reference to Candomblé as it maintains most of the characteristics that have come to be associated with a religion and because of the often pejorative connotation associated with the term "cult." See also Brown and Bick 1987, pp. 75–76; Omari 1984.

32 Póvoas 1989, p. 57.

33 Verger 1966, p. 35.

5 *Candomblé Medicine*

1 Because nearly all Candomblé followers are Catholics, priests are generally also consulted regarding questions of sin, absolution, and the great beyond.

2 Peel 1990, p. 357.

3 Maclean 1971.

4 Recited by Pai Ruy Póvoas, 1990.

5 Recited by Pai Ruy Póvoas, 1990.

6 Santos 1986, p. 39.

7 Discussions of the means by which axé is planted and maintained in the terreiro are found in Santos 1986, pp. 39–52, and Póvoas 1989, pp. 39–41.

8 There are exceptions to this two-deity rule, depending on the terreiro and the personality of the adherent.

9 Lépine 1981, pp. 11–31. Morton-Williams describes a similar situation for Yoruba followers; see Morton-Williams 1973, pp. 659–660.

10 See also Trinidade 1981, pp. 3–10.

11 There is variation among different terreiros in the colors associated with each god.

12 For an interesting description of Bahian street vendors, see Herskovits and Herskovits 1943.

13 See, for example, Parrinder 1961, pp. 41–44.

14 Recited by Ruy Póvoas in 1991.

15 See also Thompson 1983, p. 63.

16 Carneiro 1967 [1948], pp. 110–111.

17 Cascudo reports that washing the steps of the church is an ancient European custom, and that the Portuguese rather than the Africans initiated the lavagem do Bonfim. Cascudo 1954, pp. 350–351.

18 Parrinder 1961, p. 61.

19 Barros interprets -gun to mean agitation, a plant that serves to excite the deities. See Barros 1983, pp. 112–113.

20 Observations on the erê trance state were recently described by Wafer 1991, pp. 121–154.

21 Bascom 1980.

22 The price of the consultation usually depends on the stature of the terreiro. I have paid the equivalent of five to twenty-five dollars (U.S.) for a single session. In many terreiros, the charge depends on the financial ability of the client. One small terreiro in Salvador has a sign stating that all consultations are on a cash basis, "no credit extended."

23 Braga 1988, pp. 132–133.

24 Donald Pierson reported that the Dique was considered sacred to Candomblé adherents in the 1930s. Pierson 1967 [1942], p. 279.

25 On the apparent and hidden qualities of magical plants, see, for example, Stannard 1977.

26 Many of the appropriate leaf collection times are listed in Williams 1979, pp. 27–30, 142–153.

27 Although the invocation of magical powers by means of incantations is widespread, the origin of this tradition in Candomblé appears to be Yoruba. See, for example, Buckley 1985, pp. 140–146; Durodola 1986, p. 21; Maclean 1971, pp. 82–83. Verger 1995, p. 35, notes that reciting the names of the plants during their preparation gives the priest a certain power over the axé of the plant.

28 Nery 1977, p. 52.

29 Nina Rodrigues 1935 [1896], p. 92.

30 Buckley describes an indigenous Yoruba germ theory in which the illness is seen as already present in the body, but only activated when the person indulges in excesses. This concept is similar to the Candomblé concept of spiritual equilibrium, although in Brazil each person is seen as possessing the inherent potential for a particular illness due to the person's association with one or more of the deities. Pierson noted in the 1930s that at least one Bahian informant described syphilis as always being present in the body. Buckley 1985, pp. 26–33; Pierson 1967 [1942], p. 253.

31 Csordas 1987.

32 Although samambaia is a generic Portuguese term for "fern," I have only heard the word used to describe the species *Lygodium volubile* in Candomblé terreiros.

33 Freyre 1986 [1948], pp. 113–114.

34 Piso 1948 [1648], pp. 10, 73–74.

35 Martius 1843, p. 20.

36 Sousa 1971, pp. 169–172.

37 Martius 1843.

38 Court 1985. For the application of this principle by peoples of the Caribbean, see Morton 1981, p. xiii.

39 Parrinder 1961, p. 157; Oliver-Bever 1986, pp. 5–6.

40 Cardim 1939 [1584], p. 91; Piso 1948 [1648], p. 135; Sousa 1971, pp. 17–23; Vicente do Salvador 1931 [1627?], p. 35.

41 Piso 1948 [1648], p. 73.

42 Cardim 1939 [1584], p. 65; Vicente do Salvador 1931 [1627?], p. 35; Soares 1966 [1594?], p. 151.

43 Ferreyra 1735, p. 534; see also Sousa 1971, p. 210.

44 Vicente do Salvador 1931 [1627?], p. 35.

45 Cardim 1939 [1584], p. 65.

46 Letter to Padre Simão Rodrigues, 6 Jan. 1550, Nóbrega 1886, p. 81; Knivet 1625 [1591], p. 1311; Sousa 1971, p. 206.

47 Quotation from a 1742 letter, cited in Russell-Wood 1982, p. 119.

48 I observed the use of tobacco in only one terreiro. Although it is never used in the more traditional terreiros, tobacco is employed extensively in other Afro-Brazilian religious rituals and is slowly making inroads into the small, proletarian Candomblé terreiros. See, for example, Leacock and Leacock 1975.

49 Knivet 1625 [1591], p. 1310. A similar medicinal function is noted by Soares 1966 [1594?], p. 151.

50 Cardim 1939 [1584], p. 65; Knivet 1625 [1591], p. 1310.

51 Farnsworth 1988, p. 86.

52 Alfred Métraux noted that Haitian Vodun drew heavily on French magic and sorcery as well. Métraux 1959, p. 269.

53 Verger 1995, p. 72.

54 This species is referred to in Luke 11:42. See Zohary 1982, p. 90.

55 Correa 1926.

56 Cascudo 1967, p. 203.

57 Debret 1978 [1834–1839], vol. 3, p. 184.

58 Cascudo 1967, pp. 210–211.

59 Hildburgh 1908, pp. 213–224; Parrinder 1961, p. 160.

60 Karasch 1987, pp. 262–263.

61 Pierson 1967 [1942], p. 266.

62 Cacciatore 1977, pp. 129–130.

63 Hildburgh 1908, pp. 214–215.

64 Walsh 1831, p. 230.

65 Nina Rodrigues 1935 [1896], p. 185.

66 Patuá is a Yoruba term describing an object that serves to eliminate illness. See Cacciatore 1977, p. 219.

67 Kieckhefer 1989, pp. 20, 75–77.

68 Nina Rodrigues discusses his collection of Black Muslim talismans; Nina Rodrigues 1935 [1896], p. 67. See also Querino 1955, p. 119.

69 Parrinder 1961, p. 161.

70 Bastide 1978, p. 279.

71 Pierson 1967 [1942], pp. 254 and 258; Williams 1979, pp. 80–86.

72 Recited by a filha-de-santo in Ilhéus.

73 Recited by a filha-de-santo in Ilhéus.

74 Williams lists many of the Christian prayers employed to treat this and other local health problems. Williams 1979, pp. 87–112.

75 Kieckhefer 1989, pp. 69–70.

76 Russell-Wood 1982, pp. 57–58. Advertisements of African amas de leite (wet nurses) for hire were commonly listed in Salvador's principal newspaper, the *Diário da Bahia* (Biblioteca de Geografia e História, Salvador, Bahia).

77 For significance of fertility among the Yoruba, see Hallgren 1988, pp. 14–17.

78 Verger 1967.

79 Bastide 1978, p. 66.

80 Often cited as *Bryophyllum pinnatum* Kurz.

81 Burkill 1985, vol. 1, pp. 556–558.

82 Verger 1967, p. 11.

83 Oral text was recorded from Agripina Souza, who had learned them from Mãe Aninha, a famous mãe-de-santo from Axé Opó Afonjá in Salvador. Verger 1989.

84 Meek 1931, pp. 304–305.

85 Querino 1955, p. 90.

86 Costa Lima, 1963.

87 Nina Rodrigues 1935 [1896], p. 90.

88 An advertisement announcing the sale of pimenta-da-costa is listed in *Diário da Bahia*, 24 Feb. 1858, p. 3.

89 Buckley 1985, p. 62.

90 Dalziel 1948.

91 Hurston 1931, p. 324.

92 Querino 1955, p. 82.

93 Freyre 1986 [1948], pp. 334–337; Nina Rodrigues 1935 [1896], pp. 90–95; Querino 1955, pp. 80–82.

6   *Medicinal Plant Classification*

1 Thompson 1975, pp. 52–59, 89–90.

2 Recited by Pai Ruy Póvoas in 1990.

3 Cabrera 1971, p. 100; Verger 1981, pp. 122–124.

4 Recited by Pai Ruy Póvoas in 1989.

5 Voeks 1995.

6 Sandoval 1979; Williams 1979, p. 16.

7 See Ayensu 1978; Morton 1981, p. 465.

8 Thompson 1983, pp. 72–75.

9 For reference to the rounded forms of the leaves of the female deities, see Barros 1983, pp. 125–127.

10 Cravo 1984, p. 300.

11 Thompson 1983, p. 62.

12 Cascudo 1967, p. 214.

13 Dalziel 1948.

14 The features used by the African Yoruba to classify their healing flora are discussed by Verger 1995, pp. 29–35.

15 The correspondences between plants and Candomblé deities are also listed in Barros 1983; Fichte 1976; Williams 1979.

16 Anderson 1987, p. 331; Currier 1966; Laguerre 1987, pp. 70–71.

17 Colson and Armellada 1983; Messer 1987.

18 Morton-Williams 1973, p. 655; Thompson 1983.

19 Bascom 1991.

20 Verger 1967.

21 Buckley 1985.

22 Cardim 1939 [1584]; Sousa 1971.

23 Staden 1928, p. 150; also Léry 1625, pp. 1333–1346.

24 Piso 1948 [1648], p. 10.

25 Freyre 1986.

26 Cascudo 1967.

27 Nina Rodrigues 1935 [1896].

28 Camara 1988.

7 *The Candomblé Flora*

1 Bastide 1978, p. 193.

2 All liturgical species are not necessarily accessible, however, because pasture and plantation development is decreasing collection opportunities in these smaller cities as well. For example, difficulty in locating folha do ar (*Mikania glomerata*), muricí (*Byrsonima sericea*), and other species was reported by informants.

3 Jogo de bicho, or the animal game, is a type of numbers game. In principle illegal, the jogo de bicho is played semi-openly in most parts of Brazil.

4 *Diário da Bahia*, 24 Feb. 1858, p. 3.

5 Pierson 1967 [1942], p. 239.

6 Although one pai-de-santo reported that his **orobô** had successfully fruited, I never personally saw it.

7 Commercial plant preparations are much more commonly used by Umbanda followers.

8 In eighteenth-century Guadeloupe, fear of African magic led the authorities to outlaw the use of plants by slaves for any type of medicine. See Bougerol 1983, p. 85.

9 Santos Filho 1947, p. 37.

10 Cunha 1941.

11 Freyre 1986 [1948], pp. 384–385.

12 Gottlieb and Kaplan 1990; Myers 1984.

13 Coley, Bryant, and Chapin 1985; Waterman and McKey 1989, pp. 513-536.

14 Coley and Aide 1991, pp. 25–49; Levin 1976.

15 Daly 1992, pp. 224–230; Soejarto and Farnsworth 1989.

16 Abe and Higashi 1991; Coley, Bryant, and Chapin 1985; Waterman and McKey 1989.

17 Holm et al. 1977.

18 Voeks 1996. Two other studies demonstrating the relative importance of disturbed as opposed

to primary tropical vegetation for medicinal plant foraging include Kohn 1992 and Toledo et. al. 1992, pp. 99–109.

8   *African Religion in the Americas*

1 See, for example, Entrikin 1988, pp. 165–178; Kershaw 1978, pp. 6–13.
2 Rawley 1981, p. 428.
3 Bastide 1978, p. 36.
4 Figures cited in Russell-Wood 1982, p. 48.
5 Reis 1988b, p. 114.
6 See overview of major African groups brought to Brazil in Ramos 1980 [1939], pp. 11–14.
7 Verger 1987, pp. 9–13.
8 Viana Filho 1946, p. 137.
9 Viana Filho 1946, p. 71.
10 Karasch 1987, p. 12.
11 Schwartz 1985, p. 439.
12 Eltis 1987. Viana Filho (1946) fixes the average number of imports between 1800 and 1830 at 6,231 per year.
13 Métraux 1959, p. 26.
14 Pollak-Eltz 1972, p. 32.
15 Rugendas 1941, p. 168.
16 Walsh 1831, p. 219.
17 Freyre 1986 [1948], p. 4.
18 For a balanced view of plantation slave conditions in Brazil, see Schwartz 1985, pp. 132–149.
19 Rugendas 1941, p. 180.
20 Thornton 1992, p. 170.
21 Schwartz 1992, pp. 45–48.
22 Schwartz 1985, p. 400. See also pp. 355–356 and 394–402.
23 Pereira 1728, p.159.
24 Walsh 1831, p. 84.
25 Boxer 1962, p. 8; Conrad 1983.
26 Schwartz 1985, p. 134.
27 Ramos 1980 [1939], pp. 20–22.
28 Schwartz 1992, pp. 41–42.
29 Ramos 1980 [1939], pp. 20–23.
30 Schwartz 1985, pp. 348–349.
31 Kipple 1989.
32 Schwartz 1992, pp. 41–42; Thornton 1992, pp. 162–182.
33 Rugendas 1941, p. 179. Gilberto Freyre argues, however, that the slaves' diet was no worse and in some ways was more nutritious than that of the masters. Freyre 1986 [1948], pp. 50–62.
34 Alden and Miller 1988, pp. 35–109; Piso 1948 [1648], p. 39.
35 Kipple 1989.
36 Karasch 1987, pp. 25, 183.
37 Menezes 1957, pp. 67–73; Rodrigues 1934, pp. 88–91; Walsh 1831, pp. 227–228.
38 Freyre 1986 [1948], pp. 324–325.

39 Schwartz 1992, p. 41.

40 Karasch 1987, p.8.

41 Reis 1988b, p. 115.

42 The situation seems to have been similar in Suriname, where 300,000 Africans arrived in the Dutch colony between 1668 and 1823, but scarcely 50,000 survived at the end of this period. Price 1976, p. 9.

43 Herskovits and Herskovits 1943, p. 266.

44 Police records of passport requests by liberated slaves are found in the Colonial Section of the Arquivo Público do Estado da Bahia in Salvador—maço (folder) 6403, 6312, and 6308. Newspaper accounts of departures are found in the *Diário da Bahia;* see, for example, 6 Mar. 1858, p. 3.

45 Verger 1952.

46 For life histories of freed slaves returning to Africa, see Turner 1942. Sr. Martiniano was a veritable institution in Salvador, and became part of the required itinerary for all scholars studying African influences in Brazil. See, for example, Landes 1947, pp. 22–34; Carneiro 1967 [1948], p. 150; Pierson 1967 [1942], p. 293.

47 Carneiro 1967 [1948], pp. 63–65; Reis 1988a; Verger 1981, pp. 28–29.

48 Russell-Wood 1982, pp. 128–160; Ribeiro 1958, pp. 470–474.

49 Bastide 1978, p. 49.

50 Public notices of arrests for dancing in the street are listed in the *Diário da Bahia*, 25 Sept. 1857, 5 Oct. 1857, 23 Nov. 1857, and 8 Apr. 1858.

51 Rugendas 1941, p. 197.

52 Letter cited in Conrad 1983, p. 403.

53 Bastide 1978, pp. 91–92; Reis 1988b; Ribeiro 1958, pp. 474–475; Verger 1955.

54 Ribeiro 1958, p. 461; Rugendas 1941, p. 170; Antonil 1976 [1711], pp. 90–92.

55 Pereira 1728, pp. 149, 161.

56 Freyre 1986 [1948], pp. 228–229, 334.

57 Guerra 1976, pp. 169–175.

58 Nina Rodrigues 1935 [1896], pp. 172–183.

59 Bastide 1978, pp. 260–272. For correspondences between Catholic saints and African deities in Cuba, see Cabrera 1971; Sandoval 1979, p. 138.

60 Nina Rodrigues 1935 [1896], p. 182.

61 Camara 1988, p. 304.

62 For the African origin of the cross in Haitian Vodun, see Desmangles 1977.

63 Ribeiro 1958, p. 472.

64 Mathews 1987.

65 The dissolution of African religions in North America did not preclude the survival of African magic and medicine, or African contributions to the regional lexicon. See, for example, Baer 1982; Creel 1988; Hurston 1931; Jackson 1976, pp. 259–272.

66 Reis 1987 provides a thorough analysis of the major slave uprisings of early nineteenth-century Bahia. See also Ramos 1980 [1939], pp. 24–53; Schwartz 1992, pp. 103–136; Thornton 1992, pp. 272–303. For the role of escaped slave societies in cultural retention, see Barrett 1976; Price 1976, pp. 2–3; Thompson 1987, pp. 273–289.

67 Ben-Yehuda 1989, pp. 229–260; Bastide 1978, p. 131.

68 Fear of European magic among the black population is noted by Lewis 1986, pp. 66–69; Schuler 1979, pp. 65–79.

69 Maclean 1971, p. 31.

70 Sopher 1967, pp. 4–10, 88.

71 A notable exception was laterite duricrust, one of African Exu's principal icons, which to my knowledge is lacking in coastal Bahia.

72 Berlin 1992, pp. 52–78.

73 See Gentry 1993; Mori et. al. 1983; Verger 1967; Verger 1976–1977.

74 Barros says that the African *Vernonia senegalensis* was replaced by the Brazilian *Vernonia baihensis*. Barros 1983, p. 53.

75 DeBry noted in the 1600s that Gold Coast inhabitants "killed a Dutchman for cutting these trees." See DeBry 1625, p. 943.

76 Burkill 1985, p. 280.

77 Baker 1965, pp. 185–216.

78 Beckwith 1969, p. 89; Métraux 1959, p. 107; Pollak-Eltz 1972, p. 131.

79 William Bascom, unpublished notes taken in 1938 in Ife, Nigeria. In Bascom Collection, carton 7, Bancroft Library, University of California, Berkeley.

80 Parrinder 1961, p. 54.

81 Jim Wafer offers a contemporary perspective on the many faces of Iroko. Wafer 1991, pp. 166–176. Also see Carneiro 1967 [1948], p. 80.

82 This species was called **ubiragura** by the Tupinambá, a term that apparently did not survive. Sousa 1971, p. 220.

83 Nina Rodrigues 1977 [1932], p. 227.

84 Yorubas arriving in Cuba, also lacking their native **iroko**, substituted the silk cottonwood. See Cabrera 1971, pp. 149–155.

85 Verger (1995) discusses the use of 1086 species by Yoruba **babalaô**. Seventy-nine of these are used by Candomblé pais- or mães-de-santo in Bahia.

86 See, for example, Cardim 1939 [1584], pp. 62–65; Sousa 1971.

87 Martius 1843.

88 Vicente do Salvador 1931 [1627?], p. 37.

89 Verger 1995, pp. 41–46.

90 Ayensu 1978, p. 172; Gill and Akinwumi 1986; Burkill 1985, p. 88.

91 Practitioners of Santeria, another widespread New World religion derived from the Yoruba, encountered similar floristic problems in the preparation of their omiero elixir, which serves similar functions to the Candomblé abô. Andoh suggests that the twenty-one sacred ingredients used in the Cuban omiero are species that also occur in West Africa or are similar floristically—usually congenerics. Andoh 1986, pp. 23–91. (Although omiero is underlined here, it is, of course, a Spanish, not a Portuguese, word.)

GLOSSARY

Probable word origin in parentheses: ʏ=Yoruba, ᴘ=Portuguese, ᴇ=Ewe, ᴋ=Kimbundu, ᴛ=Tupi.

abafé—Medicinal and spiritual plant used among the Yoruba and Candomblé adherents. Example of the process of substituting a New World species (*Bauhinia ovata*) for a closely related African species (*Bauhinia thonningi*). (ʏ)

abô—Bath of sacred leaves employed for medicinal, spiritual, or magical ends. Essential to initiation process. Also known as banho de folhas, banho de desenvolvimento, banho de descarga, and **amaci**. (ʏ)

acarajé—Bean dumpling deep-fried in palm oil. Sold by Bahian women on street corners, this is a consecrated food pertaining principally to Iansã. (ʏ)

agô—Sacred term used by Candomblé adherents to ask permission from the deities. (ʏ)

aiê—In Yoruba cosmology, it is the land of mortals, rocks, plants, and animals. It is the material parallel of **orun**. (ʏ)

akokô—African medicinal and spiritual species, *Newbouldia laevis*, intentionally introduced to Bahia. (ʏ)

amaci—Leaf bath employed in Candomblé de Angola terreiros principally during initiation. See **abô**. (ʏ)

arruda—Medicinal and magical plant of Mediterranean origin (*Ruta graveolens*) intentionally introduced by Spanish and Portuguese to New World. Especially employed against evil eye (mau-olhado). (ᴘ)

atarê—Seeds of West African species (*Aframomum melegueta*) long imported to Brazil for magical ends. Also known as pimenta-da-costa. (ʏ)

axé—The vital force or energy of the Yoruba and related New World belief systems. Acquisition and cultivation of **axé** is the primary means of meeting Candomblé objectives. (ʏ)

babalaô—African priest of Ifá, diviner, and keeper of **odu**, the orally transmitted Yoruba legends. This religious position did not survive in Brazil. (ʏ)

babalorixá—Literally "father of the **orixás**," high priest of Candomblé, especially Candomblé de Angola and Jeje. More commonly known as pai-de-santo. (ʏ)

banho—A foliar bath employed for medical, spiritual, and magical ends. See **abô**. (ᴘ)

barracão—Large, central room in the terreiro used for major ceremonies, including public functions. (ᴘ)

Candomblé—Yoruba-derived religion in Brazil dedicated to adulation of a pantheon of African deities—the **orixás**. Focus of religion is on improving the lives of adherents, especially in areas of health and prosperity.

Candomblé de Angola—Type of Candomblé that incorporates Bantu divinities within the general Yoruba structure. It is particularly common in southern Bahia.

Candomblé de Ketu—The structural model for all Candomblé types. Usually directed by a female priestess, Candomblé de Ketu (or Keto) is especially common in the city of Salvador.

caraibe—Brazilian indigenous healer who focuses on spiritual and magical rather than medical problems. (T)

casa de folhas—Herb stands in major open markets catering both to the spiritual needs of Candomblé followers and the medicinal needs of other clients. (P)

curandeiro—Traditional healer, usually dedicated to the use of herbal remedies. Can be secular or religious. (P)

dandá—Old World aromatic sedge (*Cyperus rotundus*) used for medical and magical ends. Also known as **dandá**-da-costa, referring to its presence along the coast of West Africa. (Y)

dendê—Sacred oil of the African palm (*Elaeis guineensis*), employed principally in conjunction with animal offerings. (K)

ebó—Sacrificial offering to an **orixá**, usually Exu. After serving its ritual purpose, the offering is placed in a sacred place or, more often, along a trail or crossroads. Also known as despacho. (Y)

egun—Spirit of a dead ancestor. (Y)

erê—Child-like manifestation of deity. Appears at the end of possession trance, after the adult form of the **orixá** has returned to the spiritual universe. (Y)

euó—Religious taboo, usually in the form of food, drink, herbal preparation, location, or color of clothing. (Y)

ewe—Leaf. (Y)

Exu—Capricious messenger of the Yoruba gods. Erroneously associated with Satan by nonbelievers. (Y)

faca—Literally 'knife,' the person charged with carrying out ritual sacrifices in Candomblé. (P)

feiticeiro—A witch doctor, someone who commands power over the occult forces. Often associated by the secular public with Candomblé pais- and mães-de-santo (P)

figa—Small figure, usually made of wood, showing a clenched fist with the thumb placed between the forefinger and middle digit. Serves a protective function. (P)

filha-de-santo—Literally 'daughter of the saints.' Female Candomblé adherent who has passed through lengthy initiation process. Most of the support work of the terreiro is carried out by the filhas. Also known as iaô. (P)

filho-de-santo—Literally 'son of the saints.' Male counterpart of filha-de-santo. Also known as iaô. (P)

garrafada—Bottled medicine prepared with water or white wine in combination with various leaves, roots, or seeds. (P)

ialorixá—High priestess of a terreiro, especially in Candomblé de Ketu. More often known as mãe-de-santo. (Y)

Iansã—Hot-tempered female **orixá** associated with wind, storms, and lightning. (Y)

iaô—Candomblé adherent that has passed through lengthy initiation. Also known as filha-de-santo (female) and filho-de-santo (male). (Y)

Ifá—Yoruba god of divination whose messages are revealed by the **babalaô** priest. (Y)

Ijexá—Major Yoruba kingdom from seventeenth through nineteenth centuries, with capital at Ileshá. Name of Candomblé nation in Bahia. (Y)

iroko—West African tree (*Chlorophora excelsa*) believed to be the place of residence of the **orixá** Iroko, god of time. In Brazil, a species of *Ficus* was substituted for the African **iroko**. (Y)

Jeje—Type of Candomblé that cultivates the **vodun** spirits from the ancient kingdom of Dahomey. Structure of the religion follows Yoruba tradition closely. Common in city of Cachoeira. (Y)

jogo-de-búzios—Divination practice from West Africa. Priest interprets messages from the gods by tossing sixteen cowry shells onto a small table. (P)

Ketu—African city near the border of Nigeria and Benin. Source area for many nineteenth-century slave arrivals in Bahia. See also Candomblé de Ketu. (Y)

lavagem do Bonfim—Public ceremony carried out in city of Salvador during January of each year. Candomblé followers march to the Church of Bonfim and there wash the steps, following a Yoruba legend associated with the African deity Oxalá. (P)

limpeza—Ritual cleansing meant to purify a person or place of negative energies. (P)

Logunedé—Offspring of **orixás** Oxum and Oxóssi. Said to be six months male and six months female. (Y)

mãe-de-santo—High priestess of the terreiro, especially in Candomblé de Ketu. Same as **ialo-rixá**. (P)

mãe pequena—Literally the "little mother," second in command of the terreiro. (P)

mão-de-ofá—Person charged with ritually collecting and preparing the sacred leaves. (P)

mariuô—Inner fronds of the African oil palm (*Elaeis guineensis*), usually shredded and hung at the entrance of the terreiro. (Y)

mata higrófila—A tropical moist forest that mantles clayey, oxisolic soils. (P)

mau-olhado—A variety of evil eye, usually cast unintentionally by means of excessive envy. (P)

Nanã—Ancient female **orixá** of rain, soil, and mud. (Y)

obí—Seed of African kola (*Cola acuminata*) essential to initiation ceremonies. Also employed in divination. Although domestic **obí** is available, seeds are still imported from West Africa for Candomblé use. (Y)

odu—Corpus of Yoruba myths of creation, possessed as oral knowledge. In principle, all sacred knowledge, including use and meaning of plants, are contained in the **odu**. These myths are revealed through divination, usually the jogo-de-búzios method. (Y)

Odudua—Wife of Oxalá (or brother, depending on the legend), credited with creating the material world. (Y)

ogã—Male member of the terreiro who normally does not pass through initiation or manifest deities. He often contributes politically and financially to maintenance of the terreiro. (Y)

Ogun—Male **orixá** associated with iron, war, and revolution. A symbol of strength and resistance, his role is to clear impediments to the health and prosperity of adherents. (Y)

olho grande—Literally 'big eye,' a variety of evil eye that usually applies to financial issues. Unlike mau-olhado, olho grande is usually cast intentionally. (P)

Olórun—Distant and unknowable high god of the Yoruba. He is not worshipped directly by devotees and does not manifest during trance. (Y)

Omolu—Greatly feared male **orixá** of illness, especially as manifested in skin ailments. (Y)

orixá—One of the deified heroes of Yoruba legend. As residents of **orun**, the spiritual universe, the **orixás** direct the lives of adherents and manifest during possession trance. Normally, the head of each Candomblé follower "belongs" to two **orixás**—one male and one female. (Y)

orun—The spiritual universe: nine levels of space occupied by the **orixás**, Olórun, and the spirits of the dead. (Y)

Ossâim—Male **orixá** of sacred leaves and medicine. In many terreiros, his image has blended with that of the indigenous Tupi forest spirit Caapora, and he is perceived as female. (Y)

ossé—Weekly offering of consecrated foods made to each **orixá**. (E)

otá—Sacred rock consecrated to each **orixá**. Kept in a ceramic pot in the deity's private shrine. (Y)

Oxalá—Male Yoruba god of love and peace. Syncretized with Jesus Christ. Always dressed in white. (y)

Oxóssi—Male god of the forest and hunt. Frequently keeps the company of Ossâim. (y)

Oxum—The beautiful and vain female **orixá** of rivers and streams. (y)

Oxumarê—Dahomean deity of rainbows and good weather, adopted by the Yoruba. Half-male and half-female, Oxumarê is symbolized by the serpent. (y)

Oyo—Ancient kingdom of the Yoruba. Conquered by the Muslim Fulani and the Dahomean Fon during the nineteenth century, Oyo was the source of many of the high Yoruba priests and priestesses that arrived as slaves in the New World. (y)

padê—Offering made to Exu prior to all Candomblé ceremonies. (y)

pai-de-santo—High priest of Candomblé, especially Candomblé de Angola and Jeje. Also known as **babalorixá**. (p)

pajé—Traditional healer among Brazilian Tupi groups. Specialty was treatment of physical problems. (t)

pano-da-costa—Colorful cloth long imported from West Africa by Afro-Brazilians. Worn by filhas-de-santo during ceremonies. (p)

patuá—Small cloth amulet hung around the neck containing sacred objects, devotional messages, and plant parts. (y)

peji—Small, individual shrines containing the sacred objects and offerings of the **orixás**. (y)

peregun—Shrubby plant of Old World origin (*Dracaena fragrans*) employed in many Candomblé ceremonies. (y)

pimenta-da-costa—Seeds of West African species (*Aframomum melegueta*) long imported to Brazil for magical ends. Also known as **atarê**. (p)

quilombo—Community of escaped African slaves in Brazil. (k)

restinga—In Bahia, the heath-type forest that mantles sandy, spodosolic soils. (p)

roda—During Candomblé ceremonies, the circle of adherents (mostly filhas-de-santo) dancing to the music of each of the **orixás**. (p)

roncó—Tiny room where Candomblé initiates spend much of their time in seclusion. (y)

sacudimento—Cleansing ceremony in which the client has specified leaves passed over his or her body or is lightly whipped by the leaves. (p)

seita—House of Candomblé worship. See terreiro. (p)

terreiro—The Candomblé temple. Usually includes a barracão, separate rooms (**roncó**) for initiates, gardens of sacred plants, and often the living quarters of the priest or priestess. (p)

Tupinambá and Tupinaquim—Major indigenous groups inhabiting the coast of Bahia when the Portuguese arrived in the sixteenth century. (t)

vodun—In Brazil, the pantheon of gods or single deity (Vodun) honored by the Jeje variant of Candomblé. The Vodun belief system traces its origin to the Fon people of ancient Dahomey. (e)

Xangô—Male warrior god associated with thunder and lightning. One of the most geographically successful African gods in the Americas. (y)

Yemanjá—Female **orixá** of the sea and the patron saint of fishermen. Yemanjá's public ceremonies are extremely popular with the secular public. (y)

REFERENCES CITED

Abbiw, D. 1990. *Useful Plants of Ghana.* Kew: Intermediate Technology.

Abe, T., and M. Higashi. 1991. Cellulose-centered perspective on terrestrial community structure. *Oikos* 60: 127–133.

Abreu, J. Capistrano de. 1922. *Um Visitador do Santo Officio á Cidade do Salvador e ao Recôncavo da Bahia de Todos os Santos (1591–1592).* Rio de Janeiro: Rodrigues.

Akinjogbin, I. A. 1967. *Dahomey and Its Neighbors 1708–1818.* Cambridge: Cambridge University Press.

Alcorn, J. 1981. Huastec non-crop resource management: Implications for prehistoric forest management. *Human Ecology* 9 (4): 395–417.

Alden, D., and J. C. Miller. 1988. Unwanted cargoes: The origins and dissemination of smallpox via the slave trade from Africa to Brazil, c. 1560–1830. *In* K. F. Kipple (ed.), *The African Exchange: Toward a Biological History of Black People,* pp. 35–109. Durham: Duke University Press.

Almeida, L. F. 1975. Aclimatação de plantas do oriente no Brasil durante os séculos XVII e XVIII. *Revista Portuguesa de História* 15: 339–395.

Anchieta, J. 1933. Cartas Jesuíticas. In *Cartas, Informacões, Fragmentos Históricas e Sermões do Padre Joseph de Anchieta, S. J. (1554–1594).* Rio de Janeiro: Civilização Brasileira.

Anderson, A. A. 1983. The biology of *Orbignya martiana* (Palmae), a tropical dry forest dominant in Brazil. Ph.D. dissertation, University of Florida, Gainesville.

Anderson, E. N. 1987. Why is humoral medicine so popular? *Social Science and Medicine* 25: 331–337.

Andoh, A. K. 1986. *The Science and Romance of Selected Herbs Used in Medicine and Religious Ceremony.* San Francisco: North Scale Institute.

Andrade-Lima, D. de. 1984. A botânica da carta de Pero Vaz de Caminha. *Rodriguesia* (Rio de Janeiro) 36: 5–8.

Antonil, A. J. 1976 [1711]. *Cultura e Opulência do Brasil.* São Paulo: Companhia Melhoramentos.

Atougia. 1925 [1751]. Letter to the Royal Court. *Anais do Arquivo Público da Bahia* 14: 185–186.

Ayensu, E. S. 1978. *Medicinal Plants of West Africa.* Algonac, MI: Reference Publications.

Baer, H. A. 1982. Towards a systematic typology of Black folk healers. *Phylon* 37: 327–343.

Baker, H. G. 1965. The evolution of the cultivated kapoc tree: A probable West African product. In D. Brokensha (ed.), *Ecology and Economic Development in Tropical Africa,* pp. 185–216. Berkeley: Institute of International Studies.

———. 1986. Patterns of plant invasion in North America. *In* H. A. Mooney and J. A. Drake (eds.), *Ecology of Biological Invasions of North America and Hawaii,* pp. 44–57. New York: Springer-Verlag.

Bancroft, E. 1769. *Essay on the Natural History of Guiana, in South America*. London: T. Becket and P. R. DeHondt.

Barrett, L. 1976. *The Sun and the Drum: African Roots in Jamaican Folk Tradition*. London: Heinemann Books.

Barros, J. F. P. de. 1983. Ewé o Osányin: Sistema de classificação de vegetais nas casas de santo Jêje-Nagô de Salvador, Bahia. Ph.D. dissertation, Universidade de São Paulo, Brasil.

Bascom, W. 1938. Unpublished notes taken in Ife, Nigeria. Bascom Collection, carton 7, Bancroft Library, University of California, Berkeley.

———. 1980. *Sixteen Cowries: Yoruba Divination from Africa to the New World*. Bloomington: Indiana University Press.

———. 1991 [1969]. *Ifa Divination: Communication between Gods and Men in West Africa*. Bloomington: Indiana University Press.

Bastide, R. 1971. *African Civilizations in the New World*. New York: Harper and Row.

———. 1978. *The African Religions of Brazil: Toward a Sociology of the Interpretation of Civilizations*. Translated by Helen Sebba. Baltimore: Johns Hopkins University Press.

Beazley, M. 1990. *The Last Rain Forests*. London: Mitchell Beazley Publishers.

Beckwith, M. W. 1969. *Black Roadways: A Study of Jamaican Folk Life*. New York: Negro University Press.

Bentley, J. H. 1993. *Old World Encounters: Cross-cultural Contacts and Exchanges in Pre-modern Times*. New York: Oxford University Press.

Ben-Yehuda, N. 1989. Witchcraft and the occult as boundary maintenance devices. *In* J. Neusner, E. Frerichs, and P. Flesher (eds.), *Religion, Science, and Magic*, pp. 229–260. New York: Oxford University Press.

Berlin, B. 1992. *Ethnobiological Classification: Principles of Categorization of Plants and Animals in Traditional Societies*. Princeton: Princeton University Press.

Bernat, M., L. Martin, A. Bittencourt, and G. da S. V. Boas. 1983. Datations Io-U du plus haut niveau marin du dernier interglaciaire sur la côte du Brésil. Utilisation du 229Th comme traceur. *Comptes Rendus, Académie des Sciences* (Paris) 296: 197–200.

Bittencourt, A. C. S. P., L. Martin, and G. da S. V. Boas. 1979. Quaternary marine formations of the coast of the State of Bahia (Brazil). *In* K. Suguio, T. Fairchild, L. Martin, and J. M. Flexor (eds.), *Proceedings of the 1978 International Symposium of Coastal Evolution in the Quaternary*, pp. 232–253. São Paulo.

Black, F. L. 1975. Infectious diseases in primitive societies. *Science* 187: 515–518.

Bondar, G. 1937. A cultura da noz de kola no Brasil. *Bahia Rural* 5: 1924–1930.

———. 1949. Plantas exóticas da Bahia. *Bahia Rural* 17: 29–31.

Bosman, W. 1705. A new and accurate description of the Coast of Guinea, divided into the Gold, the Slave, and the Ivory Coasts. *In* John Pinkerton (ed.), *A General Collection of the Best and Most Interesting Voyages and Travels in All Parts of the World*, pp. 337–547. London: Longman, Hurst, Reis, Orme, and Brown: Paternoster-Row.

Bougerol, C. 1983. *La Médicine Populaire á la Guadeloupe*. Paris: Karthala.

Boxer, C. R. 1962. *The Golden Age of Brazil: 1695–1750*. Berkeley and Los Angeles: University of California Press.

Braga, J. 1988. *O Jogo de Búzios: Um Estudo de Adivinhação no Candomblé*. São Paulo: Editora Brasiliense.

Braga, R. 1968. *Pero Vaz de Caminha: Carta a El Rey Dom Manuel*. Rio de Janeiro: Editora Sabiá.

Braun, O. P. G., and R. Ramalho. 1980. Geomorfologia da Bahia. *Revista Brasileira de Geografia* 42: 822–861.

Briggs, J. C. 1983. *Biogeography and Plate Tectonics.* Amsterdam: Elsevier.

Brinkmann, W., and A. N. Vieira. 1971. The effect of burning on germination of seeds at different soil depths of various tropical tree species. *Turrialba* (Costa Rica) 21(1): 77–82.

Brown, D. G., and M. Bick. 1987. Religion, class, and context: Continuities and discontinuities in Brazilian Umbanda. *American Ethnologist* 14: 73–93.

Brown, K. M. 1989. Systematic remembering, systematic forgetting: Ogou in Haiti. *In* S. T. Barnes (ed.), *Africa's Ogun: Old World and New,* pp. 65–89. Bloomington: Indiana University Press.

Brown, K. S. 1982. Paleoecology and regional patterns of evolution in neotropical forest butterflies. *In* G. T. Prance (ed.), *Biological Diversification in the Tropics,* pp. 255–308. New York: Columbia University Press.

Brunei Darussalam. Department of Agriculture. 1992. Ministry of Industry and Primary Resources. *Medicinal Plants of Brunei Darussalam.*

Buckley, A. 1985. *Yoruba Medicine.* Oxford: Clarendon Press.

Burkill, H. M. 1985. *The Useful Plants of West Tropical Africa.* Vol. 1. *Families A–D.* Kew: Royal Botanical Gardens.

Butzer, K. W. 1988. Diffusion, adaptation, and evolution of the Spanish agrosystem. *In* P. J. Hugill and D. B. Dickson (eds.), *The Transfer and Transformation of Ideas and Material Culture,* pp. 91–109. College Station: Texas A & M University Press.

Cabrera, L. 1971. *El Monte.* Miami: np.

Cacciatore, O. G. 1977. *Dicionário de Cultos Afro-Brasileiros.* Rio de Janeiro: Instituto Estadual do Livro.

Camara, E. M. 1988. Afro-American religious syncretism in Brazil and the United States: A Weberian perspective. *Sociological Analysis* 48: 299–318.

Cardim, F. 1939 [1584]. *Tratados da Terra e Gente do Brasil.* São Paulo: np.

Carneiro, E. 1967 [1948]. *Candomblés da Bahia.* Np: Editora Tecnoprint.

Cartas Avulsos (1550–1568). 1887. Materias e Achêgas para a História e Geografia do Brasil, nos. 7–8. Rio de Janeiro: Imprensa Nacional.

Cascudo, L. de C. 1954. *Dicionário do Folclore Brasileiro.* Rio de Janeiro: Ministerio da Educação e Cultura.

———. 1967. *Folclore do Brasil.* Rio de Janeiro: Editora Fundo de Cultura.

Childs, S. T., and D. Killick. 1993. Indigenous African metallurgy: Nature and culture. *Annual Review of Anthropology* 22: 317–337.

Coelho, Judge José Augusto Beirbosa. Letters. Colonial Section, Agriculture-Piassava. Public Archive of Bahia, Salvador.

Coley, P. D., and T. M. Aide. 1991. Comparison of herbivory and plant defenses in temperate and tropical broad-leaved forests. *In* P. W. Price, T. M. Lewinsohn, G. W. Fernandes, and W. W. Benson (eds.), *Plant-animal Interactions: Evolutionary Ecology in Tropical and Temperate Regions,* pp. 25–49. New York: Wiley.

Coley, P. D., J. P. Bryant, and Chapin, F. S. 1985. Resource availability and plant anti-herbivore defense. *Science* 230: 895–899.

Colinvaux, P. 1993. Pleistocene biogeography and diversity in tropical forests of South America. *In* P. Goldblatt (ed.), *Biological Relationships between Africa and South America,* pp. 473–499. New Haven, Conn.: Yale University Press.

Colson, A. B., and C. de Armellada. 1983. An Amerindian derivation for Latin American Creole illnesses and their treatment. *Social Science and Medicine* 17: 1229–1249.

Conceição, A. J. 1979. *A Mandioca.* Cruz da Almas, Brasil: Universidade Federal da Bahia.

Conrad, R. E. 1983. *Children of God's Fire: A Documentary History of Black Slavery in Brazil.* Princeton: Princeton University Press.

Constable, O. R. 1994. *Trade and Traders in Muslim Spain: The Commercial Realignment of the Iberian Peninsula 900–1500.* Cambridge: Cambridge University Press.

Correa, P. M. 1926. *Dicionário das Plantas Uteis do Brasil.*

Costa Lima, V. da. 1963. Notas sobre uma farmacopeia Africana. *Diário de Noticias* (Salvador, Bahia), 3 Nov.

Court, W. E. 1985. The doctrine of signatures or similitudes. *Trends in Pharmacological Sciences* 6: 225–227.

Crane, P. R. 1987. Vegetational consequences of the angiosperm diversification. *In* E. M. Friis, W. G. Chaloner, and P. R. Crane (eds.), *The Origins of Angiosperms and Their Biological Consequences,* pp. 107–144. Cambridge: Cambridge University Press.

Cravo, A. B. 1984. *Frutas e Ervas que Curam.* São Paulo: Hemus Editora.

Creel, M. W. 1988. *A Peculiar People: Slave Religion and Community-Culture among the Gullahs.* New York: New York University Press.

Crosby, A. W. 1993. *Ecological Imperialism: The Biological Expansion of Europe, 900–1900.* Cambridge: Cambridge University Press.

Csordas, T. J. 1987. Health and the holy spirit in African and Afro-American spirit possession. *Social Science and Medicine* 24: 1–11.

Cunha, E. da. 1975 [1944]. *Rebellion in the Backlands (Os Sertões).* Translated by Samuel Putnam. Chicago: University of Chicago Press.

Cunha, N. S. de. 1941. *De Von Martius aos Ervanários da Bahia.* Salvador: Papelaria Dois Mundos.

Currier, R. L. 1966. The hot-cold syndrome and symbolic balance in Mexican and Spanish-American folk medicine. *Ethnology* 5: 251–263.

Curtin, P. D. 1984. *Cross Cultural Trade in World History.* Cambridge: Cambridge University Press.

———. (ed.). 1968. *Africa Remembered: Narratives by West Africans from the Era of the Slave Trade.* Madison: University of Wisconsin Press.

Curtis, J. R. 1980. Miami's little Havana: Yard shrines, cult religion and landscape. *Journal of Cultural Geography* 1: 1–15.

Daly, D. C. 1992. The National Cancer Institute's plant collections program: Update and implications for tropical forests. *In* M. Plotkin and L. Famolare (eds.), *Sustainable Harvest and Marketing of Rain Forest Products,* pp. 224–230. Washington, D.C.: Island Press.

Dalziel, J. M. 1948. *Useful Plants of West Tropical Africa.* London: Crown Agents for the Colonies.

Danielson, R. 1979. *Cuban Medicine.* New Brunswick, N.J.: Transaction Books.

Dantas, B. G. 1982. Repensando a pureza Nagô. *Religião e Sociedade* 8: 15–20.

Davis, E. W. 1988. *Passage of Darkness: The Ethnobiology of the Haitian Zombie.* Chapel Hill: University of North Carolina Press.

Davis, E. W., and J. A. Yost. 1983. The ethnomedicine of the Waorani of Amazonian Ecuador. *Journal of Ethnopharmacology* 9: 273–297.

Dean, W. 1995. *With Broadax and Firebrand: The Destruction of the Brazilian Atlantic Forest.* Berkeley and Los Angeles: University of California Press.

Debret, J. B. 1978 [1834–1839]. *Viagem Pitoresca e Histórica ao Brasil: 1834–1839.* 3 vols. Rio de Janeiro: Fontana.

DeBry. 1625. A description and historical declaration of the Golden Kingdom of Guinea. *In* S. Purchas (ed.), *Purchas His Pilgrimes, Contayning a History of the World, in Sea Voyages & Lande Travells, by Englishmen & Others.* London: William Stansby.

Denevan, W. M. 1992. The pristine myth: The landscape of the Americas in 1492. *Annals of the Association of American Geographers* 82: 369–385.

Descourtilz, M. E. 1827. *Manual de Botánica-Medica é Industrial para el Uso de los Habitantes de la Isla de Cuba y Demas Antillas.* Translated by D. R. Sagra. Havana: D. Pedro N. Palmer é Hijo.

Desmangles, L. G. 1977. African interpretations of the Christian cross in Vodum. *Sociological Analysis* 38: 13–24.

Diário da Bahia, 1857–1858. Biblioteca de Geografia e História, Salvador, Bahia.

Durodola, J. I. 1986. *Scientific Insights into Yoruba Traditional Medicine.* New York: Trado-Medic Books.

Eder, H. M. 1970. Palms and man in coastal Oaxaca, Mexico. *Yearbook—Association of Pacific Coast Geographers* 32: 41–58.

Eltis, D. 1987. The nineteenth-century transatlantic slave trade: An annual time series of imports into the Americas broken down by region. *Hispanic American Historical Review* 67: 110–138.

Entrikin, J. N. 1988. Diffusion research in the context of the naturalism debate in twentieth-century geographic thought. *In* P. J. Hugill and D. B. Dickson (eds.), *The Transfer and Transformation of Ideas and Material Culture,* pp. 165–178. College Station: Texas A & M University Press.

Farnsworth, N. R. 1988. Screening plants for new medicines. *In* E. O. Wilson (ed.), *Biodiversity,* pp. 83–97. Washington, D.C.: National Academy Press.

Farnsworth, N. R, and D. D. Soejarto. 1992. Global importance of medicinal plants. *In* O. Akerele, V. Heywood, and H. Synge (eds.), *The Conservation of Medicinal Plants,* pp. 25–51. Cambridge: Cambridge University Press.

Ferreira, A. B. de H. 1967. *Pequeno Dicionário Brasileiro da Língua Portugûesa.* Rio de Janeiro: Civilização Brasileira.

Ferreyra, L. G. 1735. *Erario Mineral.* Lisboa: Impressor do Senhor Patrarca.

Fichte, H. 1976. *Xango: Die Afroamerikanischen Religionen.* Frankfurt: S. Fischer.

Figueiredo, N. 1983. *Banhos de Cheiro, Ariachés e Amacis.* Cadernos de Folclore, no. 33. Rio de Janeiro: Instituto Nacional do Folclore.

Filgueiras, T. S. 1990. Africanas no Brasil: Gramíneas introduzidas da Africa. *Cadernos de Geociências* 5: 57–63.

Forsyth, D. W. 1983. The beginnings of Brazilian anthropology: Jesuits and Tupinambá cannibalism. *Journal of Anthropological Research* 39:147–178.

Freyre, G. 1986 [1948]. *The Masters and the Slaves: A Study in the Development of Brazilian Civilization.* Berkeley and Los Angeles: University of California Press.

Gentry, A. H. 1988. Tree species richness of upper Amazonian forests. *Proceedings of the National Academy of Sciences* 85: 156–159.

———. 1993. Diversity and floristic composition of lowland tropical forest in Africa and South America. *In* P. Goldblatt (ed.), *Biological Relationships between Africa and South America,* pp. 500–547. New Haven, Conn.: Yale University Press.

Gill, L. S., and C. Akinwumi. 1986. Nigerian folk medicine: Practices and beliefs of the Ondo People. *Journal of Ethnopharmacology* 18: 257–266.

Gomez-Pompa, A., J. S. Flores, and V. Sosa. 1987. The "pet kot": A man-made tropical forest of the Maya. *Interciencia* 12: 10–15.

Good, R. 1974. *The Geography of the Flowering Plants.* London: Longman.

Gottlieb, O. R., and M. A. C. Kaplan. 1990. Amazônia: Tesouro químico a preservar. *Ciência Hoje* 11: 17–20.

Grimé, W. E. 1979. *Ethno-botany of the Black Americans.* Algonac, Mich.: Reference Publications.

Guerra, F. 1976. Medical folklore in Spanish America. *In* W. D. Hand (ed.), *American Folk Medicine*, pp. 169–175. Berkeley and Los Angeles: University of California Press.

Haffer, J. 1969. Speciation in Amazonian forest birds. *Science* 165: 131–137.

———. 1982. General aspects of the refuge theory. *In* G. Prance (ed.), *Biological Diversification in the Tropics*, pp. 6–24. New York: Columbia University Press.

Hallgren, R. 1988. *The Good Things in Life: A Study of the Traditional Religious Culture of the Yoruba People*. Löberöd (Sweden): Plus Ultra.

Harris, D. R. 1965. *Plants, Animals, and Man in the Outer Leeward Islands, West Indies: An Ecological Study of Antigua, Barbuda, and Anguilla*. Publications in Geography, 18. Berkeley: University of California.

Hartley, C. W. S. 1976. *The Oil Palm*. Bristol: Longman.

Hemming, J. 1978. *Red Gold: The Conquest of the Brazilian Indians*. London: Macmillan.

Herskovits, M., and F. Herskovits. 1943. The Negroes of Brazil. *The Yale Review* 32: 266.

Hildburgh, W. L. 1908. Notes on some contemporary Portuguese amulets. *Folklore* 19: 213–224.

Holm, L. G., D. L. Plucknett, J. V. Pancho, and J. P. Herberger. 1977. *The World's Worst Weeds: Distribution and Biology*. Honolulu: University Press of Hawaii.

Hughes, J. D. 1984. Sacred groves: The gods, forest protection, and sustained yield in the ancient world. *In* H. K. Steen (ed.), *History of Sustained Yield Forestry: A Symposium*, pp. 331–343. Portland, Ore.: Forest History Society.

Hurston, Z. 1931. Hoodoo in America. *Journal of American Folklore* 44: 317–417.

Ibn Batúta. 1984 [1829]. *Travels in Asia and Africa, 1325–1354*. Translated by George Routledge. London: Routledge & Kegan Paul, pp. 317–339.

Isaac, E. 1959. Influence of religion on the spread of Citrus. *Science* 129: 179–186.

Jackson, B. 1976. The other kind of doctor: Conjure and magic in Black American folk medicine. *In* W. D. Hand (ed.), *American Folk Medicine*, pp. 259–272. Berkeley and Los Angeles: University of California Press.

Jackson, J. F. 1978. Differentiation in the genera *Enyalius* and *Strobilurus* (Iguanidae): Implications for Pleistocene climatic changes in eastern Brazil. *Arquivas de Zoología* (São Paulo) 30: 1–79.

James, C. L. R. 1963. *The Black Jacobins: Toussaint L'Ouverture and the San Domingo Revolution*. New York: Vintage Books.

Johannessen, C. L. 1966. The domestication process in trees produced by seed: The pejibaye palm in Costa Rica. *Geographical Review* 56 (3): 363–376.

Johnson, D. 1973. The botany, origin, and spread of the cashew (*Anacardium occidentale* L.). *Journal of Plantation Crops* 1: 1–7.

Karasch, M. C. 1987. *Slave Life in Rio de Janeiro 1808–1850*. Princeton: Princeton University Press.

Kershaw, A. C. 1978. Diffusion and migration studies in geography. *In* P. G. Duke (ed.), *Diffusion and Migration: Their Roles in Cultural Development*, pp. 6–13. Calgary: University of Calgary Press.

Kieckhefer, R. 1989. *Magic in the Middle Ages*. Cambridge: Cambridge University Press.

King, L. C. 1956. A geomorfologia do Brasil Oriental. *Revista Brasileira de Geografia* 18: 147–265.

Kipple, K. K. 1989. The nutritional link with slave infant mortality and child mortality in Brazil. *Hispanic American Historical Review* 69: 677–690.

Knivet, A. 1625 [1591]. The admirable adventures and strange fortunes of Master Antonie Knivet. *In* S. Purchas (ed.), *Purchas His Pilgrimes, Contayning a History of the World, in Sea Voyages & Lande-Travells, by Englishmen & Others*. London: William Stansby.

Kohn, E. O. 1992. Some observations on the use of medicinal plants from primary and secondary growth by the Runa of eastern lowland Ecuador. *Journal of Ethnobiology* 12: 141–152.

Kousky, V. E. 1979. Frontal influences on NE Brazil. *Monthly Weather Review* 107: 1140–1153.

———. 1980. Diurnal rainfall variation in NE Brazil. *Monthly Weather Review* 108: 488–498.

Kubitzki, K. 1977. The problem of rare and of frequent species: The monographer's view. *In* G. T. Prance and T. S. Elias (eds.), *Extinction Is Forever,* pp. 231–236. Bronx: New York Botanical Garden.

Laguerre, M. S. 1987. *Afro-Caribbean Folk Medicine.* South Hadley, Mass.: Bergin & Garvey.

Landes, R. 1947. *The City of Women.* New York: Macmillan.

Lapa, J. R. do A. 1968. *A Bahia e a Carreira da India.* São Paulo: Nacional.

———. 1978. *Livro da Visitação do Santo Ofício da Inquisição ao Estado do Grão-Para (1763–1769).* Petrópolis, Brazil: Vozes.

Leacock, S., and R. Leacock. 1975. *Spirits of the Deep: A Study of an Afro-Brazilian Cult.* Garden City, N.Y.: Anchor Books.

Leão, S. 1982. The evolution of agricultural land use patterns in the state of Bahia, Brazil. Ph.D. dissertation, University of Western Ontario.

Leite, S. 1938. *História da Companhia de Jesus no Brasil.* 5 vols. Rio de Janeiro: Civilização Brasileira.

Lépine, C. 1981. Os estereótipos da personalidade no Candomblé Nágô. *In* C. E. M. de Moura (ed.), *Oloorisa: Escritos Sobre a Religião dos Orixás,* pp. 11–31. São Paulo: Editora Agora.

Léry, J. 1625. Extracts out of the historie of John Lerivs, a Frenchman who lived in Brazil (1557 and 1558). *In* S. Purchas (ed.), *Purchas His Pilgrimes, Contayning a History of the World, in Sea Voyages & Lande-Travells, by Englishmen & Others.* London: William Stansby.

Levin, D. A. 1976. Alkaloid-bearing plants: An ecogeographic perspective. *American Naturalist* 110: 261–284.

Lewis, I. M. 1986. *Religion in Context: Cults and Charisma.* Cambridge: Cambridge University Press.

Leyden, B. 1985. Late Quaternary aridity and Holocene moisture fluctuations in the Lake Valencia basin. *Ecology* 66: 1279–1295.

Livingstone, D. A. 1993. Evolution of African climate. *In* P. Goldblatt (ed.), *Biological Relationships between Africa and South America,* pp. 455–472. New Haven, Conn.: Yale University Press.

Lovejoy, P. 1980. *Caravans of Kola: The Hausa Kola Trade, 1700–1900.* Zaria, Nigeria: Ahmadu Bello University Press.

Lovell, W. G. 1992. "Heavy shadows and black night": Disease and depopulation in colonial Spanish America. *Annals of the Association of American Geographers* 82: 426–443.

Maclean, U. 1971. *Magicial Medicine: A Nigerian Case Study.* London: Penguin Press.

Magalhães, E. G. 1973. *Orixás da Bahia.* Salvador, Bahia: Prefeitura Municipal do Salvador.

Marchant, A. 1942. *From Barter to Slavery: The Economic Relations of Portuguese and Indians in the Settlement of Brazil, 1500–1580.* Baltimore: Johns Hopkins University Press.

Martin, L., A. C. S. P. Bittencourt, G. da S. V. Boas, and J. M. Flexor. 1980. *Mapa Geológico do Quaternário Costeiro do Estado da Bahia: Texto Explicativo.* Salvador, Bahia: Secretaria da Minas e Energia/ Coordenação da Produção Mineral.

Martius, K. F. P. von. 1843. *Systema Materiae Medicae Vegetabilis Brasiliensis.* Np.

Masefield, J. 1906. *Dampier's voyages, by Captain William Dampier.* New York: E.P. Dutton.

Mathews, H.F. 1987. Rootwork: Description of an ethnomedical system in the American South. *Southern Medical Journal* 80: 885–891.

Matsumoto, E. 1983. A note on the tabuleiros in the coastal region of the Brazilian NE—A geomorphological approach. *Latin American Studies* (Occasional Paper, Univ. of Tsukuba, Japan) 6: 1–13.

Meek, J. C. K. 1931. *Sudanese Kingdoms: An Ethnographic Study of the Jukan-Speaking Peoples of Nigeria.* London: Kegan Paul, Trench, Trubneer.

Megenney, W. W. 1978. *A Bahian Landscape: An Ethnolinguistic Study of African Influences on Bahian Portuguese.* Chapel Hill: University of North Carolina Press.

———. 1991. African influences in the language of Afro-Brazilian religions. *Hispania* 74: 627–636.

Mendonça, H. F. de. 1925. *Primeira Visitição do Santo Offício ao Partes do Brasil.* São Paulo: np.

Mendonça, R. 1935. *A Influência Africana no Portugûes do Brasil.* São Paulo: Editora Nacional.

Menezes, F. de S. 1957. *Medicina Indígena (na Bahia).* Salvador: Livraria Progresso Editora.

Messer, E. 1987. The hot and cold in Mesoamerican indigenous and Hispanicized thought. *Social Science and Medicine* 25: 339–346.

Métraux, A. 1959. *Voodoo in Haiti.* Translated by H. Charteris. London: Andre Deutsch.

Milde, L. C. E. 1983. Estudo de precipitação diária: Regimes pluviometricos e modelos de distribuição para a região cacaueira do Sudeste da Bahia. Master's thesis, Federal University of Paraíba.

Mittermeier, R. A. 1986. Eastern Brazil. *World Wildlife Fund Conservation Yearbook* 1985/86: 298–315.

Monardes, N. 1580 [1574]. *Joyful Newes out of the New Found World, Wherein Are Declared the Rare and Singular Vertues of Divers and Sundrie Herbs, Trees, Dyes, Plants, and Stones.* Translated by John Frampton. London: William Norton.

Moore, H. E. 1973. Palms in tropical forest ecosystems of Africa and South America. *In* B. J. Meggers, E. S. Ayensu, and W. D. Duckworth (eds.), *Tropical Forest Ecosystems in Africa and South America: A Review,* pp. 63–88. Washington, D.C.: Smithsomian Institution.

Mori, S. 1989. Eastern extra-Amazonian Brazil. *In* D. G. Campbell and H. D. Hammond (eds.), *Floristic Inventory of Tropical Countries: The Current Status of Plant Systematics, Collections, and Vegetation,* pp. 427–454. Bronx: New York Botanical Garden.

Mori, S., B. M. Boom, A. M. Carvalho, and T. S. Santos. 1983. Southern Bahian moist forests. *The Botanical Review* 49: 155–232.

Mori, S., B. M. Boom, and G. T. Prance. 1981. Distribution patterns and conservation of Eastern Brazilian coastal forest tree species. *Brittonia* 33: 234–245.

Mori, S., G. Lisboa, and J. A. Kallunki. 1982. Fenologia de uma mata higrófila Sul-Bahiana. *Revista Theobroma* 12: 217–230.

Mori, S., and G. T. Prance. 1981. The Sapucaia group of *Lecythis* (Lecythidaceae). *Brittonia* 33: 70–80.

Morton, J. 1981. *Atlas of the Medicinal Plants of Middle America.* Springfield, Ill.: Charles C. Thomas.

Morton-Williams, P. 1973. An outline of the cosmology and cult organization of the Oyo Yoruba. *In* E. Skinner (ed.), *Peoples and Cultures of Africa,* pp. 654–677. New York: Natural History Press.

Myers, N. 1984. *The Primary Source: Tropical Forests and Our Future.* New York: W.W. Norton.

———. 1988. Threatened biotas: "Hot spots" in tropical forests. *The Environmentalist* 8: 187–208.

Nelson, B. W., C. A. C. Ferreira, M. F. da Silva, and M. L. Kawasaki. 1990. Endemism centres: Refugia and botanical collection density in Brazilian Amazonia. *Nature* 345: 714–716.

Nery, M. E. V. 1977. Psiquiatria folclórica do Candomblé. Master's thesis, Universidade Federal da Bahia.

Niane, D. T. 1984. Relationships and exchanges among the different regions. *In* D. T. Niane (ed.), *Africa from the Twelfth to the Sixteenth Century,* vol. 4 of *General History of Africa,* pp. 615–634. UNESCO. Berkeley and Los Angeles: University of California Press.

Nina Rodrigues, R. 1935 [1896]. *O Animismo Fetichista dos Negros Baianos.* Rio de Janeiro: Civilização Brasileira.

————. 1977 [1932]. *Os Africanos no Brasil*. São Paulo: Editora Nacional.

Nóbrega, M. da. 1886. *Cartas do Brasil do Padre Manuel da Nóbrega (1549–1560)*. Materias e Achêgas para a História e Geografia do Brasil, no. 1. Rio de Janeiro: Imprensa Nacional.

Oakes, A. J., and M. P. Morris. 1958. The West Indian weedwoman of the U.S. Virgin Islands. *Bulletin of the History of Medicine* 32: 164–170.

Oliveira, W. F. 1985. *A Industrial Cidade de Valença (Um Surto de Industrialização na Bahia do Século XIX)*. Salvador: Centro de Estudos Baianos.

Oliver-Bever, B. 1986. *Medicinal Plants in Tropical West Africa*. Cambridge: Cambridge University Press.

Omari, M. S. 1984. *From the Inside to the Outside: The Art and Ritual of Bahian Candomble*. Museum of Cultural History Monograph no. 24, UCLA.

Orta, G. de. 1913 [1563]. *Colloquies on the Simples and Drugs of India*. Translated by Sir Clements Markham. London: Henry Sotheran.

Paraíso, M. H. B. 1982. Caminhos de ir e vir e caminho sem volta: Indios, estradas e rios no sul da Bahia. Master's thesis, Universidade Federal da Bahia.

Parameter, F. C. 1976. A Southern Hemisphere cold front passage at the Equator. *Bulletin of the American Meteorological Society* 57(12): 1435–1440.

Parrinder, G. 1961. *West African Religion: A Study of the Beliefs and Practices of Akan, Ewe, Yoruba, Ibo, and Kindred Peoples*. London: Epworth Press.

Parsons, J. J. 1970. The "Africanization" of the New World tropical grasslands. *Tübinger Geographische Studien* 34: 141–153.

————. 1972. Spread of American pasture grasses to the American tropics. *Journal of Range Management* 25: 12–17.

Peel, J. D. Y. 1990. The pastor and the babalawo: The interaction of religions in nineteenth-century Yorubaland. *Africa* 60: 338–369.

Peixoto, A. L., and A. Gentry. 1990. Diversidade e composição florística da mata de tabuleiro na Reserva Florestal de Linhares (Espirito Santo, Brazil). *Revista Brasileira de Botanica* 13: 19–25.

Pereira, N. M. 1728. *Peregrino da America*. Lisboa: Impressor do Santo Officio.

Pierre, R. 1977. Caribbean religion: The Voodoo case. *Sociological Analysis* 38: 25–36.

Pierson, D. 1967 [1942]. *Negroes in Brazil: A Study of Race Contact in Bahia*. Carbondale: Southern Illinois University Press.

Piso, G. 1948 [1648]. *História Natural do Brasil Ilustrada*. Translated by A. Taunay. São Paulo: Companhia Editora Nacional.

Pitman, W. C., S. Cande, J. LaBrecque, and J. Pindell. 1993. Fragmentation of Gondwana: The separation of Africa from South America. *In* P. Goldblatt (ed.), *Biological Relationships between Africa and South America*, pp. 15–34. New Haven, Conn.: Yale University Press.

Pollak-Eltz, A. 1972. *Vestigios Africanos en la Cultura del Pueblo Venezolano*. Caracas: Universidad Católica "Andres Bello."

Posey, D. A. 1984. A preliminary report on diversified management of tropical forests by the Kayapó Indians of the Brazilian Amazon. *Advances in Economic Botany* 1: 112–126.

Póvoas, R. do C. 1989. *A Linguagem do Candomblé: Níveis Sociolingüísticos de Integração Afro-Portuguesa*. Rio de Janeiro: José Olympio Editora.

Prance, G. 1987. Biogeography of neotropical plants. *In* T. C. Whitmore and G. T. Prance (eds.), *Biogeography and Quaternary History in Tropical America*, pp. 46–65. Oxford: Clarendon Press.

————, ed. 1982. *Biological Diversification in the Tropics*. New York: Columbia University Press.

Price, R. 1976. *The Guiana Maroons: A Historical and Bibliographic Introduction.* Baltimore: Johns Hopkins University Press.

Purchas, S., ed. 1625. *Purchas His Pilgrimes, Contayning a History of the World, in Sea Voyages & Lande-Travells, by Englishmen & Others.* London: William Stansby.

Querino, M. 1955. *A Raca Africana e os Seus Costumes.* Salvador: Progresso.

Ramos, A. 1980 [1939]. *The Negro in Brazil.* Philadephia: Porcupine Press.

Ratisbona, C. R. 1976. The climate of Brazil. *In* W. Schwerdtfeger and H. E. Landsberg (eds.), *Climates of Central and South America,* vol. 12 of *World Survey of Climatology,* 219–293.

Raven, P., and D. Axelrod. 1974. Angiosperm biogeography and past continental movements. *Annals of the Missouri Botanical Garden* 61: 539–673.

Rawley, J. A. 1981. *The Transatlantic Slave Trade: A History.* New York: W. W. Norton.

Reichel-Dolmatoff, G. 1971. *Amazonian Cosmos: The Sexual and Religious Symbolism of the Tukano Indians.* Chicago: University of Chicago Press.

Reis, J. J. 1987. *Rebelião Escrava no Brasil: A História do Levante dos Malês (1835).* São Paulo: Editora Brasiliense.

———. 1988a. Magia Jeje na Bahia: A invasão do Calundu do pasto de Cachoeira, 1785. *Revista Brasileira de História* 8: 57–81.

———. 1988b. Slave resistance in Brazil: Bahia 1807–1835. *Luso-Brazilian Review* 25: 111–144.

Ribeiro, R. 1958. Relations of the Negro with Christianity in Portuguese America. *The Americas* 14: 454–484.

Richards, P. W. 1973. Africa, the "odd man out." *In* B. J. Meggers, E. S. Ayensu, and W. D. Duckworth (eds.), *Tropical Forest Ecosystems in Africa and South America: A Review,* pp. 21–26. Washington, D.C.: Smithsonian Institution.

Richardson, J. B. 1972. The pre-Columbian distribution of the bottle gourd (*Lagenaria siceraria*): A re-evaluation. *Economic Botany* 26: 265–273.

Rizzini, C.T. 1963. Nota prévia sobre a divisão fitogeográfica do Brasil. *Revista Brasileira de Geografia* (Rio de Janeiro) 25 (1): 33–64.

Rodrigues, L. 1934. *Anchieta e a Medicina.* Bello Horizonte: Edicões Apollo.

Rugendas, J. M. 1941. *Viagem Pitoresca Atraves do Brasil.* 3rd ed. São Paulo: np.

Russell-Wood, A. J. R. 1982. *The Black Man in Slavery and Freedom in Colonial Brazil.* New York: St. Martin's Press.

Sagar, G. R., and J. L. Harris. 1964. Biological flora of the British Isles, *Plantago major* L., *P. media* L., and *P. lanceolata* L. *Journal of Ecology* 52: 189–221.

Sampaio, T. 1955. *O Tupi na Geografia Nacional.* Câmara Municipal de Salvador: np.

Sandoval, M. C. 1979. Santeria as a mental health care system: An historical overview. *Social Science and Medicine* 13B: 137–151.

Santos, J. E. dos. 1986. *Os Nago e a Morte: Pade, Asese e o Culto Egun na Bahia.* Petrópolis, Brazil: Vozes.

Santos, R. F. A. 1962. *Chuvas na Bahia: Máximas e Mínimas.* Salvador, Bahia: Ministério da Viacão e Obras Públicas.

Santos Filho, L. 1947. *História da Medicina no Brasil (Seculo XVI ao Seculo XIX).* São Paulo: Editora Brasiliense.

Sauer, C. O. 1963. Man in the biology of tropical America. *In* J. Leighly (ed.), *Land and Life: A Selection from the Writings of Carl Ortwin Sauer,* pp. 182–193. Berkeley and Los Angeles: University of California Press.

Sauer, J. D. 1988. *Plant Migration: The Dynamics of Geographic Patterning in Seed Plant Species.* Berkeley and Los Angeles: University of California Press.

Schatz, G. E., and A. Thomas. 1993. Annonaceae: A primitive dicot family with an ancient center in Africa-South America. *In* P. Goldblatt (ed.), *Biological Relationships between Africa and South America,* pp. 86–103. New Haven, Conn.: Yale University Press.

Schuler, M. 1979. Myalism and the African religious tradition in Jamaica. *In* M. E. Crahan and F. W. Knight (eds.), *Africa and the Caribbean: The Legacies of a Link,* pp. 65–79. Baltimore: Johns Hopkins University Press.

Schwartz, S. B. 1978. Indian labor and new world plantations: European demands and Indian responses in Northeastern Brazil. *The American Historical Review* 83: 43–79.

———. 1985. *Sugar Plantations in the Formation of Brazilian Society: Bahia, 1550–1835.* Cambridge: Cambridge University Press.

———. 1992. *Slaves, Peasants, and Rebels: Reconsidering Brazilian Slavery.* Urbana: University of Illinois Press.

Scott, C. S. 1978. Health and healing practices among five ethnic groups in Miami, Florida. *In* E. E. Bauwens (ed.), *The Anthropology of Health,* pp. 61–70. St. Louis: C. V. Mosby.

Silva, B. C. N. 1984. *Comportamento das Chuvas no Estudo da Bahia: Uma Contribuição Cartográfica.* Salvador: Departamento Geografia, Universidade Federal da Bahia.

Silva, L. A., G. Lisboa, and T. Santos. 1982. *Nomenclatura Vulgar e Científica de Plantas Encontradas na Região Cacaueira da Bahia.* Centro de Pesquisas do Cacau, Boletim Técnico No. 35. Itabuna, Bahia: Centro de Pesquisas do Cacau.

Simpson, G. E. 1978. *Black Religions in the New World.* New York: Columbia University Press.

———. 1980. *Yoruba Religion and Medicine in Ibadan.* Ibadan, Nigeria: Ibadan University Press.

Simpson, G. G. 1980. *Splendid Isolation: The Curious History of South American Mammals.* New Haven, Conn: Yale University Press.

Simpson, L. B. 1937. *The Medicine of the Conquistadores: An American Pharmacopeia of 1536.* Tempelhof, Belgium: St. Catherine Press.

Smith, A. C. 1973. Angiosperm evolution and the relationship of the floras of Africa and America. *In* B. J. Meggers, E. S. Ayensu, and W. D. Duckworth (eds.), *Tropical Forest Ecosystems in Africa and South America: A Review,* pp. 49–61. Washington, D.C.: Smithsonian Institution.

Smith, R. 1988. *Kingdoms of the Yoruba.* London: James Curry.

Soares, F. 1966 [1594?]. *Coisas Notaveis do Brasil.* Vol. 1. Edited by A. G. Cunha. Rio de Janeiro: Instituto Nacional do Livro.

Soderstrom, T. R., and C. E. Calderón. 1974. Primitive forest grasses and evolution of the Bambusoideae. *Biotropica* 6: 141–153.

Soejarto, D. D., and N. R. Farnsworth. 1989. Tropical rain forests: Potential source of new drugs? *Perspectives in Biology and Medicine* 32: 244–256.

Sofowora, A. 1982. *Medicinal Plants and Traditional Medicine in Africa.* Chichester: John Wiley and Sons.

Sopher, D. E. 1967. *Geography of Religions.* Englewood, N.J.: Prentice-Hall.

Sousa, G. S. de. 1971. *Tratado Descritivo do Brasil em 1587.* 4th ed. São Paulo: Companhia Editora Nacional.

St. John, S., Sir. 1889. *Hayti or the Black Republic.* New York: Scribner & Welford.

Staden, H. 1928. *Hans Staden: The True History of his Captivity, 1557.* Translated by Malcolm Letts. London: George Routledge & Sons.

Stannard, J. 1972. Greco-Roman materia medica in medieval Germany. *Bulletin of the History of Medicine* 46: 455–468.

———. 1977. Magiferous plants and magic in medieval medical botany. *Maryland Historian* 8: 33–46.

Stedman, J. 1963 [1796]. *Expedition to Surinam*. London: Richard Clay.

Szatmari, P., J. Françolin, O. Zanotto, and S. Wolff. 1987. Evolução tectônica da margem equatorial Brasileira. *Revista Brasileira de Geociências* 17: 180–188.

Targioni-Tozzetti, A. 1855. Historical notes on the introduction of various plants into the agriculture and horticulture of Tuscany. *Journal of the Horticultural Society of London* 9: 133–181.

Taussig, M. 1987. *Shamanism, Colonialism, and the Wild Man: A Study in Terror and Healing*. Chicago: University of Chicago Press.

Thomas, W. W., and A. M. de Carvalho. 1993. Estudo fitossociologico de Serra Grande, Uruçuca, Bahia, Brasil. *In Resumos do XLIV Congresso Nacional de Botânica* (24–30 January 1993), vol. 1, p. 224.

Thompson, R. F. 1975. Icons of the mind: Yoruba herbalism arts in Atlantic perspective. *African Arts* 8: 52–59, 89–90.

———. 1983. *Flash of the Spirit: African and Afro-American Art and Philosophy*. New York: Random House.

Thompson, V. B. 1987. *Making of the African Diaspora in the Americas 1441–1900*. New York: Longman.

Thorne, R. F. 1973. Floristic relationships between tropical Africa and tropical America. *In* B. J. Meggers, E. S. Ayensu, and W. D. Duckworth (eds.), *Tropical Forest Ecosystems in Africa and South America: A Review*, pp. 27–47. Washington, D.C.: Smithsonian Institution.

Thornton, J. 1988. On the trail of voodoo: African Christianity in Africa and the Americas. *The Americas* 55: 261–278.

———. 1992. *Africa and Africans in the Making of the Atlantic World, 1400–1680*. Cambridge: Cambridge University Press.

Toledo, V. M., et al. 1992. Products from the tropical rain forests of Mexico: An ethnoecological approach. *In* M. Plotkin and L. Famolar (eds.), *Sustainable Harvest and Marketing of Rain Forest Products*, 99–109. Washington, D.C.: Island Press.

Tomlinson, P. B. 1979. Systematics and ecology of the Palmae. *Annual Review of Ecology and Systematics* 10: 85–107.

Trease, G. E., and W. C. Evans. 1983. *Pharmacognosy*. London: Bailliere Tindall.

Trinidade, L. M. S. 1981. Exu: Poder e magia. *In* C. E. M. Moura (ed.), *Oloorisa: Escritos sobre a Religão dos Orixás*, pp. 3–10. São Paulo: Editora Agora.

Turner, L. D. 1942. Some contacts of Brazilian ex-slaves with Nigeria. *Journal of Negro History* 27: 55–67.

Tyler, E. 1958. *Primitive Culture*. 2 vols. New York: Harper.

Unruh, J. D. 1990. Iterative increase of economic tree species in managed swidden-fallows of the Amazon. *Agroforestry Systems* 11: 175–197.

Vasconcellos, S. de. 1865 [1663]. *Chrônica da Companhia de Jesus do Estado do Brasil*. 2 vols. Rio de Janeiro: J. L. da Silva.

Veloso, H. P. 1946. A vegetação no município de Ilhéus, Estado da Bahia. *Memórias do Instituto Oswaldo Cruz* 44(1): 13–103.

Verger, P. 1952. Cartas de um Brasileiro estabelicido no século XIX na Costa dos Escravos. *Anhembi* 6: 212–253.

———. 1955. Yoruba influences in Brazil. *Odu* 1: 3–11.

———. 1966. The Yoruba high God. *University of Ife Journal of African Studies* 2: 19–40.

———. 1967. *Awon Ewe Osanyin: Yoruba Medicinal Leaves.* Ife, Nigeria: University of Ife.

———. 1976–1977. Use of plants in traditional medicine and its linguistic approach. Seminar Series No. 1, part 1, pp. 242–297. Ife, Nigeria: University of Ife.

———. 1981. *Orixás.* São Paulo: Corrupio.

———. 1987. *Fluxo e Refluxo: Do Tráfico de Escravos Entre o Golfo do Benin e a Bahia de Todos os Santos.* Translated by Tasso Gadzonis. São Paulo: Corrupio.

———. 1989. *Dilogun: Brazilian Tales of Yoruba Divination Discovered in Bahia.* Translated by Willfried R. Feuser and Jose Marianno Carneiro de Cunha. Ibadan, Nigeria: Shaneson C. I.

———. 1995. *Ewé: O Uso das Plantas na Sociedade Iorubá.* São Paulo: Editora Schwarcz.

Viana Filho, L. 1946. *O Negro na Bahia.* Rio de Janeiro: Jose Olympio Editora.

Vicente do Salvador. 1931 [1627?]. *História do Brasil: 1500–1627.* 3rd ed. São Paulo: Companhia Melhoramentos.

Vilas Boas, G., L. Martin, A. C. S. P. Bittencourt, and J. M. Flexor. 1979. Paleographic and paleoclimatic evolution during the Quaternary in the northern half of the coast of the State of Bahia, Brazil. *In* K. Suguio, T. R. Fairchild, L. Martin, and J. M. Flexor (eds.), *Proceedings of the 1978 International Symposium on Coastal Evolution in the Quaternary,* pp. 254–263.

Vinha, S. G. da, T. de J. S. Ramos, and M. Hori. 1976. Inventário Florestal, Diagnôstico Socioeconômico da Região Cacaueira. Vol. 7 of *Recursos Florestais.* Itabuna, Bahia: Centro de Pesquisas do Cacau.

Voeks, R. A. 1987. A biogeography of the piassava fiber palm (*Attalea funifera* Mart.) of Bahia, Brazil. Ph.D. dissertation, University of California, Berkeley.

———. 1988. The Brazilian fiber belt: Management and harvest of the piassava fiber palm (*Attalea funifera*). Advances in Economic Botany 6: 262–275.

———. 1990. Edaphic limitation of a Brazilian rainforest palm: The role of energy allocation and competition for sunlight. *Physical Geography* 11: 154–171.

———. 1993. African medicine and magic in the Americas. *Geographical Review* 83: 66–78.

———. 1995. Candomblé ethnobotany: African medicinal plant classification in Brazil. *Journal of Ethnobiology* 15: 257–280.

———. 1996. Tropical forest healers and habitat preference. *Economic Botany* 50: 354–373.

Voeks, R. A, and S. G. da Vinha. 1988. Fire management of the piassava fiber palm (*Attalea funifera*) in eastern Brazil. *Yearbook—Conference of Latin Americanist Geographers* 14: 7–13.

Wafer, J. 1991. *The Taste of Blood: Spirit Possession in Brazilian Candomblé.* Philadelphia: University of Pennsylvania Press.

Walsh, R. 1831. *Notices of Brazil in 1828 and 1829.* 2 vols. Boston: Richardson, Lord & Holbrook.

Waterman, P. G., and D. McKey. 1989. Herbivory and secondary compounds in rain-forest plants. *In* H. Lieth and M. J. A. Werger (eds.), *Ecosystems of the World: Tropical Rain Forest Ecosystems,* pp. 513–536. Amsterdam: Elsevier.

Watson, A. 1974. The Arab agricultural revolution and its diffusion, 700–1100. *Journal of Economic History* 34: 7–35.

Welwitsch, F. 1965 [1862]. Amostras de Drogas Medicinais de Plantas Filamentosas e Tecidas e de Vários Outros Objectos Marmente Etnograficos, Coligidos em Angola. *In Colectônia de Escritos Doutrinarios, Floristocos e Fitogeograficos de Frederico Welwitsch,* pp. 295–333. Np.

Whitaker, T. W. 1971. Endemism and pre-Columbian migration of the bottle gourd, *Lagenaria siceraria* (Mol.) Standl. *In* C. L. Riley, J. C. Kelley, C. W. Pennington, and R. L. Rands (eds.),

Man across the Sea: Problems of Pre-Columbian Contacts, pp. 320–327. Austin: University of Texas Press.

Williams, P. V. A. 1979. *Primitive Religion and Healing: A Study of Folk Medicine in North-East Brazil.* Totowa, N.J.: Rowman and Littlefield.

Zohary, M. 1982. *Plants of the Bible.* Cambridge: Cambridge University Press.

GENERAL INDEX

INDEX OF SCIENTIFIC NAMES